TEACHER EDUCATION AND RELIGION

TEACHER EDUCATION AND RELIGION

A. L. SEBALY, EDITOR
EVAN R. COLLINS
KENNETH S. COOPER
EUGENE E. DAWSON
KNOX C. HILL
EVERETT J. KIRCHER
HAROLD K. SCHILLING

THE AMERICAN ASSOCIATION OF COLLEGES FOR TEACHER EDUCATION - ONEONTA, NEW YORK

1959

11 Elm Street, Oneonta, N. Y.

Printed in the United States of America

Library of Congress Catalog Card Number: 59-5143

THE AUTHORS

A. L. SEBALY	Professor of Education, Western Michigan University, Kalamazoo, Michigan National Coordinator, Teacher Education and Religion Project, 1956–1958. *Editor*
EVAN R. COLLINS	President, State University of New York College for Teachers, Albany, New York
KENNETH S. COOPER	Professor of History, George Peabody College for Teachers, Nashville, Tennessee
EUGENE E. DAWSON	President, Colorado Woman's College, Denver, Colorado National Coordinator, Teacher Education and Religion Project, 1954–1956
KNOX C. HILL	Associate Professor of Humanities in the College, University of Chicago, Chicago, Illinois
EVERETT J. KIRCHER	Professor of Education, The Ohio State University, Columbus, Ohio
HAROLD K. SCHILLING	Dean, Graduate School, The Pennsylvania State University, University Park, Pennsylvania

SUBCOMMITTEE ON TEACHER EDUCATION AND RELIGION

JOHN G. FLOWERS	President, Southwest Texas State Teachers College, San Marcos, Texas, *Chairman*
EVAN R. COLLINS	President, State University of New York College for Teachers, Albany, New York
EUGENE E. DAWSON	President, Colorado Woman's College, Denver, Colorado
CHARLES W. HUNT	Consultant, American Association of Colleges for Teacher Education, Oneonta, New York
J. J. OPPENHEIMER	Chairman, Department of Education, University of Louisville, Louisville, Kentucky
GERALD READ	Professor of Education, Kent State University, Kent, Ohio
ROBERT J. SCHAEFER	Director, Graduate Institute of Education, Washington University, St. Louis, Missouri
HAROLD K. SCHILLING	Dean, Graduate School, The Pennsylvania State University, University Park, Pennsylvania
ROSCOE WEST	President Emeritus, Trenton State College, Trenton, New Jersey

SAMUEL M. BLUMENFIELD	Director, Department of Education and Culture, The Jewish Agency, New York, New York, *Consultant*
WILLIAM E. McMANUS	Superintendent of Archdiocesan Schools, Chicago, Illinois, *Consultant*
SEYMOUR A. SMITH	President, Stephens College, Columbia, Missouri, *Consultant*
KENNETH I. BROWN	Executive Director, The Danforth Foundation, St. Louis, Missouri, *Ex-officio*
PRENTISS L. PEMBERTON	Associate Director, The Danforth Foundation, St. Louis, Missouri, *Ex-officio*
EDWARD C. POMEROY	Executive Secretary, American Association of Colleges for Teacher Education, Oneonta, New York, *Ex-officio*
A. L. SEBALY	National Coordinator, Teacher Education and Religion Project, Oneonta, New York, *Ex-officio*

Preface

In recent years there has been an accelerated interest and concern by educators in public education on the place and role of religion and of courses designed to give emphasis to moral and spiritual values in the curriculum. From an examination of current literature in higher education, it is evident that many of the national associations, representing various segments of higher education, regard this area as one of great challenge and opportunity. This interest impelled the American Association of Teachers Colleges, now known as the American Association of Colleges for Teacher Education, to authorize a survey study of the status of religion as a discipline in the curriculum of the member institutions. This study, which was reported to the Association, in 1947, revealed many complex problems connected with the inclusion of courses in religion and recommended that a more searching study be undertaken.

Later two significant reports were published: *Moral and Spiritual Values in the Public Schools,* by the Educational Policies Commission of the NEA, in 1951; and *The Function of the Public Schools in Dealing with Religion,* by the Committee on Religion and Education of the American Council on Education, in 1953. These two reports provided an excellent background of material for the Committee on Teacher Education and Religion which was commissioned by the American Association of Colleges for Teacher Education, in 1953, to undertake a thorough study and to make a report of its findings and conclusions. The Executive Committee of this Association secured a grant from The Danforth Foundation to finance the study for a five-year period.

This book is an outgrowth of the Committee's study. It is, in fact, a symposium on Teacher Education and Religion. It is, however, more than a symposium because the writers held many meetings together at which times they analyzed and discussed in detail the various facets of each other's writing. Consequently, in spite of the fact that each writer is responsible for his own chapter, some of the thinking of each of the authors has influenced each chapter. In the final analysis, however, no attempt was made to change the style or ideas of any writer. Each chapter, although interrelated with the others, maintains the individual's approach, and each writer assumes responsibility for his own writing.

The book has a dual function: a discussion of where materials about religion are intrinsic to various disciplines important to prospective teachers' preparation; and a report on some of the outcomes of the Project which motivated the writing of this book. The book describes the Association's concern for the improvement of teacher education in the area of Teacher Education and Religion. Consequently, it describes the nature and operation of the Project. Two chapters, the first and the sixth, are devoted to this purpose. Four of the chapters are concerned with the teaching about religion within the following specific fields: professional education, humanities, social studies, and the natural sciences. These latter three areas are best described as general education. A final chapter summarizes the dual purposes of the book.

This Committee has not sought to give final answers. In an area as difficult and complex as this, where the possibilities of conflicting opinions and where backgrounds of understanding are so diverse, it was not likely that all of the issues could be resolved. But it was encouraging to the Committee to find that college faculties and administrators preparing teachers were willing to seek curriculum improvement in this difficult area of study.

From the modest beginnings made by the Committee and by the fifteen cooperating colleges and universities, we are encouraged to believe that with further experimentation and with the application of available scientific safeguards by competent scholars sound accomplishment is assured. It is the hope of the Committee that an increasing number of scholars may engage themselves in research and experimentation in the area of the Committee's responsibility.

The Committee on Teacher Education and Religion is indebted to many individuals, colleges and universities and to numerous associations, the number being too great to mention here, but it is under special debt to the following:

The presidents, deans, local coordinators, and teaching staffs of the fifteen colleges and universities which served as pilot institutions:

Troy State College, Troy, Alabama
Arizona State College, Tempe, Arizona
Iowa State Teachers College, Cedar Falls, Iowa
Kansas State Teachers College, Pittsburg, Kansas
College of Education and College of Arts and Sciences, University of Kentucky, Louisville, Kentucky
State Teachers College at Towson, Baltimore, Maryland
Western Michigan University, Kalamazoo, Michigan
Macalester College, Saint Paul, Minnesota
School of Education, New York University, New York, New York
State University of New York Teachers College, Oswego, New York
East Carolina College, Greenville, North Carolina
College of Education, The Ohio State University, Columbus, Ohio
Oregon College of Education, Monmouth, Oregon

George Peabody College for Teachers, Nashville, Tennessee
North Texas State College, Denton, Texas

The two national coordinators of the Project: Eugene E. Dawson and A. L. Sebaly.

The consultants to the Committee:

Dr. Samuel M. Blumenfield, Director, Department of Education and Culture, The Jewish Agency, New York, New York
Very Rev. Msgr. William E. McManus, Superintendent of Archdiocesan Schools, Chicago, Illinois
Dr. Seymour A. Smith, President, Stephens College, Columbia, Missouri

The writers who made this book possible by volunteering their services to the Association.

The four individuals who helped prepare the manuscript for publication: Joyce M. Doyle of the Central Office staff; Gertrude W. Rounds, Head Librarian, State University of New York Teachers College, Oneonta; Frank C. Householder, Associate Professor of English, Western Michigan University, Kalamazoo; and Manuel Barkan, Professor of Art Education, The Ohio State University, Columbus, for the layout work and design of this book.

The efficient Central Office of the American Association of Colleges for Teacher Education, especially the Executive Secretary, Dr. Edward C. Pomeroy.

And finally, with deep appreciation, The Danforth Foundation, which provided adequate financial support for the numerous activities directed by the Committee.

John G. Flowers, Chairman
Teacher Education and Religion
Project Committee

San Marcos, Texas
February, 1959

Contents

I

*Teaching About Religion in Teacher Education**

Many informed and conscientious educators over the country are giving careful thought to the contributions of education to the pressing and complex problems of our contemporary culture. Not the least of these problems is the relationship of education to religion. This problem has been a continuing one in the American society. Individuals concerned with the professional preparation of teachers have indicated by their declarations and actions that they are serious in their willingness to explore ways and means to teach reciprocal relationships between religion and other elements in human culture.

This book is the story, in part, of how one group, the American Association of Colleges for Teacher Education, explored for five years, through the work of fifteen pilot institutions, (1) the relationship of various subject matter disciplines to religion. More specifically, it is concerned with a discussion of the relationship of religion to three broad areas

* This chapter prepared by Dr. Eugene E. Dawson, President, Colorado Woman's College, Denver; and Dr. A. L. Sebaly, Professor of Education, Western Michigan University, Kalamazoo.

of general education: the humanities, natural sciences and social sciences; and a discussion of the relationship of professional education to religion.

Because of the nature of the subject the writers found it difficult to discuss teacher education without discussing public education and higher education, both in its general and professional aspects. The publication, however, has a limited focus directed toward an improved teacher education program.

IS THERE A PROBLEM?

At the outset the question should be posed—why the current upsurge in the study of the relationship of teacher education to religion?

1. *The need to prepare teachers who are knowledgeable about religion.* There is a belief on the part of some that most teachers are not prepared to deal adequately with religion as it arises in a natural way in day-to-day teaching. One conclusion, for example, of the American Council on Education's Committee on Religion and Education, in 1953, about the preparation of public school teachers, was that its inquiry provided "no evidence that more than a very small percentage of them have received any special professional preparation for dealing with religion in the schools." (2) If this charge is true, then the problem becomes one of colleges and universities doing a better job of preparing teachers to deal with questions about religion whenever they come up naturally in the subject matter of the discipline which a teacher is teaching. The contention is that teachers, in order to be professionally competent, must possess insight and knowledge of the religious dimension in human experience. They must become acquainted with the role of religion and religious institutions in our civilization.

2. *General education and religion.* General education would seem to connote many things for many people. (3) It could be defined as any plan "to extend or to fulfill the common edu-

cation needed by a person to be a man and a citizen in our society."(4) Troyer and Pace noted that general education for prospective teachers is "not essentially different from general education for all other college students."(5) They concluded, however, that it had special significance at the college level and for the prospective teachers, "because teachers, more than other persons, have a responsibility for transmitting the culture to young people and for being themselves good specimens of the culture."(6) Some have argued that relating religion to education is in accord with the philosophy and practice of general education at its best. Ernest Johnson has summarized this argument by concluding that the "enterprise of general education includes the confrontation of growing persons with spiritual values and influences in accord with their actual magnitude in the culture and the general estimate of their importance in the life of the community."(7) The conclusion is that teachers need to be sensitized to all aspects of their cultural heritage.

3. *The interest is due to a felt need for ethical judgments.* There are those who are contending that much of this interest is due to a widespread felt need for ethical judgment and behavior in a day when social progress is said to have been far outdistanced by technological developments. Certainly it is no overstatement to suggest that people are increasingly concerned over the problems pertaining to interpersonal relationships—nationally and internationally. The last devastating war, the ever-present threat of a new one—these conditions, and many more, make us constantly sensitive to faulty interpersonal relationships and ways by which they might possibly be improved.

The writer has been primarily concerned with articulating some of the factors said to be responsible for precipitating the current concern for religion in teacher education. Actually, these are variables which have doubtlessly contributed to the general upsurge of interest in religion in various categories of educational experience and beyond the context of teacher education. It must be reiterated, however, that it is the purpose of this volume, as well as the Project which the volume partially describes, to focus attention on the study about religion in teacher education.

It is evident that colleges preparing teachers were conscious of their limitations in the general area of relating religion to teacher education from the conclusions of a study of "Religious Practices in State Teachers Colleges."

> There is little doubt that the American philosophy of separation of church and state is an all-pervading, never forgotten influence in shaping religious practices in our teacher training institutions. As a by-product of this philosophy, we have the statutory restrictions on sectarian teaching in tax-supported schools, which apparently is interpreted in many instances as a ban on all religious instruction or even extramural religious activity. . . . one gets the impression of caution from analyzing responses to the inquiry. The administrators seem to feel they are teetering near a precipice in this field. . . . this Committee is of the opinion that religious practices in the state teachers colleges lag far behind the religious interests of the administration of the colleges. In still other terms, it would appear that there is indisputable evidence of religious interests in the vast majority of these colleges but that religious practices and procedures tend to be desultory and restricted, unsystematic, if not even timorous in form of expression. As previously indicated, it would seem that this discrepancy between interest and practice emanates from the American philosophy of separation between church and state, and the related notion in popular thinking that religious activity and instruction are synonymous with denominational activity and instruction. Faced with these two hurdles, there appears to be a very real tendency for the colleges to 'play the game safely', and, in the main, develop only enough of a religious program to appease those with outstanding religious interests while not offending those with any particular sectarian bent. (8)

"TEACHING ABOUT" RELIGION

What is the evolution of this concept, "teaching about" religion, and what does it mean? In clarification of what is meant by this phrase and in discussing the background of this particular approach, it is necesary to understand the position of two important national bodies in American education about this point.

The Educational Policies Commission of the National Education Association and the Committee on Religion and Education of the American Council on Education came to virtually the same conclusion that the public schools could teach objectively *about* religion without advocating or teaching any religious creed. It is important to understand the positions of these two groups because their conclusions influenced to a high degree the structuring of a design for the AACTE's Teacher Education and Religion Project. Rather full reference is made to the American Council on Education's definition because it is the one which influenced to a great degree the work of the AACTE's Subcommittee on Teacher Education and Religion. As it will be observed later, however, the scope of the AACTE's work was much more limited in its aims.

Position of the Educational Policies Commission. The Educational Policies Commission, in 1951, expressed the following opinions about the relationship of public education to religion. "The public schools can teach objectively *about* religion without advocating or teaching any religious creed. To omit from the classroom all references to religion and the institutions of religion is to neglect an important part of American life. Knowledge about religion is essential for a full understanding of our culture, literature, art, history and current affairs."(9)

Position of the American Council on Education. For the past several years the Committee on Religion and Education of the ACE has concerned itself, in its words, with "the problem of how to find a way to give due recognition in public education to the place of religion in the culture and in the convictions of our people while at the same time safeguarding the separation of church and state."(10) The solution to this problem, the ACE believed, was one which "requires the charting of a middle course between the existing situation and adoption of expedients which are unwarranted."(11) The ACE took the stand that "the school has a responsibility for fostering appreciation of religious elements in the culture," (12) and that "total orientation toward religion as part of the culture is better accomplished if religion is not abstracted from those fields of study, however designated, in the curriculum of which it is a part."(13) The ACE's Committee on Religion and Education had taken the position that "the systematic study of religious history, of comparative religion, and even of religious doctrine may fit very well into the elective program of a state university, but even there it is no substitute for the study of the religious phases of the major academic disciplines."(14) In the opinion of the ACE's Committee a major part of the problem was "the achievement of a fuller understanding on the part of the people at large of the inherent limitations with respect to religion under which the tax-supported educational institutions must operate."(15) The solution to the problem, the ACE believed, was a "factual study of religion as the best solution confronting public education in dealing with religion."(16) But the Council pointed out that publication of the report in which this conclusion was stated "should not be understood as formal endorsement" of it.(17) The ACE defined factual study of religion, in 1953, in this way:

> Factual study of religion is characterized by deliberate aim and definite plan to deal directly and factually with religion wherever and whenever it is intrinsic to learning experiences in social studies, literature, art, music, and other fields. The aims of such study are to develop religious literacy, intelligent understanding of the role of religion in human affairs, and a sense of obligation to explore the resources that have been found in religion for achieving durable convictions and personal commitments. These aims arise from the requirements of general education which, to be effective, must view culture, human life, and personality whole.(18)

It should not be assumed at this point that the ACE Religion and Education Committee were the only advocates of this approach to the study of religion in either public (19) or higher education. (20)

DESIGNING THE TEACHER EDUCATION AND RELIGION PROJECT

The individuals in the American Association of Colleges for Teacher Education who designed the Teacher Education and Religion study were familiar with the declarations of the Educational Policies Commission and the Education and Religion Committee of the ACE. Policy-making groups within the AACTE reached the following agreements as a basis for the design of its Teacher Education and Religion Project: (21)

1. It is the proper function of colleges and universities preparing teachers to teach an intelligent understanding of the role of religion in human affairs.
2. The area of study was defined as teaching *about* religion —a factual study of religion whenever and wherever it is intrinsic to learning experiences in the various fields of study.
3. The aim of the study was intelligent understanding of the role of religion in human affairs.
4. The study was "not to emphasize the development of religious literacy among prospective teachers in the sense of the great organized religious beliefs of the world and their principal tenets."
5. The study had further limitations in that it was not to seek "the development of a sense of individual commitment in encouraging students to explore the resources of religion as a basis for durable conviction."

The AACTE study was to be an academic enterprise, one which was limited in scope to curricular affairs; one which was concerned with where religion was intrinsic to the various disciplines taught by college and university teachers in teacher education institutions.

On December 1, 1953, the American Association of Colleges for Teacher Education's Subcommittee on Teacher Education and Religion adopted the following statement to describe the nature of the national project in which it was engaged; that:

> The chief purpose of this study of Teacher Education and Religion be to discover and develop ways and means to teach the reciprocal relation between religion and other elements in human culture in order that the prospective teacher, whether he teaches literature, history, the arts, science or other subjects, be prepared to understand, to appreciate and to convey to his students the significance of religion in human affairs. (22)

Those responsible for the Project consciously steered away from attempting any definition of religion in the study. They were realistic enough to know that there are many, many definitions of religion and that there are numerous manifestations of religious experience. They were interested in considering religion where they found it and where it seemed to complete the picture which they had been studying. They were aware that in recent years an extraordinary growth in religious interest and activity has taken place in the United States. In essence, then, the study which they had designed was based upon the assumption that there was need to do a better job of preparation of teachers in the area of teacher education and religion. The Subcommittee members understood that they were not engaged in a study in religion; rather, the study was concerned with the "reciprocal relationships" of religion and the humanities, natural sciences, social sciences and professional education courses, as such would relate to more effective preparation of teachers.

AACTE PROCEDURE

For those unfamiliar with AACTE procedures, a brief explanation is necessary. After a study is defined, the Association's approach is completely decentralized. In the case of the TER study fifteen colleges and universities were selected from among the fifty-seven which had applied to be in the Project on a formal basis. The Central Office served as a coordinating agency and a clearing house. It provided staff assistance through publications and visits of the coordinator and consultants.

Such a decentralized plan permitted broad latitudes of action at local institutional level. The Subcommittee of the Association responsible for this study at no time viewed itself, nor wished to be viewed, in a position of attempting to establish a program of action for local institutions. Each college and university was free to pursue its own course of action. Yet each had to be willing to cooperate within the frame of reference of the study. However, all action was voluntary.

ACTIVITIES OF THE TEACHER EDUCATION AND RELIGION PROJECT PILOT INSTITUTIONS

The fifteen colleges and universities selected to serve as pilot institutions, on the whole, focused attention on two broad areas: general and professional education courses.

Within the area of general education the three sets of disciplines which lent themselves most effectively to the study were: the humanities, the natural sciences, and the social sciences. The second area of activity related to professional education courses. Many educators believed that such courses as Philosophy of Education, History of Education, and Foundation courses were logical places to treat the many and varied problems pertaining to teacher education and religion.

Each pilot institution remained free throughout the study to develop its own methods of approach. Consequently there were considerable variations and several institutions became interested in developing, or refining, such courses as History of Religion, Sociology of Religion, or Religion in Twentieth Century America. There was not anything approximating complete agreement on what facets of "teaching about" religion in general education courses should be emphasized or what methods should be employed. These varied opinions and approaches have been a strength of the Project and allowed for much experimentation.

An examination of some of the activities on pilot institutions' campuses indicates the variety of approaches which were used in the Teacher Education and Religion study. The following descriptions of activities, illustrative of differing approaches, were submitted by the various coordinators in pilot institutions.

Course Developments[23]

"Several of our general education courses were explored for content relevant to religion. As a result of these explorations we concluded that the humanities and the social sciences seemed to offer the greatest opportunity for implementing the purposes of the Project. Most of our work has therefore been concentrated in these areas. The two courses in which we have been particularly interested are: Survey of Western Civilization, and Introduction to the Humanities.

"Dr. Robert W. Coonrod, Chairman of the Department of History and Political Science, writes as follows concerning the course, Survey of Western Civilization:

> No organized staff attempt has been made in the history work to approach the problem of religion with particular reference to teacher education. However, at least half of those who are studying to be teachers here have come into contact with our course, *Survey of Western Civilization.* This course emphasizes the history of ideas. Of first-rank importance are, of course, religious ideas. The students are urged to develop a historical approach to the understanding of religion. That is, they are asked to differentiate between that which can be established as objective fact, and that which must be resolved through religious experience. They are encouraged to trace the development of religious concepts and to assess the significance of such ideas on modern civilization. Students are invited to think through their own religious heritage in the hope that two things might be accomplished:

[23] *Arizona State College,* Tempe, by Dr. Herbert Gurnee, Professor of Psychology.

> 1. a better understanding of the historical development of social institutions and practices might lead to a more rational approach to modern living; and 2. a better definition of experiences which are purely religious in character might lead to a strengthening of faith of the individual which, in turn, might make that individual a more valuable member of society.

"Introduction to Humanities is a year course for eight semester hours of credit. Four periods in the development of western European civilization are chosen for study: the ancient world (Greece particularly), the medieval world, the Renaissance, and the post-Renaissance or modern world. In each of the four periods the prevailing idea or attitude of the times is presented as the central unifying factor. The accomplishments in the fields of art, music, literature, or philosophy (including religion) are shown in relation to the prevailing attitude.

"Dr. Dorothy C. Schilling, Chairman of the Department of the Humanities, reports as follows:

> In each of the time-thought units, the subject of religion takes its historical place in the works and attitudes studied. The unit of the ancient world, prevailingly rational in attitude, contains frequent references to and discussions of religion. The philosophy of Plato is related to its time, to earlier religions, and to subsequent Christianity. The content of Greek tragedy is presented as religious belief, and the drama festivals as a phase of religious worship. Art presents the sculpture of the gods and myths relating to them, and the architecture of the temples is related to the worship conducted within them. The medieval unit, concentrating on the spiritual view of life, is almost totally concerned with matters about religion. Philosophy treats of St. Augustine's *The Confessions* and *The City of God*. Dante's *Divine Comedy* is the text for literature; art presents the Gothic cathedral as the supreme expression of man's spiritual aspiration; music centers attention on the music of the church, including (since the lecture comes at Christmas time) a presentation of Christmas carols.
>
> The humanistic attitude is chosen as the unifying idea of the Renaissance. Attention directed to this-worldly affairs does not necessarily exclude a continuing interest in spiritual matters. Music shows harmonic development continuous from the church music of the Middle Ages, and in the evolution of musical instruments the perfecting of the pipe organ for church use. Art presents the Christian and pagan religious paintings of Leonardo and Michelangelo. Philosophy considers the in-

terests and ideas of Francis Bacon with inevitable reference to ethics, religion, and religious reform. Shakespeare's *Romeo and Juliet,* the lovers star-crossed in the pagan sense, contains incidental religious references usually medieval in tenor.

The final unit of the second semester, the post-Renaissance, deals with modern man in his search for new values, chiefly spiritual values. Goethe's *Faust,* the art of the eighteenth to the twentieth century, the music of the modern world, Somerset Maugham's *Of Human Bondage,* Albert Schweitzer's *Out of My Life and Thought*—all are filled with major and minor expressions of religious subject and interest.

"In the construction of the humanities course we have been concerned with the development of value attitudes. It seemed to us that the attitudes we developed would be more important to our students than any specific facts we might teach them. We therefore spent some time trying to define the attitudes we thought desirable. Eventually we came up with certain concepts which, although not completely satisfactory, nevertheless provided us with at least a working basis from which to construct an attitude scale of 120 items. We are making various exploratory studies with this scale."

A Voluntary Forum on Teacher Education and Religion [24]

"A voluntary forum on Teacher Education and Religion was held in December, 1954, which eighteen faculty members and forty-five graduate students and public school teachers attended. There the Project was described and some tentative principles were conceived. From the minutes of that meeting the following excerpts reveal the mind and consensus of the group:

We are too much on the defensive, often needlessly, in many areas. An example of this is the doctrine of separation of church and state, an area in which our teachers are often uninformed. When they are well informed the pressures can be lessened. It is necessary that such pressures as these be eased. Teachers should know enough history, sociology and political science, etc., to be able to explain to critics and to misguided enthusiasts, who criticize the school for its stand, the sound relationship which should exist between church and school.

[24] *University of Kentucky,* Lexington, by Dr. James Gladden, Professor of Sociology.

Teachers should know enough about religion and the community to see religion as a vital factor in American tradition. Secular public schools have hardly hindered the growth or progress of the churches in America. At least the statistics reveal that United States churches compare favorably with those in nations with established or monopolistic churches. Foreign church leaders and other visitors are struck by this picture of church strength and vitality in America. Our voluntary system has also provided better financial support for our churches. Teachers should know these things, and have an understanding of the reasons behind them.

How can we cope with this general problem? How shall we educate teachers that they will not be led into unnecessary controversy and pressure, but will be able to teach objectively and confidently on any relevant area or deal with any needed subject matter?

The question before us is 'What account should be taken in the area of religion in teacher education?' We should consider the implications for all major areas: humanities, physical sciences and social sciences.

"Why is this important? What should be done? There are several possibilities. One is that the College of Education could take a stand independently. But our approach should be broader than this. The responsibility extends into those other colleges of the University which contribute to teacher education. Upon some important considerations we stand together, for example, in opposition to sectarian religious indoctrination in teaching. But this does not imply that we should completely withdraw from the whole area of religion. We are concerned that this be a comprehensive and scholarly background so that teachers will be prepared to guide students through various areas of literature, history, and other social studies, etc., by an intellectually honest approach, presenting the various backgrounds impartially so that pupils may know and understand the problems in which religion is a part."

Area Conferences [25]

"During the month of March, 1957, the four area teacher training institutions of Michigan cooperated in sponsoring

[25] *Western Michigan University*, Kalamazoo, by Mr. Leonard Gernant, Associate Director of Field Services.

four conferences for public school teachers and administrators on 'Problems Relating to Religion in Public School Education.' The original impetus came from Western Michigan University, which is one of fifteen pilot centers established under the Teacher Education and Religion Project of the American Association of Colleges for Teacher Education. This Project aims at improving teacher education, and it has encouraged the pilot centers to study the question whether certain problems relating to religion might be met more effectively if prospective teachers were alerted to them while they are in college.

"Several members of Western's Teacher Education and Religion Committee became interested in making an informal survey of the experiences and opinions of teachers in various communities. A committee on 'Conferences for Public School Teachers' was appointed, and, under the direction of Otto Yntema, Director of Field Services, the committee invited the other regional colleges to plan a series of four meetings on the problems arising in the area of religion. Eastern Michigan College, Central Michigan College, and Northern Michigan College joined Western in order to canvass each section of the state. Cordial response on the part of the Field Services Divisions of these schools resulted in four conferences which followed identical programs and procedures. In each case the aim was to gather information. It was specifically stated in the invitation that the conferences would be limited to exploration, in the hope that perhaps future meetings might deal with those problems teachers considered most significant, with the aim of 'doing something about them' rather than just describing them.

"Twenty-three groups of ten to fifteen members each discussed the theme of the conferences under the three general headings: 1. Problems Originating From Children; 2. Problems Originating From Faculty and Administration; 3. Problems Originating From the Community.

"Not all groups covered the whole of this territory, but since the starting-point was different for different groups, fairly adequate coverage was obtained. Each discussion group included a person who kept a running record of problems as they were raised."

Faculty Writing Project[26]

"As a result of campus activity and the surveys made, a group of faculty members, mostly TER committee members, but not exclusively so, decided to issue a college bulletin, *Religion in the High School Curriculum.* After the publication of the bulletin a session, based on the work of the Project, was held at Meredith College. Interested professors from the state of North Carolina as a whole were invited. The bulletin also was followed by faculty-student-town seminars in which the Greenville Ministerial Association participated. These seminars led to the development of a two-week workshop for teachers held at East Carolina College in June, 1957. The workshop, offered for credit, was favorably received, and was highly successful as an experiment which East Carolina College offered again in the summer of 1958. Radio and television programs were also devoted to the discussion of ideas and the controversies raised by the Project and its findings."

Reorganization of General Education Courses[27]

"There has been a careful and systematic reorganization of the courses in our general education program. Let me emphasize that our general education program actually antedates the Teacher Education and Religion program, but the latter has had a modifying influence on the former. The third quarter of the Humanities sequence is devoted to a study of the great philosophies and religions of the world. This is a unique course

[26] *East Carolina College,* Greenville, North Carolina, by Dr. Leo W. Jenkins, Vice-President.
[27] *George Peabody College for Teachers,* Nashville, Tennessee, by Dr. William H. Vaughan, Registrar and Professor of Education.

and the student has the opportunity to read extensively in the great religious literatures of the world.

"The second course in the Humanities is devoted to the study of the great music and fine art of the world. Here it is both fitting and proper that sacred music should be emphasized and studied. Also the place that religious themes occupy in the fine arts is a part of the humanities. When one reflects that the humanities are required of our undergraduates, it is evident that we consider the place of religion is very important in the college curriculum.

"There are other classes in which the place of religions and religious movements is vital to education. As an example, another required course of our undergraduates is 'Our Basic Heritage.' This contains the major ideas and movements that have been handed down to us from our forefathers. Such a course would be incomplete without some reference to religion and religious ideas that have become a part of the fabric of our culture."

Workshop on Religion in Teacher Education [28]

"The theme of the workshop held June 14–16, 1956, was 'The Responsibility of Professional Education for Religion in Teacher Education.' This workshop was also jointly sponsored by North Texas State College and the national Project.

"The opening address of the workshop was given by Dr. H. Gordon Hullfish of The Ohio State University. Sectional meetings of elementary school teachers and secondary school teachers and administrators discussed a wide variety of topics, such as the question of Bible readings in schools, prayers in school programs, religious holidays, and factual teaching about religion in the curriculum. One of the conclusions reached was as follows: 'Our responsibility as a teacher-training institution

[28] *North Texas State College,* Denton, by Dr. A. M. Sampley, Vice-President.

is to produce people who are literate on questions of religion and who realize the values which religion has brought to our democratic culture, but we can leave to the church and home those things pertaining to particular faiths and creeds.'

"An important feature of this workshop was a series of demonstration meetings in which teachers observed in actual practice the use of resources and methods of presenting material about religion in language arts, social studies, and music. Demonstrations were held at both the elementary and the secondary levels. The participation of high school pupils helped to illustrate the resources of the secondary school curriculum in dealing with religious materials."

Faculty Seminar [29]

"These weekly study sessions have served a number of functions, the first and foremost being to promote a climate of attitude and understanding conducive to a study of objective religion and its relation to teacher preparation. It was felt from the beginning that the study was not one that could or should be hurried. A great deal of exploration and clarification was necessary to satisfy a state institution and its faculty that the Project was concerned with a legitimate educational problem. The seminar session revolved around such areas as published literature, relation of religion to various academic disciplines, religion and general education, and student and faculty reactions to the Project.

"The weekly seminar provided the focal point around which all other activities of the Committee revolved."

Faculty Seminar [30]

"We also organized a faculty seminar. This became and remained the central feature of our project. Over the succeeding

[29] *Kansas State Teachers College*, Pittsburg, by Dr. J. D. Haggard, Professor of Mathematics.

[30] *College of Education, The Ohio State University*, Columbus, by Dr. Donald P. Cottrell, Dean, College of Education.

months, the seminar came to involve 35 members of our staff, drawn from seven different departments. Meetings were scheduled bi-weekly, except for vacation periods, up through December, 1956. There were 45 sessions in all, each for two or three hours. Prominent in the core of the group were staff members from the central administration of the College.

"We did not think of the seminar as an action committee but as a group for the expression and exchange of personal views on value questions having to do with the professional development of ourselves and teacher education. In respect to religious denominations, we were a heterogeneous group, but in respect to our mutual feelings for our work and life together, we sensed a common bond. It was the further meaning of the common bonds which we found most profitable to explore together, using our deepening understanding as direct personal benefit to ourselves and as indirect benefit, as well, to the cause of teacher education and religion. Though books and formalized views were useful, on occasion, what was most helpful was our personal efforts to give expression to our own ways of thinking and feeling, speaking spontaneously in the give and take of good conversation. We relied on our conviction that religion, at its best, is something that communicates between teacher and student as a quality of basic relationships to life, intrinsic in the whole outlook and bearing of the teacher and student. Good conversation in the seminar was a way of honoring our beliefs on this score."

Course Additions [31]

"We were able to add two courses to our college offerings: An Introduction to Philosophy, and Comparative Religions. A proposal to offer an integrated Fine Arts unit with emphasis upon its religious aspects is still pending."

[31] *Oregon College of Education,* Monmouth, by Dr. Charles R. McClure, Professor of Humanities.

Multiple Approaches[32]

"At Oswego a variety of techniques has been used to approach the broad question of the place of religion in teacher education. Under the direction of Professor Seward Salisbury, a study was carried to completion to determine 'the extent to which the present generation of college students reflects the widespread interest in religion which seems to characterize American culture at present.' In addition to this study two Teacher Education and Religion Conferences were sponsored at Oswego and proved to be stimulating to those interested in the success of the Project. At the first of these, in 1956, Dr. A. L. Sebaly, National Coordinator, discussed the philosophy, activities, and achievements of the Project as carried forward at the various pilot centers. At the second conference, in 1957, Dr. John L. Childs, Teachers College, Columbia University, gave the keynote address on the topic, 'Education in a Multi-Religion Society.' At both the 1956 and 1957 conferences outstanding public school administrators, supervisors, guidance personnel, and classroom teachers served as consultants and panelists at sessions devoted to discussing with classroom teachers who were attending the regular summer sessions the practical, everyday problems which arise in situations of some religious significance for pupils, teachers, and parents. Of particular interest to the educators who attended the conferences were problems arising out of conflicting views of science and religion, released time for religious instruction, morning prayers, the reading of passages from the Bible, the teaching of moral and spiritual values, humanism, religious holidays, cooperation with religious institutions, and religious freedom of teachers."

[32] *State University of New York Teachers College,* Oswego, by Dr. Francis P. Hulme, Professor of English.

A Survey of Student Attitudes and Values [33]

"Does the whole experience of going to college really change the values, goals, and ambitions of the student? The Troy researchers sought an answer to this persistent and disturbing question. It completed a thorough investigation of the beliefs and values of 1017 of its own freshmen, sophomores, juniors, and seniors.

"The testing instrument used in the attitude survey consisted of about 80 multiple choice items designed to give us socio-economic data about our students; to discover their responses to questions about religious dogma and denominational practices; and then to ascertain opinions which would by the answer chosen reflect the attitudes and the value preferences of the respondents. The questionnaire was constructed with the greatest care; and, in order that we might make useful comparisons, it purposely contained items identical with those in surveys and polls used elsewhere. The 1017 schedules when filled in were shipped to Cornell University's testing laboratory for processing, coding, and result-tabulation.

"Our next problem on the home front was to present to our whole faculty the conclusions to which the statistical study seemed to lead, and to make this presentation with such force and impact as would draw forth a vigorous response and a desire to act further. The familiar shock technique was used, three statistically-minded non-committeemen and the college president being invited to serve on a panel for an hour and a half summary of the mimeographed report. Here again we felt that we succeeded. The responses were forceful and varied, the audience only with the greatest reluctance withholding its comments until the panel members could complete their remarks. It was a brisk evening we had, to be sure.

[33] *Troy State College,* Troy, by Dr. Frank P. Rainwater, Professor of English.

"Upon invitation, faculty members later submitted to the coordinator of instruction their written observations about the attitude survey report, their comments upon it, and their alternate interpretations as to the meaning of the questions and the implications of the answers. Also the coordinator of instruction met separately with each of the nine departments, thus giving 53 of the 55 teaching members of the college the opportunity to voice whatever personal opinions they wished about the import and meaning of the 'Attitudes and Aspirations' study. These responses and opinions have all now been written up and placed in the hands of department chairmen and others."

Conference on Religion and the Humanities[34]

"The Macalester College Conference on Religion and Education held on April 26–27, 1957, was devoted to a discussion of the topic, 'The Humanities Teacher: His Function in Treating Religious Ideas in Humanities Courses.' Participants were invited from four Twin Cities colleges besides the sponsoring institution: The University of Minnesota, the College of St. Thomas, the College of St. Catherine, and Hamline University.

"The purpose of the Conference, it was announced, was to help humanities teachers to do better that which they all do, sometimes haphazardly, in their courses. As the program stated:

> In one way or another, nearly every day the humanities teacher discusses religion with a variety of students, most of whom have pronounced ideas on religion, if not definite religious commitments. Because he deals with religious ideas constantly, he presumably needs now and then to criticize his performance. For such criticism this conference intends to afford a formal occasion. The proposed critical examination of presuppositions, provisional enunciation of principles in the light of which practice can be guided, and the exchange of practical information regarding the classroom treatment of religious documents and works of art—these, we hope will correct and fructify our teaching.

[34] *Macalester College,* St. Paul, Minnesota, by Arnold H. Holtz, Assistant Professor of Education.

"'The plan of the Conference was built on the convictions that searching papers delivered by the best available persons and that practicable suggestions for teaching offered by successful teachers would best serve the announced purposes.

"'The first paper, 'The Believer as Teacher,' was delivered by Professor Herbert Slusser of the College of St. Thomas. In this paper were set forth the intellectual presuppositions of the Christian teacher and the peculiar advantages of the religious believer in dealing with religious ideas in humanities courses. The second paper, complementary to the first, was 'The Unbeliever Teaching Humanities.' Presenting this paper in one of his last public appearances, Joseph Warren Beach, Professor Emeritus of the University of Minnesota, was at his learned and witty best in explaining the not inconsiderable virtues and usefulness of the responsible religious unbeliever in discussing religious ideas. Professor Beach, speaking in the liberal tradition of Mill and Arnold, established the point that the unbeliever, granted his respect for his subject and his students, can often by his open-mindedness and freedom from specific religious commitment better deal with religious ideas in the classroom than the believer.

"'The last major paper, 'The Limitations of Humanism,' was delivered by Professor Robert J. Ames of the Humanities Program of the University of Minnesota. Professor Ames, in analyzing the dialectic of secular humanism, advanced the thesis that the humanistic outlook by its very nature, even at best, led progressively to the spectator view of life, uninvolved, ironical, irresponsible; at worst, humanism, denying the transcendental element in man, declines readily into inhumanism.

"'The major address of the Conference was given by Father Martin Jarrett-Kerr of the Anglican Community of Resurrection. Father Jarrett-Kerr, in speaking of 'The Death of God,' drew from his wide knowledge of modern English and

Continental letters to reveal characteristic signs of the decline of the sacramental view of life and the belief in God. From novelists, poets, philosophers, and psychologists, Father Jarrett-Kerr quoted lines showing a low view of man, disgust with the world, spiritual malaise, and the abortive search for satisfying absolutes to fill the place left by the demise of God.

"The following shorter papers, some more or less practical in nature, were given: 'Three Versions of the Mass: A Study in Contrasts,' Professor Glenn Glasow, the College of St. Catherine; 'Miracles, Mysteries, and Moralities in the College Theater,' Professor James Carlson, Hamline University; 'The Use of Recordings in Humanities,' Professor F. Earl Ward, Macalester College; 'The Qualifications and Responsibilities of the Teacher Dealing with Non-Christian Religious Ideas,' Professor David White, Macalester College.

"Terminating the two-day session was a paper contributed by Professor Alburey Castell, Chairman of the Department of Philosophy, University of Oregon, and one-time organizer and head of the Humanities Program of the University of Minnesota. This paper, 'The Liquidation of Secondary Ignorance,' was read for the author by Professor Daniel V. Bryan of the University of Minnesota."

Field Study [35]

"One of the more promising things about the work of the local committee is the proposed field project to be part of the operation in the spring of 1957. We are fortunate in that the college has seen fit to release one of our sociology professors to give full time to the carrying out of the project. The purpose of this experiment has to do with a deliberate attempt to test in the field certain assumptions that have prompted the

[35] *Iowa State Teachers College*, Cedar Falls, by Dr. Harold E. Bernhard, Director of Bureau of Religious Activities and Professor of Religious Literature.

Teacher Education and Religion Project from the very beginning.

"That the 'teaching about' religion or the handling of topics with religious content in the public schools of America is generally being poorly done seems to be the basic assumption underlying the current Teacher Education and Religion Project of the American Association of Colleges for Teacher Education. Gathering the evidence to test the validity of this assumption is the principal concern of the Iowa State Teachers College Education and Religion Committee in setting up this project.

"There is further concern with the validity of the TER Project assumptions that topics with religious content, such as those that might be found in the study of history, or art, or literature, or any other academic area, are generally poorly taught because teachers either (a) purposely ignore or evade such topics or (b) they are too ignorant of the facts of religion to teach about them adequately.

"A second important purpose of this inquiry is to gather information which will identify the specific situations in the public school classrooms in which topics with some religious content cause problems. It is believed by the local TER committee that a report detailing such situations would be of considerable value to prospective teachers as well as to many practicing teachers.

"Since the quality of the teaching in this area cannot be readily ascertained in a direct fashion by means now available to this committee, evidence that bears indirectly on this basic question will be sought. The statements of teachers regarding the means of handling these topics, the attitudes and knowledge possessed and the pressures felt by them will furnish data for a judgment of the quality of the teaching. At the same time this information should furnish an explanation of the behavior of school teachers regarding the teaching of topics with religious content.

"This study is essentially a case study of the knowledge, attitudes, beliefs, observations, and behavior of a number of public school teachers in a selected set of schools.

"Information for this study will be sought by interviewing each teacher selected. A schedule of specific questions with appropriate probes will be used in the interview to elicit and record pertinent information.

"In addition each teacher in the school district will be asked to answer an inventory of religious knowledge, which is being prepared especially for this Project. The inventory completed by interviewed teachers will be collated with their interview form in the interest of gaining further insight into that particular respondent's behavior. All the forms together will be used to gain understanding of the general level of religious knowledge among the public school teachers of Iowa and to furnish a point of reference for the scores of the respondents to the interview. This inventory will also be administered to selected groups of Iowa State Teachers College students in order to establish another reference point for the study.

"It is expected that this study then will shed some definite light upon the validity of the assumptions underlying the national TER Project and at the same time furnish some guidance for the work of Iowa State Teachers College and other colleges in the task of preparing teachers for the public schools of America."

A Multiple Approach [36]

"This cursory review of the activities of our committee and faculty indicate that a wide variety of techniques was employed in carrying forward a program of work designed to

[36] *State Teachers College at Towson,* Baltimore, Maryland, by Dr. Mahlon H. Hellerich, Professor of History.

meet the objectives of the Project. A partial list of these techniques would include the following:

Study (exploration of issues, problems, possible courses of action)
- Reading of pertinent books and pamphlets
- Discussion within the Committee
- Use of consultants and lecturers in conference with individual instructors, in meetings with departments and with the entire faculty
- Meetings of an informal faculty discussion group
- Discussions with Schoolmen's Advisory Committee
- Intervisitation with another pilot center
- Regional and national workshops

Curriculum Enrichment
- Studies of required courses in both general education and professional education sequences to determine materials about religion taught in said courses
- Studies of elective courses in both general education and professional education sequences to determine materials about religion taught in said courses
- Organization of new elective courses in religion on a nondepartmental basis
- Giving assistance to departments and individual instructors as they organized new elective courses dealing with religion and/or added materials about religion to existing courses
- Providing lecture series on religion for entire college community

Research and Evaluation
- Use of opinionnaire to ascertain student reaction to Project, to ascertain alumni reaction to Project, to ascertain student and alumni reaction to elective course—Religion in Contemporary America
- Use of questionnaire and personal interviews to gather

information on teaching about religion in the curricula
Use of test and control groups to gain information about religious values of our students and the effectiveness of teaching in the course—Religion in Contemporary America
Development of a test instrument to test knowledge of various religious bodies in the United States
Communicating the results of our experience
Through articles in professional journals
Through articles in student newspaper and literary magazine
Through workshops
Through appearances of committee members on programs of professional associations."

ISSUES RELATED TO "TEACHING ABOUT" RELIGION

In trying to realize the aims and objectives of the Teacher Education and Religion Project, those participating have encountered numerous problems, some of a highly complex nature. Very substantial questions have been raised. It would have been nothing short of sophistry on the part of those participating in the study to have indicated that there was complete agreement that the "factual study" of religion or the "teaching about" religion are methods completely devoid of limitations. In pointing to some of these issues perhaps additional insight may be gained regarding the whole matter of teacher education and religion.

1. *What is meant by the term "teaching about" religion?* This question is a basic consideration. Few of those who were involved in the Project contended that this phrase was a perfect solution as far as terminology is concerned. As a term it seemed to be somewhat more free of the limitations of other terms, although there have been those who have preferred to speak of the "factual study" of religion or again of the "proper

educational account of religion." And some would have preferred "a study about religion." A case might be made that the phrase "teaching about" religion does not mean the same as factual study. Or that to seek where religion is intrinsic to sets of disciplines such as the natural sciences, the humanities, or social sciences is an entirely different problem from "teaching about" religion. The phrase did not lend itself to as neat a definition as some observers would have liked. The AACTE operated on the principle that whatever belonged within the content of a course should be taught. However, these questions could be raised: What determines the content of a given divisional or subject matter area? Individual faculty preference? The textbook? Consensus among scholars in the field? Student need? Much discussion has revolved around the term "teaching about" religion which has been used in the Teacher Education and Religion Project. (37) With all limitations, however, the term has appeared to be a happy choice.

2. *There is hardly a need for "teaching about" religion.* This argument was advocated by those who believed a satisfactory amount of such teaching has taken place over the years and hardly needed to be accepted. Faculty members teaching in the social science and humanities areas often expressed this opinion. There is need apparently for more extensive status surveys to find out what is being done. Some observers believe that securing this information is a first priority in studying the relationship of religion to teacher education. (38) If "teaching about" religion is currently at a high level, this would mean that textbooks and materials are adequate and pedagogical methods effective and there would be little need for further explorations. The last chapter considers some of the challenges facing teacher education. Many questions need answering. How have our schools of teacher education treated religious references when intrinsic to the study of subject matter in the various disciplines? What have prospective teachers been told about the attitudes teachers should bring to their discus-

sions concerning controversial subjects concerning religion? What do prospective teachers know about the kinds of questions children will be asking once they meet them in classroom situations? How do textbooks consider some of these areas of instruction? Do they treat the reciprocal relationship between religion and particular subjects and do they do so accurately?

3. *The anticipated lack of ability of college teachers to "teach about" religion in an objective and unbiased manner.* It has been argued that teachers are susceptible to the same biases and motivated by the same subjective variables as are others, and it is unrealistic to expect even an approximation of objectivity in implementing such a program.

Those involved in the experimental study recognized that for such teaching to be effective, capable and emotionally secure teachers would be demanded, not only those who are able to acquire a better understanding of the beliefs and practices of others, but those who are able to understand reasonably well why they feel and believe as they do. What needs to be remembered is that such considerations are basic in treating other areas of the curriculum as well. It should be reiterated that this was not a project in religion but rather teacher education and that it did not involve young and immature children but college and university students and not young and inexperienced teachers but college and university teachers.

4. *There was little in the study that would contribute to the student's moral and spiritual development.* Some observers have pointed out that, in their opinions, the study was too limited. The argument was that should it be entirely possible to accomplish the aims of the study, to maintain an objective opinion, and to refrain from personal commitment on the part of students, there would be little remaining in the process that would contribute to each student's moral and spiritual development. Such a project becomes little more than innocuous. It became evident that some wished for a program that would result in "conversions" or "commitments."

5. *Little is accomplished in the way of giving students or prospective teachers a greater understanding of the role of religion in human affairs.* The "teaching about" approach to religion was related primarily to general education courses or regular courses within the various disciplines. Some observers indicated they preferred a more direct approach to the problem. They contended that what was needed were formal courses in religion where the major tenets of all the world's great religions could be given emphasis. Some educators and instructors, who have been inclined to sympathize with this point of view, have done so because they thought such a position affords a more exhaustive treatment of the subject. Still others contended for such an approach because they thought it enabled them to avoid having to consider explosive topics within their own courses. There were likewise spokesmen of various religious denominations who indicated interest in the possibilities of such a procedure. On the other hand, it was the prevailing opinion on the part of the majority of those involved in the Teacher Education and Religion Project that such a procedure of establishing separate departments of religion was beyond the scope of the study and was an individual campus problem.

The questions and problems treated in this section represented only a few of the more important questions which were encountered during the time the study was in progress. Additional problems could be listed. There are philosophical questions which might be considered. (39) There were questions relative to the feasibility of such an approach in view of already over-crowded curricula in our institutions of teacher education, or again questions relative to the availability of curriculum materials for such teaching. These latter questions and concerns are treated more extensively in subsequent chapters of this volume which relate to "teaching about" religion in the humanities, natural sciences, social sciences, and professional education courses.

A Minimum of Criticism of the Study

As the Teacher Education and Religion effort began, there was a certain amount of apprehension and concern among those who were to participate, lest this effort result in suspicions and even hostilities, if not from religious groups, then from individuals and organizations dedicated to preventing any semblance of religion from entering the classroom. It is not difficult to understand why such apprehensions prevailed. In a pluralistic culture such as ours, the ever-present dangers are that there will be violations of the principle of the separation of the church and state, or that religious liberties will be jeopardized and that individuals or groups within the framework of the public school will embark on sectarian crusades for the purpose of winning devotees. Some observers had reservations about the Teacher Education and Religion study. It was satisfying and reassuring to the Association, therefore, to note a very minimum in the way of criticism of the activities of the Project. While there was no universal agreement as to the significance of the activity or even the validity of the recommendations and experiments, the skepticism advanced was on the whole a healthy skepticism.

EDUCATORS WILL NEED TO PROMOTE AND FACILITATE AN EVEN GREATER AMOUNT OF COMMUNICATION

A second point which should be emphasized is that the study has not been terminated—the problems have not been resolved. Experimentation must continue, and as educators continue to deal with the total problem of teacher education and religion, they will need to promote and facilitate an even greater amount of communication, not only among representatives of all segments of education, but between educators and religionists, the laity and professionals, students and teachers. Better communication will not resolve all differences and difficulties, but neither will the absence of such a climate of understanding represent a solution to the problem. Colleges and universities need to examine further their responsibilities as well as limitations for preparing teachers who are competent to teach intelligent understanding of the role of religion in human affairs. The Teacher Education and Religion Project has made a beginning in a difficult area of study.

VARIOUS LEVELS OF EDUCATION INFLUENCE TEACHER EDUCATION

Prospective teachers in this country today obtain their professional preparation in colleges and universities which are higher educational institutions. The greater number of these individuals intend to teach in elementary and secondary schools. Consequently, those who prepare teachers are cognizant that teacher education programs are subject to influences which arise not only from problems within higher education but from elementary and secondary schools as well.

It is evident that the problems of relating education to religion in the elementary and secondary schools are different from problems faced by institutions of higher education in doing the same tasks. Compulsory education for the relatively immature presents a different situation from that which arises in teaching mature students who are attending higher educational institutions for the purpose of preparing themselves to be teachers. Colleges and universities which prepare teachers face responsibilities of forming judgments as to what the higher educational institution's role is in a free society. The next chapter discusses this point in greater detail. The issues as to what either general or professional education should be in teacher education institutions are far from settled. At the same time much of what has been done in the preparation of teachers in higher educational institutions has been directed by focus on compulsory public school educational problems.

It is not the purpose of this book, or this chapter, to attempt to resolve the numerous problems which arise at the compulsory school or higher education levels. It must be recognized, however, when one begins to consider where religion is intrinsic to various sets of disciplines, he should keep in mind the many variables which influence to a greater or lesser degree the type of pre-service instruction prospective teachers will receive.

2

Teacher Education and Religion *

PART I

It is common knowledge that the nations of the world differ greatly in their various beliefs. But nations differ from one another also in another more subtle and more significant way, the unanimity of belief insisted upon or the diversity of belief allowed for. Nations requiring uniformity of belief commonly assume that a one-philosophy or a one-religion state is the clear prerequisite for either cultural coherence or social stability. On the other hand, nations tending toward cultural diversity as commonly believe that their strength lies in providing for the freedom of thought which results in cultural pluralism.

Cultural Pluralism, the Condition of Religious Freedom

The framers of our Constitution were confronted by a problem which even today has not been finally resolved. Heretofore, it was customary for a civilization to identify its

* This chapter prepared by Dr. Everett J. Kircher, Professor of Education, The Ohio State University, Columbus.

source of authority in order that it could know its center. It was customary to locate the source of authority in order that it could know its center. It was customary to locate the source of authority in a person, in a class, in a political party, in a clerical group, in a certain philosophy or in a particular religion. There is a clear if primitive logic about this. It stands to reason that a nation, like a person, ought to have a final point of reference. Yet for good and sufficient reasons our founding fathers refused to locate such a point. Rather than establishing any reliable source of authority, they willfully set up a balance of power which confused the source of authority. They chose cultural pluralism over any religious or philosophical monism. Insofar as they were able, they made it impossible for any one formal system of thought or belief to dominate the social order. As they conceived it, a state of freedom expresses itself in and depends upon the inalienable right of every man to do his own thinking and follow the dictates of his own conscience relative to the ultimate meaning of life. That many would abuse this freedom they fully understood, but in this imperfect world they chose this as the lesser evil.

As a serious and positive position, this was a radical departure from the dominant mentality of both their time and ours. Many were hesitant to endorse it and many endorsed it hesitantly. It sounded then as it does now, to many, like a compromise among faiths rather than a positive faith itself. Of course it had the remarkable virtue of assuring freedom to each particular faith, but this balance of power among the faiths appeared to be no faith at all. The most that could be said for it was that it was a *modus vivendi* that provided a variety of demonstratively true faiths but was not itself truly a faith. Thus it would appear that the free society anticipated by our Constitution is religiously and philosophically neutral. It positively refuses to sponsor one system of belief over another. Admittedly if most of our people are theists, and even

Christians, the culture tends to take on this flavor from the overtones of their thought. Even so, the neutralist obligation is so strong that these Christian theists in power refuse to make a theistic or Christian commitment the condition for exercising the franchise. One's freedom to participate in determining the destiny of our people is equally great whatever his belief. Our tendency is to draw the line only at the point of "clear and present danger" to the state.

Is Cultural Pluralism Rationally Defensible?

Such a society scarcely lends itself to rational defense as rationality is commonly conceived. As long as men of intellectual integrity are free to differ, and do, the over-all scene cannot be said to be characterized as logically self-consistent. It would appear that the free society embraces a variety of logically coherent systems but is not itself characterized by logical coherence. It is the condition of clear and particular beliefs but appears itself not to be a clear and particular belief. Moreover, it proposes not to promote one belief at the exclusion of others, for if we attempt to identify the faith of a free society with any one of the logical systems of authenticated belief within it, all other particular systems of belief are endangered. It would therefore seem that when democracy is conceived as a state conducive to the emergence of fundamentally novel ideas, this very state perpetuates cultural diversity. Implicit in this is a fact that man in all the callings of life both high and low has always resisted, for it detracts from his self-esteem. This fact is that there are apparently absolute limits to human rationality and there are most certainly practical and strategic limits. Particularly the academic man involved in secular debate of theological controversy cannot bring himself to face the fact that finally all knowledge runs out. Yet this is the final acknowledgment of intellectual and religious maturity. As Robert E. Fitch has said,

> . . . we should have purged ourselves by now of the delusion that there is some one true method that is self-certifying and self-correcting. The Thomist believes this of his method; John Dewey believed it of his version of the scientific method; the Communist believes it of his dialectical method of internal criticism. But the obvious fact is that no method can confer infallibility on man . . . we require cooperation and competition between logical methods. (1)

Some will smile at the paradox of the Christian scholar's identification of the source of John Dewey's implicit dogmatism, but it is characteristic of the scholar at his best to know that no rational scheme finally encompasses the whole truth and no method for attaining it is exclusively adequate. The recognition of this fact by any university or any society leaves each individual free to choose his own belief but not free to claim that his particular philosophy is the finally right one for all or the uniquely democratic one of the many. The historic and widespread tendency to equate one's own particular belief with a public state of virtue or of freedom always endangers freedom or virtue whether that philosophy is John Dewey's naturalistic pragmatism or Thomas Aquinas' Christian scholasticism. Of course the universal acceptance of pragmatism would not endanger the freedom of the pragmatist nor scholasticism the freedom of the scholastic, for each defines freedom within the thought patterns of its own system. However, when freedom is not defined as a way of life dictated by a system of philosophy, but as a way of life moving to unpredictable ends that emerge out of the cross-fertilization of a diversity of philosophies, the very diversity becomes the critical condition of the creative emergence.

All of our philosophical systems themselves emerged in this manner, and all original theology, for this is the condition of originality. We can only conclude that freedom and all novel forms of the good cannot finally be defined nor captured in a logical system, for freedom derives from an extra-rational sentiment. This sentiment is characterized by a respect for all rational systems of proof and truth, and by a faith in the somehow rightness of all disciplined speculative thought —a right to be, a right to be heard and a right to make a difference in the world. The prominent prohibition respecting freedom of thought is this, namely, that no concept brings with it into the world the right to dominate the world; and no concept, however fortified by the process of reason, in any way accumulates this right. A state of freedom reveals itself in a kind of unending pilgrimage upon which a wide diversity of men embark and upon which they bear themselves toward one another with disciplined imagination and sufferance to the end of mutual enlightenment.

There are many throughout the world, and some in our own country, who lament the fact of our avowedly pluralistic culture. At best, they say, cultural pluralism is a way-station on the road to the good society. At worst, it is a positive block to the attainment of the good society. As a way-station, it is thought of as a kind of compromise situation that will probably have to be endured until we can get widespread commitment to a system of genuinely authenticated truth. Many prominent representatives of each of the major systems of thought are in agreement on the fact that diversity of belief is no belief at all. It is simply self-evident to such men that when any society or social institution claims eulogistically to embrace a rich diversity of philosophies, what it really is embracing is an intellectual hodge-podge. From their point of view, the whole thing is a bit ludicrous to contemplate, a society deriving its values and taking its direction from numerous differing and conflicting philosophies forever contending with one another. This is surely a picture of the man mounting his horse and riding off in all directions. Even when the members of such a society are not contentious, the whole situation is untenable, for they then gather in confused and sentimental groups and credulously pledge vague agreement in the very midst of all their unresolved differences. Neither the committed behavior on the one hand nor the academic mind on the other finds such an ambiguous state of affairs very congenial. The first insists upon a clear and solid belief. The second must at least insist upon logical consistency. And both are commonly prepared to correct this lamentable state of affairs, the true believer with his own true faith and the scholar with his own true theory. Yet, after each has thus exercised his freedom, the result is again diversity.

The Two Unresolved Beliefs in American Culture

The foregoing may serve to point up a critical fact in American history, namely, that we are a people with two largely unresolved beliefs. We believe in freedom of thought and conscience, and the inevitable pluralism which eventuates from the exercise of this freedom; and we believe in the limitations of thought to fundamental truth and the common acceptance of that truth throughout the social order. We believe in freedom of thought and cultural pluralism; and we believe in the authority of truth over man and in cultural monism. Whenever freedom of thought and conscience is endangered by the surreptitious spread of Marxism, pragmatism, or some evangelistic particularism throughout the public schools, we hold forth for cultural pluralism. No one truth may be taught to all! The freedom and rights of the individual conscience are set above what we then call "the so-called truth" of any one body of believers. But whenever we look out upon the nation or the world and behold the waste and suffering of a struggling humanity at cross purposes with itself, we put truth above man, call upon man to embrace "a common faith" and realize the benefits of cultural coherence. On the one hand there must be freedom and diversity. On the other, there must be a common authority and homogeneity. Some men stand radically for the former. Some stand conservatively for the latter. Together they tend to constitute the tenuous balance that characterizes most societies that recognize the limited validity of each. Could it be that the wise in every culture stand in a state of tension between the two, both in their own lives and in the cultural conflict around them? Could it be that theirs is the function of mediation between authenticated truth and emergent truth when these are in conflict?

There is abundant evidence indicating that when the religious or political conservative holds violently for an authenticated concept and sets up prohibitions to its slightest change, he is exaggerating the unanimity of mind among the true believers and the state of perfection of the concept in his own mind. At the very moment of his intransigence scholars whom he reveres the most are very likely enriching the thought with overtones that had not occurred to him. Yet there is a psychological and sociological advantage to his emotionally charged exaggeration of the authenticity of his truth. It provides the conditions for a firm commitment by the mass of mankind whose mentality does not yet allow for a sufficient commitment in the absence of this very exaggeration. One of the leadership necessities of those ministering to the common man appears to be the consistent exaggeration of the finality of the truth to which they bear witness. Constantly bordering on the sin of pride, all leaders, from doctors of medicine to doctors of theology, are required by the public to presume to understand more perfectly than they do the truths they hold. If this public stance is not maintained, their followers move down the street to one who professes to represent unqualified knowledge without any disturbing humility or hesitation.

When the religious, political or educational liberal holds violently to novel ideas as inherently superior to all traditional ideas, when he deprecates authenticated truth as the dead hand of the past upon the present and glorifies the most recent innovative thought as the best, he is commonly exaggerating both the novelty of his concept and its power to bring forth its utopian promise. Again, at that very moment scholars whom he respects are probably tracing the history of his "new" notion and contemplating its probable ultimate effects, rarely Utopia. His exaggeration of the adequacy of his thought comes very naturally to him because it has come to him so recently in the heat and the excitement of creative thought, yet this gives no guarantee either of adequacy or of truth. If he is a zealous liberal, his disparagement of all things traditional often keeps the public from discovering how much he wants his view to become a tradition. Much of this is at the sacrifice of intellectual honesty but, again, it serves a psychological and sociological end, for the mass of mankind, as yet at least, responds only to exaggeration and over-simplification. Traditional truths must be made to seem more outmoded than they are, and the new truths more clear, simple, and adequate than in fact they are.

We are implying, of course, that the person serving primarily to conserve established values is, if he is wise, also sensitive to his limited understanding of those values and conscious of their inevitable imperfection as entertained by the finite mind of man. His study and self-examination never cease, and his faith is mature enough not to require an exaggeration of his knowledge to fortify his faith. And we are further implying that those persons primarily concerned with the re-examination and reconstruction of our established values and authenticated truths, if they are wise, will be sensitive to the fact that they do themselves spend much effort conserving and disseminating authentic values, that were it not for a certain permanence of established values personal emotional health would be impossible and cultural continuity unthinkable.

Finally, it is for the most enduring values attainable that both the wise liberal and conservative are in quest. Hence, the two faiths in American culture are always in tension but not necessarily in conflict. The conservatories of theological systems of thought do not propose to lose them nor let them stagnate any more than quite other conservatories of established symphonic works intend to lose them or let them stagnate. Both are constantly alert for more authentic interpretations and for varying degrees of innovation, provided the original not be lost. Similarly the wise liberal in institutions of liberal learning will recognize that without repositories of truth and value, he would lack the substantial stuff with which the creative and critical mind deals—substantive systems of belief forming diverse patterns in culture.

Social Institutions Expressive of Our Two Faiths

We have spoken of the two faiths in American culture, the faith in freedom and the faith in commitment—freedom of the individual for independent and novel thought leading to cultural diversity, and commitment to an authenticated system of belief leading to cultural unity and coherence. We have attempted to equate this with the liberal mind given primarily to the reconstruction of inherited values and the conservative mind given primarily to the perpetuation and dissemination of those values. We have pressed the point that while these two mentalities are often in conflict in culture, both the conserving and innovative mind are necessary in the free society and that the conservatives and the liberals at their best recognize this fact. It is suggestive to continue this parallelism to social institutions. Are there social institutions that are primarily concerned with commitment to established truth and other institutions that are primarily concerned with the critical re-examination of these claims to truth? Are there social institutions that meet the two dominant needs of men, the need to believe and the need to inquire, the need to associate with the like-minded and the need to associate with those of unlike minds, the need to embrace knowledge in the form of a commitment and the need to embrace it simply for enlightenment?

Without too great straining to fit the categories, we may reasonably say that there do appear to be many such social institutions. They do not appear to have been self-consciously evolved to serve these ends, and they do not stay as properly in their categories as the theorist could wish, but their dominant function is still distinguishable. The number of societies, unions, parties and institutions characterized by common belief is legion. Varying greatly in discipline, each has a central purpose and belief, or pattern of purposes and beliefs, to which each member owes his loyalty. He is pledged to public commitment and the furtherance of the views of the organization. Internal dissension there may be, but whether religious denomination, political party or labor union, if the members do not pull together, the association soon dissolves. Too many to enumerate are the benefits from the association of the like-minded. In all such associations, loyalty to fellow members and to their common beliefs is their highest virtue and primary obligation.

We now may ask if there are any social institutions in which men come together not primarily because they are alike but because they are different. Are there any institutions in which the primary goal is to embrace as great a cultural diversity as possible? One must concede that such institutions are relatively rare. One thinks of leagues of nations, of the United Nations, or better, of UNESCO; yet these are not very convincing. Members of such organizations already have a primary allegiance. They may believe that such organizations are necessary to overcome strife or they may believe that they should come together to see if they can unite on some universal principles and thus overcome their troublesome diversity, but the great majority of them cannot be said to gather to celebrate the *benefits* of their diversity.

The liberal universities of the world, on the other hand, may be just such institutions. When living up to their finest traditions, they constitute a community of scholars representing as wide a range of disciplines as possible, and within each discipline a generous range of philosophies. It was in this tradition that the department of philosophy at Harvard in the time of James, Royce and Santayana met to select an addition to their staff and agreed that the addition should enrich the department by representing a philosophy different from any of theirs. He was to be competent and scholarly of course, but also he must be different. To be so literal about this as to insist that no two members of a university or staff entertain the same philosophy would be ridiculous of course. But to have men all of the same philosophy would leave us with a parochial, not a liberal university. Here, then, is one institution that believes the life of the mind depends upon a rich diversity of thought. Ideally, all languages and all cultures are studied with the teachers themselves often drawn from those cultures. History, literature and philosophy are variously and diversely interpreted. The musical, pictorial and plastic arts are variously conceived. Mathematics and the sciences are not only studied but in process of creation. Ideally, again, these disciplines cross-fertilize both in the student body and in the staff. Truth is the goal and enlightenment is the product, and in the midst of cultural diversity the university is also a distinctive kind of community providing for what Hutchins has aptly called "the great conversation."

It is interesting to note the suggestive parallel here between the university and the free society. Both embrace many social and religious philosophies and both hold it a point of honor never wholly to subscribe to any one of these. The university not only promotes the study of the customs, beliefs and organizations of knowledge of the world, it encourages into being those large organizations of thought which represent man's major attempts to capture the truth. It does not even dismiss those who feel that they have finally captured it. However, it steadfastly refuses to commit itself exclusively to any one rendition of truth. Rather, it continues its sponsorship of criticism.

A liberal university is unalterably pluralistic not because it does not know any better but because this is the best it knows. Within the university are many coherent organizations of thought that are logically consistent and make over-all sense. But taken as a whole, the university itself is neither coherent, nor logically consistent, nor does it literally make over-all sense. From time to time this is more than the systematic academic mind can bear, and an academician will seriously propose the adoption of some one central philosophy by the university, hoping thereby to rescue it from its faithless dilemma by urging his own commitment upon it. But to acquiesce in any such proposal would sound the knell of liberal learning.

The Mutual Accommodation of Cultural Variants in the Public School

Perhaps the only other avowedly pluralistic social institution of any magnitude in American culture is the public school. Its sponsors have always felt that there was some particular virtue in the fact that it is open to all of the children of all of the people. Ideally, and oftentimes in fact, the public school in the United States embraces the complete range of social diversity relative to race, religion, sex, and levels of intelligence. Sometimes exchange students are present from other nations as they more commonly are in our institutions of higher education. This adds one further note of diversity and is considered that much more desirable.

What is the positive virtue associated with this cultural pluralism? Our history and the literature on this subject show very clearly that we are seeking to resolve one of the oldest problems of mankind. *We are seeking the mutual accommodation of man to man.* If strangeness, artificiality and misunderstandings tend to occur between the sexes because of their differences, we have inclined to the notion that to work, to play and to plan together will help to resolve the conflicts that arise from these differences. If alienation and hostility arise because of the natural differences of race, we have come to feel that daily living together will relieve these tensions. So also with the different levels of inherited ability. These are all inevitable and proper differences, and it should be self-evident that the public school does not aspire to change them nor presume to correct them. The races, the sexes, the variations in ability and temperament are differences which promise to be with us permanently.

Are ideological differences as native to mankind and as inevitable as these? Is it also in the nature of things for man to differ philosophically, religiously? Or if it is only an unfortunate tendency for mankind to differ ideologically, should we attempt to correct at least this one difference in the human family in the interests of insuring the brotherhood of mankind? Is it possible that, unlike our differences in race or sex, our ideological differences might all be resolved? Many have answered affirmatively, that it is indeed unfortunate we are confronted not only with inferior races but inferior religions, and indeed an inferior sex. These differences, it has been held, must be corrected where possible and where this is not possible, the inferior variant must be subordinated to the controlling dominant. This, in effect, would do away with the wrong one. Hence races have been officially subordinated, and sexes, and classes, and religions. And the whole problem is still far from being resolved. Yet the central tendency of public education in the United States is clear even though often violated and often contested. It has assumed that the natural variations of man, including his pronounced ideological differences, are not to be eradicated by the public schools but accepted by them. They are not to be deprecated by the public schools but, in fact, to be respected. They are not to be considered an obstruction to education; they are to be viewed, rather, as the condition of education. This is popularly sensed but not widely understood.

The reason this view is not widely understood is that it is a very difficult insight that, as a people, we are still struggling to attain. We know how to embrace a tribalistic, a parochial, a partisan belief absolutely. Some know how to entertain a noble and elevated commitment sacrificially. But most of us still don't know how to feel, behave and think when confronted by a different, an alternative, a conflicting commitment. We know what we believe and what we are opposed to, but we don't know how to conduct ourselves in the presence of a sincere and dedicated opposition. In the final analysis, we don't know how to conduct ourselves emotionally or intellectually under the conditions of cultural diversity. The all-too-common result is that we doggedly affirm and we resolutely attack. We understand the requirements of commitment better than the requirements of freedom. In a land given to both faith and freedom, we have more clubs, societies, parties, denominations involving us in a common commitment than we have institutions cultivating in us the capacity for the mutual accommodation of our differences. It is here that the public school and the liberal college may play a distinctive role. They may substitute enlightenment for hearsay relative to our differences, facilitate the creative accommodation of those differences, and introduce a sense of responsibility for the mutual sufferance of differences lying beyond our powers of rational resolution.

The forbearance and sufferance of others whose activities and interests are at variance with ours is a form of accommodation that contributes to the maturity and character of every man. Learning to respect a man of faith in a faith different from our own adds a deeper dimension to faith. Yet accommodation through forbearance, significant as this is, is not the primary benefit of cultural pluralism in our public schools. The primary benefit is to be found in the creative engagement of the differences. It is this cross-fertilization of the sufficiently different through which the mind gives birth to the energizing ideas of every age. This is why it is the *sine qua non* of every institution of liberal learning that it engage the widest possible variety and fear like the plague an official or state declaration of a single unifying ideology.

The public school in a free society is ideally designed to promote a climate of fruitful inquiry and a spirit of mutual accommodation. The quality of life sought is ethical, some would say religious. It contributes to the good life in a unique way but in a way endorsed by all high religion. It teaches what institutions of faith and commitment also seek to teach but, in one respect, are not designed to teach as effectively. Each has its own province and neither can properly do the work of the other. There is a better reason than a practical or pragmatic one for the separation of church and state.

Most mature religious or secular philosophies have a provision for loving their enemies, for embracing their opposites or for engaging differences. But the history of particular beliefs reveals that this is the redeeming element that too commonly drops out of the empirical church and sectarian religion. Conflicts at every level creep into daily living because the positive and dogmatic commitment outweighs the religious admonition to love, to suffer and to forbear. The sin of pride, the inertia of habit, and inordinate self-love conceal themselves in an arbitrariness of orthodox commitment, and war in the spirit prevails. In theology, as in philosophy, it does not lie within the nature of any logically consistent system of thought to approve what it precisely disapproves. Moreover, there is a human tendency for homogeneous groups, along with all the good they do, to stand with over-weening pride upon the niceties of their limited human logic and upon the comfort of their ingrained habits. This is the paradox of life, that every man must have a commitment which he commonly must celebrate with others of like mind, but this common commitment which is so necessary to mental health and the life of the spirit, and so necessary as a religious and ethical foundation and center for most men, all too often loses its spiritual vitality and, in the course of time, becomes ingrained, matter-of-fact and arbitrary.

In order to foster the growth of the human spirit in general, and the faith of the individual in particular, the public school and the liberal college must, paradoxically, confront the student with the faith of man in its manifold forms, provoke each to a reassessment of his own faith and drive each back into the vitalities of his own ideological tradition. He then entertains his faith in a different spirit from one who simply inherits his beliefs and who has heard only vaguely that there are others, for he has gone through the hazard of living with others, of learning to respect them, and of learning about their faiths. He has had an adventure in enlightenment in which he has also heard his own faith sympathetically presented to others, of seeing his friends' faces lighten with understanding, of discovering himself at home with them in a new and deeper sense. And now he has two homes where the light of love falls—his church, his synagogue, his mosque, his temple—and his school. He has discovered the brotherhood of man and wholesome acceptance under a new condition, under the condition of cultural diversity. Especially if his is a minority faith, he suddenly discovers a new dimension of freedom.

Official religious bodies are sometimes more sophisticated in these matters than many professional educators are prepared to believe. Unmitigated and unenlightened sectarianism does not always characterize the thinking of the confessed sectarian. For instance, in a section on "The Church and School Among Free Peoples," we hear the Presbyterian Church saying,

> There are certain principles common to the Church and to the public schools. Motivated by these principles the Church has become increasingly responsible in strengthening its support of the public school which:
>
> 1. Views the intrinsic worth of the child as the object of its deepest devotion and

2. Acknowledges that all truth can stand questioning and can only be shown to be true when questioned, and thus insists that the search for truth must be undertaken and unfettered. (2)

. . . .

The public schools in particular are shaped by the deliberate effort to respect the integrity of every child and to encourage the widest freedom and discussion in the child's search for truth. Having this character, they are an unrivaled agency for meeting the needs of all our people individually and our national society as a whole. (3)

There are, of course, both lay and clerical minds that would prefer their religion safe rather than vital, sheltered rather than challenged, inherited rather than achieved. For let us confess that intellectual and social confrontation of differences does provoke modification in all innocent and sheltered parochialism. Any good theological seminary does the same. But religious scholars of the major faiths appear to be growing in the conviction that their particular faiths enjoy a vitality and strength in the free society that they lose in the one-religion state even when their own particularism is the official faith. As Radhakrishnan says:

A study of other living religions helps and enhances the appreciation of our own faith. If we adopt a wider historical view, we obtain a more comprehensive vision and understanding of spiritual truth. Christian thinkers like St. Thomas Aquinas were willing to find confirmation of the truths of Christianity in the works of pagan philosophers. (4)

PART II

Discovering the Universal Human in the Universal Public School

Upon his return from Europe the then President Conant of Harvard wrote with heightened insight upon the intangible influence of our public school system in American culture. What impressed him was what he, like the rest of us, had grown so accustomed to it that its significance tended to be lost upon him. He spoke of the unconscious and mutual accommodation of class, cast, race, religion that tends to take place silently in the public schools. We are reminded that those differences in the human community that constantly threaten social alienation, misunderstandings and conflict are often softened at their source in a way that we no longer appreciate. Simply the physical fact of living, working, playing together appears to establish a sense of the common humanity among the most divergent of men. They discover what the anthropologists have recurrently discovered among the wide racial and cultural variations of primitive peoples. Being men, they all know gentleness, and loyalty, and wonder; they all know fear, and hope, and faith; they all know hate, and envy, and greed. And they all live in a universe they did not create, over which they do not have adequate control and the final end and purpose of which they do not wholly understand. Living together with a responsibility for mutual accommodation to one another in the public school appears to develop a sense that all partake of the universal human traits in about the same proportions, and it becomes very difficult for their elders to prove, as they sometimes attempt to do, that a certain race is not wholly human, that a certain religion is believed in only by evil or ignorant men, and that certain social classes lack virtue, or industry, or intelligence. The elder is talking about Joe or Mary, and the child may not answer back, but he is not persuaded. He may agree not to marry the difference, but he won't agree not to respect it. The public school has worked its subtle alchemy within him and he will never be the same. The Negro leadership knows this great truth and knows that racial prejudice cannot be removed with the best-intentioned argument. But let the children live together under the responsibility of mutual accommodation, and the common humanity of races is proved beyond all argument.

Concerning the common humanity of man as a transcendent value to be sought throughout the world, Robert Ulich illuminates the subject with these words:

> What matters is that all, an Arabian horseman and an American flyer, a Chinese child and a French schoolboy, a Communist worker in Russia and a mechanic at a Ford plant, can have hours in their lives when they no longer are Arabian or American soldiers, Chinese or French youth, Communist or democratic workmen, but men in whom love and responsibility suddenly burst forth with a power beyond the contingency of cultures, nations, and political systems. Not only through truth, but also through action men can become the vessel of the ground of being, wherever they live.
>
> If men of diverse backgrounds were not given the possibility of uniting in a common ground, there would be no humanity in the deeper sense. For by the term humanity we mean not merely the sum total of all human creatures, but a value: men overcoming the differences of languages and cultures by their sense of unity. (5)

This discovery of at-oneness with those distant from and different from us is a manifestation of the religious dimension of man. It is in this high sense that the public school is religious in its intent. Like all human institutions, the school has often failed in this aspiration and defeated its own purpose. Yet with all its failures we must still confess that the professional stance of teacher education and of teachers in the last generation has been touched with an ethical overtone which has come to characterize our public schools. They are places where it is widely taken for granted that young people will grow in mutual respect for one another and in the gradual accommodation of their differences. This has been the great achievement, on the ethical side, of the last generation, and credit goes to none more than to the thought and teaching of John Dewey and the progressive educator. Where we are still failing in too large a measure is in the religious enlightenment of our teachers.

The Lack of Religious Enlightenment in Teacher Education

There is little doubt that our teachers' knowledge of the religious beliefs and practices of the children they face in the classroom is seriously limited. Most departments of education, like the colleges and universities that house them, make relatively little provision for the religious enlightenment of their students. A prospective teacher may enter many of our major universities and colleges with an essentially innocent and folklore understanding of the role of religion in Western Culture. He may also be essentially ignorant both of his own religious tradition and lamentably misinformed about others. If he wishes to repair these defects in his general education, the university is commonly unable to help him. It proffers adequate enlightenment in most other major concerns of the culture; but in this one, if he comes ignorant, he often leaves in essentially the same condition.

This is something of an exaggeration, for knowledge is ideally all of one piece, and if any student has studied one field thoroughly, he has touched upon all the rest. But practically speaking our teachers are as religiously illiterate as they are either because those subjects and those core experiences which largely constitute their education were not studied deeply enough or the topic was quietly avoided even when it was relevant to the subject in hand. There has been a good deal of this latter for two reasons.

One reason for the relatively silent treatment of religion in secular institutions of learning is traceable to the earthly church and its churchmen. Many of these have felt that religion is not to be treated as one of the liberal disciplines of the university to be studied primarily for enlightenment; rather, it has been considered a subject to be studied only under parochial auspices for commitment. It is thus held to be more properly a subject for belief than for inquiry. Looked upon in this light, even a sympathetic and appreciative treatment of religion leads merely to "knowledge about" rather than "faith in." Many institutions of higher learning have taken the churchman at his word and formal offerings in religion have been deleted from the curriculum.

There is at least one other discernible reason for the absence of a study of religion in teacher education. Many secularists, humanists, and naturalists have translated essential religious teachings into secular, professional and academic language and have made these the substance of the good life in schools of teacher education. The gospel of love is translated into mutual respect for the persons and ideas of others, and teachers are taught to create an atmosphere of affectionate understanding and permissiveness in the classroom. Forbearance and sufferance reappear in professional language as accommodating our interests to those of others in such a spirit as to maintain good will and a democratic spirit in the group. The sin of pride becomes an admonition to remember the limitations of one's own desires and arbitrary convictions in order to correct one's own faults and limitations. Loving one's enemies is reintroduced as the paradox in the free society of cherishing the propriety of honest opposition in all things from sports, through political views, to ultimate commitments, and the need for mediation of all conflict, interpersonal, national, and international. Even the worship of a finally unknown God is translated into an act of secular faith and becomes a wondering, thoughtful and dedicated inquiry into the ultimate mystery of knowledge and the meaning of life. Many a churchman has sensed that in his academic and professional life he finds a reinforcement of his sectarian faith, and that in his sectarian worship he finds the ultimate sanction for his secular ideals. And many of naturalistic and humanistic bent have found their faith in secular philosophies which embody their own ennobling ideals.

Judeo-Christian Ethics and Religiosity Often Permeate the Public School

The active ethics of Christianity do literally and properly permeate the public school, but the ultimate sanction of the Christian religion must not. And Christian ethics commonly permeate the public schools because most of the teachers are Christians, and those who are thoughtfully and genuinely religious live their religions day by day. Their personalities permeate the school and determine the atmosphere of the classroom. Ideally, they are not preaching religion and they are not teaching religion but are, in varying degrees, the living embodiment of it. As one comes to know such teachers, he discovers that he is dealing with people of indubitable religious quality. One cannot prove this as he lives with them over the years and watches their influence on young people; he rather knows it in the same incontestable way that one knows he is loved over the years. And one often discovers the religious quality of such teachers before he discovers the particular religion or sect to which they belong. Many are committed churchmen and some strangely are not but are reminiscent of the prophets, essentially unchurched, but dedicated and solitary seekers of the way. In either case, children who have the privilege of living with them come to know the joy of life generously lived, richly shared, and thoughtfully ordered. Such people partake of the health-giving qualities of Jesus of Nazareth, the great teacher and healer of both body and soul. Perceptive parents are forever grateful to give their children into the hands of such as these, for in their hands the children's fears and anxieties are quieted, their faith in themselves and their world restored, their physical health improved, and no one knows how much of virtue is insured for the future. These exemplifications of a living faith constitute the spiritual substance of education at every level, but we are left in doubt whether one sect of the Christian faith is productive of more persons of religious quality than another. Indeed, there is reason to question whether the Christian religion elicits more of this quality than Judaism, or whether Judaism holds a higher percentage of genuinely religious persons than Buddhism or Islam.

Gandhi, not a Christian, was a convincingly religious man in the eyes of many authentic Christians. Many who knew John Dewey speak of his essentially religious quality. We think of Martin Buber and of Albert Schweitzer in this way also. And rare is the public school system that does not contain within it humble but spiritually convincing teachers as unheralded by the world as piety commonly is. This recalls again the second reason why there is so much of what the Christian thinks of as Christian ethics in the school. Most of the Judeo-Christian ethics are universal, adopted almost in their entirety even by the humanists.

Growth in personal, social, or intellectual maturity hardly sounds like a concept embodying the ethics of the Judeo-Christian tradition to many churchmen. Is it not true, however, that, beginning with the sand box in the kindergarten, the child is progressively encouraged in parochial and public schools alike to become less and less egocentric. He is taught to consider others and share his little possessions. As he moves through the educational system, he is asked to enlarge his understanding and his sympathies to include others quite different from himself. In literature at all levels he is asked to live sympathetically within others' lives and realize life from many perspectives. In all his general studies he goes abroad, so to speak, and lives with all the peoples of the world with a kind of affectionate regard to the end that his original egocentricity is transcended, and he becomes a more understanding, more cultured and more compassionate man. Inasmuch as the end and aim of all education worthy of the name is wisdom and virtue, many of our great-hearted humanistic teachers in the public school and in the teacher education colleges conduct themselves in relation to their students in such a way that all are convinced of their essentially religious quality. Such persons viewed from the Christian perspective appear to be Christian and to be having the effect on others that one would expect from Christians. Likewise the naturalist often mistakes the Christian teacher for a good naturalist and is amazed to learn that the teacher bears himself thus toward the students and the world upon the basis of a Christian rationale.

Considering the pluralism of the public schools and of the American culture, many teachers have discovered that the ends of religion are better served by *being* religious rather than *talking* about it or literally *teaching* it. This is not all there is to religion, for worship in ceremony and in song, and commitment to a deposit of particular beliefs are also the condition for religious living for many. Yet the separation of church and state as a general working policy in the history of our country appears to indicate that school is the place for all the non-sectarian ethical living and religious quality we can attain and the church is the place for sectarian teaching and worship.

Too often the public schools have not lived up to this ideal, indeed, not even held such an ideal. Instead of being secular in the best sense, they have been secular in the worst sense. There have been schools and teachers colleges whose influence has been culturally divisive. They have defeated their own high purposes by being anti-religious, anti-church, anti-God. They have both deleted religious subject matter from subjects in which it properly occurred, and at other times have gone out of their way to deprecate things religious. But considering the dominance of Judeo-Christian thought in both small and in large communities throughout this country, one wonders if such conditions are as common as some would have us believe.

A perceptive statement on this whole problem has been made by one Christian group which will find support from many of the more discerning in each of our major faith groups.

> . . . Some feel that because a school does not teach a particular belief, proclaim a special theological tenet, nor yet engage in a special religious exercise, such omission is evidence of its godless nature. We believe it must be remembered that the inclusion of an overt observance of religion does not necessarily provide any institution with a dynamic religious character.
>
> . . . .

> We object, therefore, to unwarranted criticism heaped upon the schools without adequate understanding of the position that the schools hold in the structure of our society. Lack of understanding of their front-line importance and ingratitude for the deep dedication of the average school teacher who clings to profound respect for the child, home, and church have led to the voicing of the reckless charge of "godlessness" in the public schools. (6)

PART III

This chapter has taken the position that cultural pluralism is the condition of the free society but that pluralism leads only to conflict and disunity unless men believe in and have developed a competency for mutual accommodation. This calls for the development of both an intellectual dimension and a religious dimension. On the intellectual side, it calls for knowledge of alternative beliefs and philosophies, the capacity for reconstructing our ideas responsibly, and the ability and disposition to engage in disciplined controversy. On the religious side, it calls for the capacity for seeing the good in life as often transcending or contradicting one's personal interests, and it calls for a religious maturity that provides for the sufferance of one's opposition without malice. To attain freedom in diversity requires a religious quality of life manifesting itself in the spirit of the interpersonal engagement. When human relations are touched with charity, the participants discover that they are free in a way that cannot be legislated, a freedom in the midst of stimulating intellectual exchange equalling the freedom of solitary thought. Only men characterized by some such implicit religion can really enjoy freedom of inquiry in the presence of honest difference. When this religious quality is absent, ulterior motives obtrude, and the impulse to dominate another with one's own ideas defiles the free flow of thought. One then engages in the power struggle with ideas as his weapons and the defeat of his adversary as his end. In such contests we have the show of intelligence and the power of thought revealed, but freedom of inquiry is commonly lost to the spirit of containment and conquest.

Three Conditions for Cultivating and Freeing the Human Spirit

We have suggested three ways in which the schools may reasonably expect to free the human spirit. First, schools which enroll the rich range of diversity in our culture must use this cultural variety as an educational resource by employing it as an aid both in enriching learning and by promoting the spirit of mutual accommodation. Second, the teachers of the future who are more informed about the religious beliefs and practices in American culture must employ this knowledge in such a way as to teach a mutual respect for one another's beliefs without attempting to commit students to one belief over another. Third, the schools of the future must strive to attain a more convincing religious dimension by putting more teachers in the classroom who are characterized by religious quality and hence more inclined to communicate implicit religion to their students.

The three conditions for freeing and cultivating the human spirit are, then, the acceptance of diversity of belief as desirable, the furtherance of religious enlightenment and the manifestation of more implicit religion. If one wishes to promote these three conditions in teacher education, one might discover that providing for ideological pluralism in the faculty is primarily an administrative concern, that providing for religious enlightenment is primarily a curricular matter, and that the cultivation of a religious quality is primarily a problem in methodology. Whether the administrative responsibility is carried by the dean alone or shared with the staff, one of the deliberate administrative concerns is providing for a balanced variety of views on the faculty. With respect to religious enlightenment, courses may be added to the curriculum or present course content may be modified in order to provide substantive knowledge in the subject matter of religion. Implicit religion, on the other hand, is elicited by one's mannner or method of teaching. Ideally, the proper method calls for a spiritual relationship between the student and teacher and is characterized by an imaginative flowing out of contagiously held ideas whose overtones bespeak both a compassionate concern for the person of the student and for the spirit of learning. This is the "I-Thou" relationship in education so perceptively defined by Martin Buber. (7)

If these are the conditions for bringing "the religious" into public education, then colleges interested in the more adequate education of teachers must ask themselves how they may impart to their students the qualities of mind and the knowledge they wish to see in the public school children of the nation. The answer to this falls into two parts, the general and the specific, or better, the intangible and the tangible.

In what has come to be the big business of education, we naturally tend to restrict ourselves to the what and the how, forgetting that the spirit in which the what and the how are imparted is the intangible which determines the success of our teaching. The demand for an increased emphasis upon religion in our schools stems more from a desire to change the character of our students for the better than from a desire to increase their factual knowledge of religion. What is widely sought is a more convincing religious quality in their lives. It is a failure in virtue that disturbs the nation. This may very well be related to knowledge about religion but it is not synonymous with it. When we look into teacher education, therefore, our inquiry must be directed both at the institution's ability to teach the relevant factual knowledge of religion as well as its capacity to impart a religious quality to its students. This is to say that in teacher education as in public education, we are interested not only in knowledge but in character. Before looking at the more specific changes a college should make in order to increase the religious knowledge of its prospective teachers, we will consider one of the intangibles of a teacher education faculty, its character.

The Character of the College and the Teaching of the College

We discover that suddenly our inquiry sounds unprofessional, for the self-assessment of a staff with respect to its own character is one of the unmentionables of teacher education. Yet it is the character of a staff from which emanates the over-all atmosphere or temper that envelops the students throughout the college. Every institution has a character of its own, an intangible environment which is as important a factor in the student's preparation for teaching and for living as the tangible environment. This character may greatly promote or largely defeat the ostensible purposes of teacher education. If we wish to prepare teachers who have a religious dimension, who come to look upon the cultivation of their own characters as indispensable to effective teaching, the character of our college must be of such a nature that it elicits this spiritual dimension in the students.

The first disturbing fact we immediately confront is that the direction in which the values of students are changed is not always under the control of the faculty. Sometimes students are actually inclined toward values contrary to the faculty's explicit intent.(8) It is understandable, however, that a failure of morale on the part of a staff would be communicated to the students regardless of avowed staff ideals to the contrary. When a staff is lacking in the capacity or genuine desire to maintain a spirit of mutual accommodation in the midst of its differences, it may verbally espouse forbearance or cooperation, but it may really be teaching the opposite by example. The spiritual demoralization of a staff results from a variety of things, but nothing deteriorates the character of any faculty more than the academic power struggle. With the academic man this often takes the form of dominating his colleagues with ideas, or the whole college with an idea. The result is represented in the language of elevated aspiration in many cases, but the faculty is actually suffering from a form of academic authoritarianism. As would be expected, a pecking order is often established which would be more appropriate in a barnyard than in a teachers college.

From time to time the academic power struggle breaks out into the open and the battle is joined between persons, departments, areas. Hostility and anxiety abound even when the struggle is covert. Many faculties, Christian-realist and pragmatist-progressive alike, have tacitly accepted this state of affairs while openly professing doctrines which deplore it. Much of the problem arises from the notion that man is morally obliged to make the "right" view prevail or dominate rather than maintaining a balanced variety of views. On every faculty as in every nation there are, of course, a plethora of "rights." Man not only has the animal impulse to dominate but he also has a belief that it is good for him to dominate when he is "right," and he is "right" an inordinate amount of the time.

The students are quick to sense conflict, tension, and hostility among members of a staff. Sometimes they find themselves in between and get hurt. Sometimes they smile inwardly to see how small such reputedly big men are. Sometimes they are bewildered and watch the show with disbelief. Its effect on students is doubtless as varied as the students themselves, but of one thing we can be reasonably sure. They are learning two things from their professors. They are learning the religious or the democratic theory of life formally, and they are also learning how life is *really* lived. They probably become more like their professors in both respects. They develop greater intellectual and social sophistication, and they mature a "realistic" view of how differences of opinion really are resolved in the battle of life. A veneer of culture and religious theory, skills with which to make a living and this kind of worldly wisdom is what they have learned at college.

It is not commonly thought of in this way, but a failure of character on the part of a faculty manifests itself as a failure of mutual accommodation. In the midst of their differences they cannot forbear, they cannot suffer one another. A course on religion is easily added, or units on religion in a number of courses, but to put on a living demonstration of forbearance and generous accommodation would call for a change of character. This, many staffs not only cannot do, they cannot want to do. This simply is not a professional concern; it is one of the intangible unmentionables. Yet, with respect to effective education, as well as the religious dimension of a college, it is of the essence.

Moreover, this is an almost universal professional objective *of* the college *for* the primary school and the public school in general! The pupils, it seems, are little egocentric animals that must learn to share, to cooperate and to work together in good spirit. Their differences must be accepted and not fought over. One of our enduring beliefs in education is that schools are designed to cultivate not only intellectual competence but intrinsic character. Teachers must reveal what we have chosen to call an intrinsic religious quality in order to impart it. This has come to seem reasonable to the professional educator. However, it appears somehow less reasonable to call attention to the failure of character on a college faculty and to want to do something about it.

The Administrative Agent and the Religious Dimension of the College

On the assumption that the administrator is desirous of cultivating the implicit religious dimension of the college, he becomes the primary agent for bringing it about. If he is himself a person of convincing integrity and is respected by the staff more for what he is and knows than for the power he has, he can sometimes accomplish as much with a college faculty as a teacher can with his pupils. He represents in himself the intangible he wishes to impart. Depending always upon the character potential of the staff, the wise administrator who is characterized by religious quality can create an atmosphere in the college by simply *being* what he is—so also the principal of his school and the teacher in his classroom. This indispensable intangible is an unquestioned power for good. The administrative mind at its best is balanced, thoughtful, judicious, and humane. Those who bring their problems to it know the resolution will be just and humane, and they come without anxiety or its counterpart, hostility. A spirit of give and take, of live and let live, grows within the staff. That half of the faculty's energies often consumed by anxiety and conflict flows into productive work. Barriers to communication on the staff are lowered and ideas are shared for common benefit rather than for the purposes of conquest or the ideological domination of others. The mental health of the staff improves.

Above all, a new disposition emerges with respect to staff differences. They discover that when entertained in a thoughtful, judicious and understanding manner, their seriously held differences actually enrich the program. They come to entertain the notion that the difference is not necessarily a threat, that a balanced *variety* of views are necessary if one really wishes to *educate* students. Only then does a student have the opportunity to listen to a representative range of well presented views. Only then is he introduced to the fact that the art and science of education is still very much unsettled, that there are very suggestive differences of opinion on curriculum, on method and on philosophy. With the background of such experiences the student is enabled to step into the problems and participate in the controversy. He has taken the most productive stance possible and one that should continue for the rest of his professional life, critical deliberation on the conflicting issues of education.

Only when we conclude that it is not possible to *educate* teachers, on the theory that they become confused and frustrated by the different views current in the profession, is it commonly considered most expedient just to *train* them, i.e., shield them from the whole problem and indoctrinate them in one best view of curriculum, method and philosophy. This enables the staff to present the student with a preplanned integration and then to conclude that the student will have an integrated view to guide him in his later professional life. When this view is held, it is logical to oppose the emergence of internal differences arising within the staff or the appointment to the staff of those who represent an alternative view of certain phases of the educative process.

Since, as a matter of fact, one educational party line cannot be maintained in the state universities of a free society, the avowed intent to limit freedom of inquiry by letting one mentality dominate the college creates the fundamental conflict that, to the best of our knowledge, cannot be resolved. It is the conflict between cultural pluralism and cultural monism. If our own society has decided anything it has decided that the latter is wrong. As was pointed out earlier in the chapter, no liberal university supported by public taxation may properly hold such a view. When it is attempted, as it frequently is, conflict and suffering result, and freedom of inquiry is jeopardized. This is the reason why the administration of a college must aim at cultivating the greatest diversity practicable, make room for every honest difference it can, and sincerely regret it when freedom to differ must be limited. Such an administrative intent makes the members of the staff feel that they are as free as practical circumstance will allow. However, it takes time to cultivate on any staff what some are destined never to attain, an intellectual and cultural sophistication which allows for the productive engagement of earnest difference.

Faculty Responsibility for the Engagement of Earnest Differences

It goes without saying that the administration alone does not have full responsibility for the cultivation of this disposition and this talent. Any staff member who holds himself to this standard improves the character of a faculty. And one of the finest ways in which the religious dimension of a staff is revealed to students is in a professor's disposition toward another of the student's professors with whom he has fundamental differences of opinion. If the students learn from each that the offerings of the other are important to their educational development and if each reveals a warm appreciation for the other's mind and integrity, the students will look forward to engaging the difference with anticipation and freedom from frustration and anxiety. Of course, charity toward one's intellectual adversaries does not preclude a good healthy tussle, just as sportsmanship in competitive games does not. Indeed, contests engaged in the right spirit often make friends of our adversaries. They should, for without an able and ingenious competition we could not learn the art either of intellectual or of physical fencing. But to make either an art rather than a battle, the spirit of sportsmanship toward one's opposition must obtain, for the spirit of sportsmanship requires, in the last analysis, that one care more for the engagement itself than for victory.

It is instructive to note that one who has matured a sense of sportsmanship prefers a competent opposition in deference to whom he may lose rather than incompetent adversaries over whom he can always win. This is interesting, for it means that he cares more for an opposition from whom he can learn than from one unable to challenge him to improve his skills, invent new ideas and cultivate new powers. The reason for this is that learning is fun too, often more fun than conquering another with one's wit or physical prowess. This is a manifestation of the religious dimension of life to be sought in physical education. One must learn to sustain an affectionate regard for what he is literally fighting, but what he is not fighting in the spirit. This is one of the forms which charity takes whether it is revealed in contests on the playing field, in faculty disputes or in a dynamic and positive administration.

There is reason to believe that much of the public has not yet learned to live at this level. It wants games that it can treat as little wars. It wants political contests carried on as angry fights characterized by abusiveness and hostility toward the opposition. It wants headlines to read, "Candidate Scores Victory." And it seems to prefer that professional debates in education be carried on with inordinate presumption on the part of each and mutual deprecation of one another. The wise and judicious mind is not very exciting to the mass of mankind that is drawn more to conflict than to mediation. But implicit religion manifests itself on a faculty only in the degree that its members mature the capacity to embrace other than their own ideas compassionately. And it is also revealed in the willingness to endure much that we cannot understandingly embrace.

Charity always transcends what we can rationally endorse. And since each of us rationally encompasses so small a portion of all there is, charity, forbearance and sufferance constitute the spiritual cohesive, binding man to man in a brotherhood beyond literal understanding. This is why implicit religion in human relations is absolutely essential in the free society. Its presumed absence in the communist state constitutes the fundamental difference in the quality of life between the free and the slave state, the liberal and the authoritarian university. If only avowedly Christian and democratic persons and nations were less inclined to rob others of their freedom in our own covert and cultivated pursuit of power, the distinction between the communist and the free state would be as clear to all as it now appears to us. Cultivating the capacity for mutual accommodation with all that this implies is the high aspiration of the schools in a free society. This on the one hand and disciplined knowledge on the other constitute the two indispensable ingredients of teacher education.

The Need for Religious Enlightenment in Teacher Education

We turn now to the problem of religious enlightenment, the problem of providing the prospective teacher an opportunity to gain an adequate knowledge of religion. Knowledge, like virtue, is something we never seem to have enough of in teacher education; but, as has been indicated earlier, our ignorance of religion and the role it plays in modern society is most impressive. That our teachers need a greater understanding of the influence of religion in the experience of children and in our culture would appear to be almost self-evident. There are many hopeful signs that we are beginning to repair this deficiency, (9) but the road to success in this matter appears to be long and difficult. The single most difficult barrier is the widespread attitude toward the study of religion current in most institutions of higher learning. It simply is not looked upon as an appropriate area of inquiry. It is neither one of the liberal disciplines nor one of the social or physical sciences. On the face of it, it would appear as if there really were no place for the study of religion in public institutions of higher learning.

Many academic men and many clergymen in the past have taken essentially this view. Particularly the Protestant clergy in the tradition of pietism have not looked upon religion as a proper subject of inquiry. This may very well be one of the reasons that Protestant Christian realists have not associated themselves with the national Philosophy of Education Association. They do not prepare papers for the national or regional conferences. Neither of the two yearbooks (10) of the National Society for the Study of Education which devote a chapter to each proposed philosophy of education in the United States contains a chapter presenting the views of the commonest single ideology in American culture. Each contains a competent chapter presenting the Catholic view, and each contains a chapter on Christian idealism. The more recent volume offers a sympathetic interpretation of the Marxist philosophy of education.

It is true that the history of this society shows a dominance of naturalistic thought, but it is equally true that the Catholic scholar and clergy have long been active participants and respected members and, like the Christian Idealists, brought their thought before the professional educator. Indeed, the presidency of the national association has been held by the Christian Catholic and the Christian Idealist. The result of this is that these philosophies have become a part of the academic working knowledge of the educational theorist. They appear in our educational textbooks in the area of theory. Why the Protestant scholar and clergy have absented themselves from the regional and national philosophy of education societies is a question that is more easily asked than answered. It could be answered that no *one* can speak for *all* of the Protestants, but this is equally true of almost all the philosophies represented in the association. Perhaps the Protestant scholars address themselves only to the church-related colleges, attend only their own educational conferences and write only for their own professional publications. Even their textbooks are written as if they were to be read by those already committed, written *by* those within the faith *for* those within the faith. This kind of parochialism makes them unsuitable for use in the liberal universities or colleges of a pluralistic society.

The results are clear. Their absence as persons at the conferences and the absence of their thought in the profession of education has become so customary as to be accepted without question. In educational theory, Protestant thought is not present and is not missed. In most courses in education it is omitted because it simply doesn't exist in the thought of the educator. It is included in history of education courses because it has a history, but it is omitted from courses in contemporary educational theory because it has no contemporary representation. Since most of the members of the profession are at least nominal Christians, it tends to get into the profession by osmosis. But the seeping in to the education of teachers of the Protestant Christian sentiment is not the way to introduce it in an institution of learning. Like everything else in the university, it must come in as, or be directly related to, an intellectual discipline, or it should stay out.

If religious thought is to be incorporated into teacher education in a significant way, it must come, initially, from significant religious scholars. In order to change the prevailing apathy of our dominantly secular colleges toward religious thought, there must appear at least one religious philosopher of genuine intellectual power and an abiding interest in public education. This is what John Dewey had, and his language and thought patterns have filtered down through the whole educational system. The power of ideas is inestimable. If a shift in the established thought patterns and sentiments of a profession are to be brought about by design, it can only be initiated by a great idea contagiously set forth. If a Reinhold Niebuhr had directed a portion of his intellectual powers and dynamic personality to the life-long task of creating a comprehensive Christian philosophy of education, it would have been discussed and debated throughout the last decades of teacher education. The literature in the profession would reveal that religious thought had become intellectually respectable. Theological concepts would have become a natural part of our professional language. Such a preoccupation with public education would establish a precedent which many young theologians would follow. Teachers colleges could then draw upon both secular and religious sources, and the students would discover the wide areas of agreement as well as certain of the inevitable differences. The profession would be enriched and an atmosphere created in which it would seem as natural to our teachers to take a course on Contemporary Religious Issues in American Culture as it would to take a course on Contemporary Political Issues.

The Religious Scholar and the State University

There are many who would hesitate to see distinguished religious scholars on the staff of a tax-supported institution. They suspect that those who want more religion in teacher education don't really want religious enlightenment, that this is simply the first step leading to the inclusion of the whole body of religion, sectarian instruction, worship, and ideological domination of education by theistic religious philosophies. This is a matter of practical judgment on which informed minds will take alternative views. It is unfortunately true that a great majority of those asking for more religion in teacher education and in our public schools are still thinking in sectarian or partisan terms. The Religious Education Association, a national organization made up of representatives from each of the major faiths, maintains a sophisticated but firm belief in what they have called "the sacred image of man" which they contrast with "the secular image of man." The sacred image of man as represented in the Judeo-Christian perspective is the image of man that they believe should be entertained by the state schools, teachers colleges and universities in American culture. Like the pragmatist-progressives in their day, they can see nothing wrong with the domination of the public schools by one philosophy just so long as this is the *right* philosophy.

Speaking to the national conference of this association, Professor Freeman Butts presented what many will doubtless consider the definitive statement for the profession on this question.

> This convention says there are two principle types of images—the secular and the sacred, and presumably we must choose between these as prototypes for education. We are asked to choose between the image of man as a creature of nature or a creature of God and to focus our attention for educational purposes upon one or the other. But I believe we cannot resolve the crisis or controversies in education by reaffirming this opposition or by hardening an antagonism between the religious and the secular.
>
> For the purposes of public education in a free society I think we need to look for another image or set of images. The image we need to find or to create anew is the image of the *free man* as he has been illumined from diverse sources over the centuries. The image of the free man . . . has sources in all branches of the family of man, in many religious faiths as well as in the secular life of the people. . . . From whatever source comes illumination for the image of the free man from that source should we draw to portray the goal for public education in America. (11)

Acknowledging the propriety of all partisan groups to press their own ends upon the state or the state schools, this chapter and this volume are convinced that the domination of public education either by a secular or by a sacred philosophy or faith would violate not only the spirit of liberal learning but of all high religion as well. It is admittedly difficult to argue for more religious enlightenment in education when the religious partisans are calling for total ideological conquest. Yet, they are not unlike other partisans throughout the culture. Each seeks the ear of the school for its own purposes. It would appear that our public institutions of higher learning are going to continue to resist such pressures successfully. The present chapter inclines to the notion that religious professionals do not constitute a clear and present danger to teacher education and that religious scholars should therefore enjoy the freedom of expression extended to other scholars. This clearly does not mean freedom to indoctrinate in tax-supported educational institutions.

To recapitulate, our purpose is never to be attained in any significant degree until 1. a religious scholar or scholars capture the imagination of the professional educator with illuminating contributions to education, 2. teacher education faculties put on better demonstrations of forbearance in their interpersonal relations where differences of opinion obtain, and 3. religious scholars are appointed to positions in colleges of education or the university at large and contribute to professional education from the resources of their own major discipline. But none of these things is going to happen tomorrow. Indispensable as they are, none of them can be simply decided upon and put into effect except the last, and it is not reasonable to suppose that this will occur to any significant extent in the near future.

A Popular Alternative to the Appointment of Religious Scholars in the University

An alternative to the appointment of religious scholars on the staff has been attempted by many colleges. Since there are many sincere churchmen in our colleges and universities, and their sentiments are of the best, it is often argued that these should get together and form a nucleus that an interested administration could develop. This looks promising at first glance, but the results are likely to be pretty dismal. The reason is that their religious feelings, interests and opinions are not entertained at an intellectual level. They clearly are not in command of an organized body of religious knowledge, yet they are surrounded by colleagues who, like themselves, are in command of other intellectual disciplines. In an institution of higher learning, they are simply incongruous. They commonly embarrass themselves out of being in as quiet and unobtrusive a manner as possible. This tends to reinforce the notion entertained by the rest of the faculty that religion is grossly out of place at the college level—and, as commonly conceived by such lay churchmen in the college, it most assuredly is. What we sometimes forget is that religious ideas entertained at the level of well-meaning volunteer groups in teacher education would be considered equally inadequate in comparable theological seminaries.

PART IV

Possible Next Steps: Inclusion of the Judeo-Christian Perspective in Philosophy of Education Courses

Granted, many attempts to advance religious enlightenment in teacher education have failed, and granted the prospect is not good for making the fundamental changes that would assure full success, there are still many approaches to the problem which show promise of limited success. In those colleges offering courses in philosophy of education, the educational philosophers should attempt to overcome the all-too-common limitation of their own preparation by studying religious philosophy for the same reason they study other philosophies—to enable them to give an appreciative and insightful presentation of the major interpretations of the Judeo-Christian view of life, and to develop suggestive implications for education. The whole meaning and purpose of education changes, as well as the significance of particular educational practices, when the educative process is looked upon through the eyes of different educational philosophers. Effective teaching cultivates an appreciative awareness of each, a sense of the integrity of each, and an appreciation for the contributions of each.

Looking at the problem strictly from an educational point of view, it is indefensible to omit the Judeo-Christian perspective. If one believes in teaching in terms of the experience of his students and wishes to capitalize upon their interest, one can walk right into their lives with the presentation of this philosophy. The presentation of every other position becomes more meaningful and more interesting for many students if one can present them in relation to a philosophy of life about which they already have some knowledge and a great deal of curiosity.

For those students who choose some interpretation of the Judeo-Christian perspective from which to view education, their professional life takes on enormously greater meaning and significance to them. Just as with students who identify themselves with other philosophies, their teaching becomes a means for realizing their most deeply felt understanding of the ultimate meaning of life. Students for whom a naturalistic philosophy is more congenial are also benefitted not only because they are informed but because they find themselves in an atmosphere which inclines them to an enlightened entertainment of a philosophy which they might otherwise lightly deprecate.

A course in comparative philosophy of education favors but does not assure the cultivation of a sentiment of accommodation. This is imparted more reliably by the instructor through the spirit in which he entertains each philosophical position. If in his own study he has captured the inspired vision of each, has had his own understanding lighted up by each, and if each casts a light on the teaching profession from a perspective not attainable by the other, all of this can be revealed in his teaching. Students find convincing truth and integrity in each, and they discover that the wise and good of the world are not all of the same persuasion. Most students discover that they have a kind of indwelling preference for one view of life over another, and such teaching of alternative views leaves them free to discover their own preference with a realized respect for the preference of others. When the educative process is so conceived, sufferance and forbearance under the conditions of cultural diversity are the natural fruits of enlightenment. Such teaching imparts both knowledge and a disposition toward knowledge which are the fundamental conditions of the accommodation of man to man.

History of Education: The Sacred or Secular View of Man?

In those institutions where there are offerings in the history of education, the intent of the teaching is essentially the same, although the content and organization are largely different. History of education can be taught as secular or as religious propaganda, and it very commonly is. Taught by an avowed or unwitting secularist, the evolution of Western thought is interpreted by secular criteria. The emergence of ideas and events which mark the growth of secularism and the decline of religious thought is considered to be progress. When taught as religious propaganda, the ideas and events of history are slanted in such a way as to lead to the opposite conclusion, that true progress only occurs when religious thought and institutions enjoy ascendancy over secular movements and institutions. The secularist and the religionist are often equally desirous to have history taught from a predetermined point of view. Each wants history honestly presented and is opposed to propaganda, which is the opprobrium each applies to the approach of the other.

The history of education professor in the tax-supported college cannot properly present history from either perspective exclusively. Like the philosophy of education professor, he most assuredly has a right to his own personal interpretation of history, but he does not have a right to impose his choice upon others. If he makes history of education live for his students, it will be because it already lives in him. Historical figures live in him, and he makes them and their ideas and their times live again for the students. This means that he must bring to life not only the persons, ideas, and movements which he approves; but, equally, he must bring to life the protagonist of as many views as his learning and imagination will allow. He does not resolve the conflicting educational views, trends, and movements for the students; he introduces students to them and puts them in possession of alternative resolutions. On the great issues of life history presents the great and diverse answers.

It is probably true that history of education in the state college and university has been taught dominantly from the secular point of view. Many sincere churchmen in the university have paradoxically taught history in this way. What we must become more aware of is that there is an intellectual dimension to religion in which concepts and principles are entertained with imagination and vitality. With no religious scholars on the staff, this becomes very difficult to realize. Yet to make history of education really live, religious principles of interpretation must be focused on the human scene. This illumination must be made to shine forth both from the past and from the present. An educational historian not in command of basic theological concepts can neither elicit them from the pages of the past nor focus them upon the problems of the present. But one who is so prepared can reveal the role of religion in culture in such a way as to give it an importance in the minds of students. This the avowed secularist can scarcely do even if he covers the same period, events, or men.

The history of education also affords opportunities to touch upon the fundamental beliefs of the great religions of the world in relation to contemporary beliefs. Contributions to the substantive knowledge of prospective teachers relative to religious beliefs and practices can be properly made by both history of education and philosophy of education. Religious knowledge is appropriately imparted in history of education courses wherever it is relevant to the fuller understanding of the subject in hand, and it may very well be more relevant than we have realized.

Educational Sociology and the Religious Dimension of Society

In educational sociology the student is again introduced to the fact of cultural pluralism and the problems of social accommodation. In fact sociology might be thought of as a science of social accommodation. Although educational sociology as one of the social sciences is dominantly secular, and properly so, it can still make very significant contributions both to the religious quality of students and to their religious enlightenment. Again, religious quality is imparted by the spirit in which inquiry is carried forward. Emotionally tinged prejudices and arrogant convictions are simply out of place in sociological inquiry. Students who come to this study properly disposed discover themselves in an atmosphere where controversial subjects are thought about rather than fought about. It is this contemplative spirit, this restrained forbearance, this spirit of inquiry, which we hope will take up residence in the prospective teacher and finally manifest itself in his own teaching.

Educational sociology is a study of social values, forces and institutions in relation to education. Religious institutions and their influence upon the social order and upon education are a natural subject of inquiry. This is an essentially secular study, as are many in the church-related college, but it should not be carried on from the point of view of an avowed secularist or an avowed religionist. When teaching for enlightenment, one does not aspire to proselytize. Approached in this spirit, students in a course in educational sociology may very properly study contemporary religions and religious institutions and their influence on the social order. In such courses more could be done to introduce our students to the religions which their future pupils will bring to their classes. Churches of the major faiths could be visited and upon such visits the clergy could define their essential beliefs, explain their religious ceremony and state their personal or the official church position on controversial social problems. Experiences of this nature tend to leave the prospective teacher with a more intimate feeling for the differing religious experiences of his pupils. If his aspiration is to teach in terms of the experience of his pupils, this knowledge is as relevant as any, yet it is often neglected.

As the realization grows that teachers should know more about contemporary religious beliefs and practices, there is every reason to believe that the educational sociologist will be entirely amenable to an increased emphasis upon those aspects of this subject that fall naturally within his discipline.

Religious Concepts and Secular Research in Sociology

There is one further consideration with respect to sociology that an inquiry of this nature cannot afford to overlook. As in all the dominantly secular studies, fundamental religious values are often entertained by the secular mind, but they are formulated in essentially secular terms. The sociologist, Pitirim A. Sorokin, is one of twenty international scholars contributing to a recent volume in which each author presents the best of his thought selected by each from his own writing. In Sorokin's chapter he speaks of his sociological research oriented to what many would consider religious values. The subject for inquiry is whether certain religious teachings can be empirically verified. To this end he says,

> In 1948, Mr. Eli Lilly and the Lilly endowment on their own initiative offered $120,000 for my studies on how to make human beings less selfish and more creative. This generous offer led to the establishment of the Harvard Research Center in Creative Altruism in 1949, which I am directing now. (12)

He believes that we learn about truth "not only from empirical scientists and logical thinkers, but also from great religious and ethical leaders like Buddha and Jesus, Confucius and Lao-tse, and from the creators in the fine arts like Beethoven and Bach, Homer and Shakespeare, Phidias and Michelangelo." (13) This reveals an acknowledgment not possible for the avowed secularist or dogmatic naturalist. He is saying that truth eventuates not only from the empirical or scientific studies. He goes on to say, however, that he is a scientist, and his professional concern is with empirical validation, although he also honors inspired religious and intuitive sources of truth. The findings of his research center reveal an interesting combination of the sacred and the secular.

> . . . Without a notable increase of unselfish, creative love (as ideally formulated in the Sermon on the Mount) in overt behavior, in overt interindividual and intergroup relationships, in social institutions and culture, there is no chance for a lasting peace and for interhuman harmony, internal or external.
>
> Our studies show also that this unselfish, creative love, about which we still know very little, potentially represents a tremendous power. (a) It can stop aggressive interindividual and intergroup attacks; (b) it can transform inimical relationships into amicable ones; (c) love begets love, and hate generates hate; (d) love can tangibly influence international policy and pacify international conflicts. In addition to these effects an unselfish and wise (adequate) love manifests itself; (e) as a life-giving force, necessary for physical, mental, and moral health; (f) altruistic persons live longer than egoistic individuals; (g) children deprived of love tend to become morally and socially defective; (h) love is a powerful antidote against criminal, morbid, and suicidal tendencies, against hate, fear, psychoneuroses; (i) love performs important cognitive and aesthetic functions; (j) it is the loftiest and most effective educational force for enlightenment and moral ennoblement of humanity; (k) it is the heart and soul of freedom and of all main moral and religious values; (l) its minimum is absolutely necessary for the durable existence of any society, and especially, for a harmonious social order and creative progress; (m) finally, at the present catastrophic moment of human history an increased "production, accumulation, and circulation of love-energy," or a notable altruization of persons and groups, institutions and culture, especially an extension of unselfish love of everyone for everyone in mankind, is a necessary condition for the prevention of new wars and for the alleviation of enormously increased interindividual and intergroup strife.
>
> With a notable increase of our knowledge of love, its potentialities can be used for the service of mankind in immeasurably greater proportions. (14)

Sorokin is doing secular research on some sacred religious concepts. His conclusions concerning the good life, like Riesman's and many another, when introduced into a course like educational sociology or the social foundations of education help reveal to prospective teachers the religious character of secular inquiry when carried on with intellectual integrity. Like all scholarly inquiry at its best, it is not secular in the sense that it is hostile to the sacred. Similarly, religious scholarship at its best is not hostile to this kind of secular inquiry even when the Sorokin studies so tend to indicate that a purely ideological belief in God or in the credo of any of the great religions brought about in the process of conversion sometimes does but more commonly does not change the convert's overt behavior toward his fellow man in any tangible way. A study of educational sociology which focuses sociological knowledge on religion can convincingly contribute to the kind of religious enlightenment needed by our teachers.

The Social Foundations of Education to be Treated Similarly

Offerings in the social foundations of education have taken the place of philosophy of education, history of education, and educational sociology in many colleges, especially in those not offering a graduate program in these areas. These courses are variously organized but it is commonly understood that those who teach them are reasonably competent in at least these three fields. All that we have said of the individual areas treated separately applies when they are reconceived and combined into one course. It should be noted that just as history and philosophy can be taught for propaganda purposes, so can social foundations. For all its objective and impartial sounding title, the social foundations of education have often been taught by avowedly naturalistic social scientists who impart not only social foundations but a partisan world-view as well. Since this is not as obvious a form of indoctrination as the straightforward teaching of a naturalistic philosophy of education, it sometimes becomes the most strategic means for the indirect indoctrination of teachers into a kind of nameless but positive secularism in which religious thought and institutions are either not mentioned at all or are introduced in a context which artfully deprecates them. Properly taught, social foundations is ideally designed to impart understandings of religious beliefs, organizations, and institutions as vital forces in the social order.

Religious Problems Loom Larger in the Lives of Children Than in the Thought of Educational Psychologists

Educational psychology in its various forms, primarily a secular study, sometimes becomes exclusively secularistic. Whether treating of the nature of the mind and of learning, or the psychology of adolescence, or child development—naturalistic theories of mind have often been treated as self-evident truths. William James was not the last to question the adequacy of a wholly naturalistic conception of mind. There are sophisticated and alternative conceptions of mind in contemporary thought which should be acknowledged in order that the student be freed to make his own decision on a problem that is still controversial and unsettled.

In the psychology of adolescence as variously conceived at the present time, it is perfectly clear that religious concerns are an enormously greater factor in the development of the adolescent than they are in the thinking of the professors of adolescent psychology. Why this disparity? One can only conclude that the prevailing climate of teacher education has been of such a nature in the last generation that the religious aspect of children's growth, development, and social maturation has often been unconsciously slighted. We have tended to act as if one of the most important factors in the lives of perhaps half of our children simply did not exist. This is probably to be accounted for in part at least by the secularist tradition in much psychological thought. One thinks of Freud's psychoanalysis, Watson's behaviorism, Koehler's organismic psychology and Dewey's interactionism, and the range is from mechanistic to naturalistic. Their contributions have been great and the results of their teaching often good, but since so large a portion of our culture is oriented to a sacred image of man it would seem wise to attempt an acknowledgment of an alternative view of man in educational psychology.

The chronological study of children's physical development and the relatively consistent emotional and psychological development which attends physical growth, has contributed much to our understanding of children. This kind of research has revealed many pertinent facts about child development that are invaluable, but it has inevitably tended to treat physical growth as the primary object of study and social influences affecting emotional and psychological development as secondary. This could easily be exaggerated, for environmental influences are held to be very important; however, they are not commonly treated as primary. This tends to impart an overtone of physicalism to the study. So conceived, it is difficult to attain a balance between modifications in child nature caused by physical development and those caused by the social environment. It is therefore often difficult for those who teach courses in child development to make the connection between the emergence of emotional traits related to developmental stages and learned emotional traits communicated to the child by his society. A case could be made for the emergence of a rudimentary kind of implicit religion in the chronological development of the child, the desire to be loved, and perhaps the impulse to love, but a much stronger case could probably be made for the cultivation of intrinsic religion by parents and teachers self-consciously seeking to instill this quality. Religious institutions and their teachers propose to nourish this to maturity. Child development adequately conceived studies the child in relation to the social forces which come to a focus in him along with the forces that are released in him by his stages of development. Religious influences often become marked at a relatively early age. A greater knowledge of contemporary religion and the part it plays in the lives of children should take its proper place in our child development offerings of the future.

Religious Concepts and Secular Research in Psychiatry

Educational psychology is widely understood to be primarily concerned with the psychology of learning, with the attitudes and circumstances that promote or retard it. The implicit assumptions of this study are commonly secular as are the insights and understandings that it seeks to communicate. This is proper, but an exclusive emphasis upon the secular tends to promote the secularist presumption. It would be a first step and a welcome relief from exclusive secularism if educational psychologists would give more thought to employing critical religious concepts that certain students of psychology and psychiatry have found enormously helpful in the understanding and management of children and of men.

Like Sorokin in sociology, Erich Fromm in psychiatry makes the easy transition from the secular to the sacred vocabulary of the student, and employs this vocabulary and the sentiments it elicits to evoke understandings uniquely significant for teacher education. With respect to the importance of the context in which learning takes place successfully, Fromm endorses the widespread notion that an understanding of the child as well as of the subject matter is important. However, by the introduction of what many would call an essentially religious concept he reveals a whole new dimension to the understanding of one's students and one's subject matter. Indeed, he adds a whole new dimension to what we must come to mean by an adequate understanding of our students. Reminiscent again of the "I-Thou" relationship between teacher and pupil as defined by Martin Buber, Fromm says:

> My thesis is that you do not understand another person unless you are related to (love) him. You can understand objects in the natural sciences, and you can understand a person in medicine *or to some extent in psychology,* as any object with which the scientist is confronted, *but you cannot understand a patient deeply, or for that matter any human being, without being related to him.* If you only look at him intellectually as an observer, from observer to object, you can see quite a few things but you cannot really *understand* him. (15)

Fromm then proceeds to develop further the distinction between objective knowledge or "knowledge about" a subject and a real understanding of a person or subject.

> If I give myself to this person, to *experience* him in his uniqueness and his full reality, suddenly this person becomes real . . . I know his past and his present because it is all there and at that very moment I feel one with him. And at that very moment you might say I love him because I have stopped judging; I see him. . . .(16)

Unfortunately, most of our psychological understandings of persons and their learnings are of such an objective nature that,

> . . . in our culture, in which we speak a lot about teamwork and togetherness and all such things, actually people are as alone as they could be any place in the universe. Few people are sufficiently concentrated and sufficiently willing to put themselves into the other person, even to really listen.(17)

To approach both learning and pupils with love not only relieves loneliness and advances understanding in the student; it does the same for the teacher. One approaches the objects of knowledge and the subjects of instruction "creatively, with all his sense, with his whole personality." With the teacher, as with a psychiatrist, "Something goes on in you. And, in fact, as always in life, if we help somebody else, we help ourselves . . . I mean by love—full realism—the ability to see the person as he is. That means not only intellectually but with the whole person—from center to center, not from periphery to periphery . . . I do not believe we have any complete knowledge about any other person except in the act of love."(18)

When one considers how much instruction in teacher education, in all education, is matter of fact and not lighted by imagination, i.e., by a creative rendition flowing from one's very being; and when one considers how much of the education of teachers is characterized by empty verbalisms and superficial group action and pseudo-democratic committee work—the significance of the religious dimension in teaching and learning can hardly be overestimated. The analytical objectivity of science is not opposed to the synthetic immediacy of the poet's knowledge or selfless religious love or the unself-conscious inquiry of a child, but it is distinguishable from these. It is an important half of learning but only half; the other half is in the love of learning. In education it takes both objective analysis and love, both of learning and of children, to meet the full human requirement. Yet the very mention of the existential, of the *religious,* dimension in education is commonly the occasion for embarrassment. The reason for this is that disarming creative love always embarrasses matter-of-fact men until it reduces them to themselves. More often, professionally objective, legalistic and official minds stare down innocent, unauthenticated, outgoing love without which no culture can long endure, and no person. Yet it is not long before these matter-of-fact and professional aggregates of bone and flesh surreptitiously slip away to a wholesome or clandestine private love or psychiatric couch as necessary compensation for the self-imposed and tragic deprivation suffered by all proper and professional men whose daily work is not lighted by the lamp of love.

If psychological and psychiatric insights into the needs of human nature reveal that an absence of wholesome, outgoing love in the home, in the school and at work results in emotional and physical illness beyond the possibility of self-repair, surely this theme should be developed in educational psychology. And surely the most instructive analogy should be developed between the atmosphere conducive to mental health in relation to the psychiatrist and to the teacher.

Religion as One of the Liberal Disciplines of the General College

With respect to religious enlightenment, the college of liberal arts in the university or the general education division of the teachers college is the ideal place to teach religion as one of the general studies. (19) Depending upon the size of the institution which somewhat governs richness of offerings, one can envision such courses as History of Religion, Religions of the Middle and Far East, The Influence of Religious Ideas on Western Thought, Comparative Religion, Contemporary Religious Beliefs and Practices in American Society. Whether or not a department of religion were to evolve, the course would be taught precisely as any other of the general or liberal studies. They would be taught essentially for enlightenment, and the professors would be altogether natural members of the academic community. They would not be selected on the basis of their religious commitment but on the basis of scholarship and teaching competence. Their area would be looked upon as one of the liberal disciplines or general studies contributing scholarly knowledge to the areas of literature, philosophy, the schools of music, fine arts, etc. One can well imagine that certain courses would be required by many of the professional schools—education, medicine, law, and schools of social work. The professors themselves might, or might not, profess a formal religious commitment.

Adequately staffed, a department of religion so conceived would raise the level of religious inquiry in the university community above its often deplorable and anti-intellectualistic level. It would set a tone of objectivity, reasonableness, and mutual respect in discussion of religious differences. Its effect on uninformed grass-roots religious emotionalism would be similar to the effect of a good political science department upon uninformed grass-roots political emotionalism. It would teach our prospective teachers by example how the spirit of learning, the spirit of inquiry, transforms raw controversy and conflict into educative material. Prospective teachers would gain both substantive knowledge and an insight into how to handle that knowledge to keep it from degenerating into irresponsible controversy. In courses properly taught they might reasonably be expected to discover how religion must be treated in their own classrooms of the future. In short, they would learn that when religion is treated *educationally*, it takes on the only form allowable in the state educational institutions of a free and pluralistic society.

The Contributions of the Liberal Studies to the Religious Dimension of Teacher Education

We have become accustomed to speaking of teacher education rather than teacher training as the conviction has grown that a teacher needed more than training. For many of us, however, the new term has replaced the old without changing our original conception. Teacher education must more and more be thought of as the education of a person as well as his professional preparation for teaching. These flow together but they are distinguishable. In the larger universities it is common to require the prospective teacher to take well over half of his work in the liberal arts college, sometimes nearly all of it. Of course some of this time is spent developing competency in the subject or subjects he wishes to teach. But a substantial amount of it is spent in courses designed to contribute to his general or liberal education. Concerning the contributions of a liberal education to teacher education, the professional educator has been strangely silent. Yet we evidently believe these contributions are significant. We might speculate a bit about those aspects of a liberal education designed to contribute to the religious enlightenment of a student and to elicit also a religious quality or dimension.

Organized knowledge of religious beliefs and practices so necessary to the teacher are doubtless best gained in a department whose offerings are primarily directed toward religious enlightenment, but this portion of the education of the teacher can never be a substitute for his general or liberal education. The maturation of the religious dimension also requires an involvement in the liberal arts and the sciences. In the sciences properly taught the student learns not only the positive value of the scientific method but its limits. As revealed in the chapter in this volume given to this subject, science leads us to the edges of verifiable knowledge from which one looks out with wonder and religious awe upon the vast unknown beyond all human knowing. It is hoped that the student will be influenced by the discipline of science from working within the substantial body of verified knowledge and by the wisdom of science which comes from standing within this discipline in order to attain a new vision of man in his universe, of the known and the limitations of all knowledge. It is entirely reasonable to assume that when science is properly taught it positively contributes to the maturation of religious understanding.

It is similarly felt that the humanities cultivate a sensitive awareness of life through art, music, poetry and history imaginatively entertained. The liberal studies are not only designed to elicit appreciative responses but to extend the range of appreciative understanding. They do this in part through cultivating the aesthetic sensibilities, the refinement of which may very well be one of the conditions of mature religious understanding and expression. This is suggested not only by theorists in the field of higher education but also by the fact that so much of man's worship is enhanced by the arts of architecture, pictorial and plastic art, poetry, music, ceremony and ritual. If so much religion has found expression through the arts, it is only reasonable to assume that the cultivation of aesthetic discrimination is the clear condition for an appreciative understanding of all religion finding expression through aesthetic form.

Significance of the Three General Education Chapters in this Volume

The three chapters in this book on science, history and the humanities are evidence of the fact that the original committee of educators who planned it recognize both that a general education is indispensable in the education of teachers and that it plays a particularly important role in their religious education. These are especially important chapters for anyone considering an increased emphasis upon religion in teacher education. There are at least three reasons for this. The first is that it is the function of the scholar in the major areas of learning to supply the substantive knowledge that our teachers subsequently are expected to impart to their students. This is as true of religious knowledge as it is of any other. The second reason for giving serious attention to these chapters is that they deal with religious knowledge and religious sentiments educationally. In reading them one discovers what it means to treat the subject of religion with intellectual integrity. Their intent is to reveal no bias for or against the sacred or secular image of man. There is no suggestion that freedom of inquiry is in any way jeopardized or that any one of the liberal studies should be subverted to any "higher" value, religious or other. The third reason they demand serious consideration is that they reveal the religious dimension of liberal learning for the sufficient reason that when adequately conceived, liberal learning reveals this dimension. These chapters thus attest both to the intellectual dimension of religion and the religious dimension of intellectual inquiry.

The liberal studies so conceived constitute a link between all high religion and the life of learning. They lead to a reinforcement and a maturation of one's commitment or to a thoughtful reconstitution of such a commitment. In his "Idea of a University" Cardinal Newman speaks of those moments given to dedicated inquiry into the meaning of life as moments almost indistinguishable from religious worship. For Meland, a cultivation of the aethetic sensibilities through a study of and an involvement in great art, music and poetry elicits a sensitive awareness which is the condition of the fullest development of the human spirit.

> Participation in the resources of creative art and poetry can have constructive and deepening effects in preparing the sensibilities of the individual for effective inquiry into the issues which concern the reconstruction of faith.(20)

> While it is true that aesthetic experience may not be equated with religious devotion, nor counted on necessarily to lead to it, one must recognize that moral zeal and religious dedication, when informed by aesthetic sensibility and appreciation, take on a dimension of human goodness which combines qualities of perceptiveness, proportion, leading ultimately to discernment. In the matter of religious orientation there is perhaps no greater or more indispensable power than discernment. . . . The difference between a religious mind cribbed and cabined within its own unclarified and undisciplined emotions, and a spirit that is free and forgiving is often a matter of sensitivity, proportion, and vision. These the aesthetic ground of experience, under certain circumstance, can provide; . . . and it is difficult to see how it could be attained except through the exercise of the appreciative consciousness. (21)

It is clear from what Meland has to say about the function of the humanities and the fine and musical arts that professional schools of theology depend upon the liberal studies for the education of the clergy quite as much as other professional schools of the university.

> A university which takes as its aim the culture of the human spirit will lift the humanistic studies to their proper place in the curriculum as the organizing core of instruction and charge it with the responsibility of clarifying the meaning of man in his full stature as a human being. (22)

It must be noted that Meland is not asking that the humanities be taught in accordance with Christian or sectarian doctrine, nor that they be taught from the point of view of an avowed secularism, but that they be taught with the acknowledgment that all knowledge runs into wonder rather than completion, that the arts reach into the mystery of life beyond the limits of rational analysis. He is seeming to say that learning pursued with utter honesty requires a kind of selflessness, a reaching out in quest of the ultimate ground of life and an encouragement to each to formulate his faith in the light of disciplined thought and cultivated sensibilities. It is interesting to note that in many Protestant church-related colleges and in the Catholic and Jewish universities as well, one often comes upon just this kind of sophistication. Such teachers of the liberal studies even in religious universities believe it is a wrong use of the liberal arts to interpret them in such a way that they tell a moral or teach a doctrine. Doctrinal instruction, they contend, is located in the theological faculty.

The Religious Liberal and the Liberal Educator Scarcely Distinguishable

It must also be noted at this point that there are representatives of relatively liberal Protestant thought who tend to identify a serious and sustained inquiry into the meaning of life with the religious pilgrimage. They look upon institutionalized religion as secondary to the interiorization of religion. They see crystalized religious doctrines and established religious customs as blocks to an emerging faith. In the spirit of Emerson, they believe that God reveals himself reliably in every generation in which he is earnestly sought. Dedicated inquiry into the meaning of life is for them a religious pilgrimage. The life of learning and the life of the spirit are synonymous. As Floyd H. Ross, professor of world religions at the University of Southern California, has expressed it,

> Creative impulses stirred into activity by the impact of a personality of unusual depth or integrity—a Socrates, a Gautama, a Lao-tse, a Jesus—have a tendency to fall back into conventionalized patterns when the relationship that originally evoked such responses has been put into a new perspective by the passage of time or by the death of the teacher. New spiritual insights lapse back into trite moralisms or theological clichés. The teachings of the master are crystalized in order to pass them on to later generations. That which had within it the seeds of a permanently continuing revolution becomes externalized in the form of new laws to abide by, new teachings to be indoctrinated, new principles to expound endlessly . . . Spontaneity, or the urge of the human spirit for freedom from all legalisms whether old or new, shrivels up once again, and fear wins the victory over faith in the very name of faith.(23)

If this vital and emergent conception of religion were widely held, there would be no need for a distinction between teaching for commitment to an inherited deposit of beliefs and teaching for enlightenment. The fundamental purpose of the school and the church would be the same. The basic distinction between the two institutions would be erased. Worship would find its expression in a life of creative self-transcendence. The implications for education are incorporated in the very view itself.

> William James spoke of the human tendency to have faith in someone else's faith. But this is not faith; rather, it is a denial of faith in the mature sense and—when found in adults—evidence of acquiescence in authoritarianism. He who has had any contact at any time with an authoritarian family situation where the child is cajoled or coerced by many devices into finding the sole basis for authority for his life in the will of the parent realizes in part how such subservience to the will of the dominant personality lays the groundwork for authoritarianism. Unless the child is guided through each learning situation in such a way as to discover progressively how the real basis of authority must be found in terms of his own inner life and his maturing relationships with others, the child will probably always tend to be a disciple rather than a fellow seeker. Certainly the history of every religious movement indicates that *disciples* are a much more common phenomenon than *pilgrims* or explorers of the way. The very training and psychological quirks that make one a disciple rather than a seeker predispose one to be a leaner or clinger—clinging to the ideas of master, teacher, friend, or guru. . . .
>
> The evidence is rather clear that some such process as this took place in the fellowship of friends who clustered around Jesus of Nazareth. (24)

How variously scholars of unquestionable integrity interpret not only religion but the Christian religion. It appears that freedom of conscience inevitably results in religious pluralism also. Each choosing his own particular leaves us with variety. The thesis developed here is that, in the education of teachers, more of the wide variety of religious beliefs be made known to them and that an appreciative awareness of each be cultivated in them, this without predisposition toward one over another.

An Attempt at Reconceiving the Terms of the Dilemma

This chapter could have taken many forms. The form it has taken is the result of certain facts, an unresolved problem in American education and a conviction. The critical facts appear to be that a very large portion of the best minds in our institutions of higher learning, including schools of education, reveal a notable lack of enthusiasm for religious education in our public schools or in released-time programs when it is church-sponsored. Some serious religious scholars have always questioned the propriety of introducing sectarian religious instruction into the schools in any way that would result in the recurrent and regular segregation of students on the basis of their beliefs. On the other hand, lay churchmen who have not probed deeply into the problem are substantially in favor of it. These are joined by a substantial majority of the Protestant clergy and by the professionally trained religious educators. Between these two stand the public school administrators and teachers in quandary—often affirming, sometimes denying the relevance of religion in public education. And if sectarian instruction is what the public and the clergy means by religious education, our state universities and teachers colleges have clearly decided that this whole project does not lie within their province.

American education is therefore at an impasse over the problem of religious education as we have commonly conceived it. Up to the present time, resolutions of the problem are apparent rather than real. One faith-group takes over in the homogeneous community. Varying percentages of the school population are released to sectarian instruction while the remainder of the students and all of the staff keep up the appearance of school in full session. In some schools religious subjects are assiduously avoided. The avowed secularist has his solution. The avowed religionist, his. Between the two lies the vast range of practical patched-up compromises. Teachers colleges show the same range of contrary convictions and confusion. It is little wonder; both are representative of our public state of mind. The greatest temptation facing anyone who attempts to deal with this problem is the temptation to go on rearranging the familiar patches in the crazy-quilt.

This chapter represents an attempt at reconceiving the terms of what has become an irreconcilable problem and suggesting a resolution. It has recognized the role of commitment in culture and the role of enlightenment. It has acknowledged the educational dimension of religion and the religious dimension of education. It has attempted to reveal the church and the school as properly complementary. It has asked for the incorporation into teacher education of a proper portion of religious knowledge as well as a more convincing religious quality. It has suggested that only that portion of religion which is *educational* be introduced into educational institutions. This not only resolves the problem for education but for religion, for what certain religious scholars and a majority of scholarly churchmen in our liberal universities see more clearly than the lay religionist and much of the local clergy is enormously important for the future of religion. They are properly apprehensive about using or involving the compulsory education system in the propagation of sectarian belief. They recall what others forget, that our forefathers sacrificed inordinately to find a haven free from persecution by sectarian faiths enjoying state encouragement in a number of different countries. And they note that we have enjoyed this blessing for so long a time we have forgotten the danger to religion that lurks in using the coercive secular laws of the state for fostering the things of the spirit.

If teacher education colleges in the past generation in this country had attended more to the religious enlightenment of their students and had restricted themselves less exclusively to the thought and language patterns of a non-theistic scientific naturalism—it is altogether possible that the churches would not have been driven to the only recourse that lay within their grasp. Their demand for sectarian religious education in the schools, and when possible in teacher education, is a reasonable and democratic demand for just as long a time as the secularist insists on dominating the educational system and excluding, neglecting or deprecating the religious dimension in American culture. Those of a theistic orientation in this country should not be asked to accept this state of affairs in the public schools and teachers colleges of the land, and there is every indication that they don't intend to.

The Supreme Court, doubtless aware that certain of the Christian sects are every bit as ambitious to dominate the public schools as any secular philosophy, has nevertheless been concerned that the hand of the state not be laid upon the mouth of those who ask for reasonable representation of their views in the public schools of the land. Torn between these and other related concerns, their rulings, to say the least, have been ambivalent. The secularist cannot count on this body to uphold the wall between church and state if the state teachers colleges and the public schools persist in one or another form of secularist parochialism. The time has come for American education to reorient its thinking on this matter and, with the help of enlightened religious scholars, provide for the religious education of our teachers for the same reason that we provide for the rest of their education. On no other controversial front has the educator hoped to solve a social problem by neglect or by withholding knowledge. Our teachers' ignorance and our educators' continued neglect of this rapidly growing problem can only result in mounting misunderstanding and unnecessary conflict in the years to come.

3

*Religion and the Humanities in Teacher Education**

The problem to which this book is addressed is a practical problem. It is not concerned with reconciling conflicting theories, but with finding practicable ways and means of interrelating religion and public education. The problem is shared by people holding a wide variety of views about religion and about education, a variety which must be accepted, if the problem is viewed as practical instead of theoretical.

A PLACE FOR RELIGION IN EDUCATION

I have tried, in keeping this feature of the problem in mind, to refer this chapter's discussions to certain attitudes toward the problem of religion and education, attitudes which are likely to bear most strongly upon the ways in which the problem can be practically dealt with. I shall accordingly advocate, for public education, what I shall call a humanistic interpretation of religion—I might almost say as well, a religious interpretation of the humanities. This interpretation

* This chapter prepared by Dr. Knox C. Hill, Associate Professor of Humanities in the College, University of Chicago, Chicago, Illinois.

tries to take proper account of the attitudes toward our problem which are significantly practical, and it is hoped that by taking proper account of these attitudes we can develop fruitful reciprocal relations between what is religious and what is humanistic, and that we can do so without doing violence to traditional attitudes toward religion and education in the United States.

Few if any thoughtful people believe that education should be purely intellectual. There are, however, many who look with alarm or suspicion upon any move which would give emphasis to the role of religion in public education. These people are not characteristically unsympathetic to religion; on the contrary, they include many who are zealously in favor of religion. It is people like these, rather than those who are hostile to religion, whose views particularly need to be taken into account when we approach the problem of religion and education. If we can gain their cooperation, there should be comparatively little difficulty in solving the problem.

Those who profess to be in favor of religion and who nevertheless object to teaching of religion in the schools maintain a position which can easily fall into serious inconsistency. The view advocated in this chapter is intended to help prevent this position from becoming thus inconsistent.

There are two propositions which American educational policy accepts. First, the aim of education is to make men better—not better in some particular respect, but better as men. Second, religious teaching of a doctrinaire sort cannot be carried on in the public schools. Neither proposition can be accepted in a sense which runs counter to the spirit of the other proposition. We cannot pursue the moral end of education by choosing religious means toward that end. We cannot be so vigilant in keeping religious teaching out of the schools that we discourage the attainment of the moral end of education. The problem is one of finding modes of education which have deeply moral tendencies, even religious tendencies, but no doctrinaire character. The humanities offer magnificent opportunities for developing in the minds and hearts of students dispositions and attitudes which are morally good, and they make it possible to do this without resort to religious indoctrination.

The two propositions can be closely interrelated by enunciating another one: the public schools should not merely be allowed, but are in fact obligated to teach their students to take religion seriously. Two things are involved. First, whatever attitude toward religion a student ultimately takes, it should be an intelligent attitude. If he commits himself to a particular doctrine, he should do so intelligently. If he decides that no doctrine is acceptable to him, he should do so intelligently. This may be put in another way by supposing that a student's education is a good one, and that, among other things, it strongly influences him to abandon "the faith of his fathers." I should defend such an education on the ground that, in this student's case, he could hold to his traditional faith only by resorting to a blind adherence to a doctrine he had merely inherited; this would involve an abandonment of intelligence, and education must be opposed to this. On the other hand, if his education encouraged him to lapse into a passive disregard of his inherited faith, not an open repudiation but an inactivity coupled with a verbal insistence that he still held the faith, he is abandoning his faith not out of conviction, but because of a sort of spinelessness which cannot be approved. It is within the province of the public schools to encourage students to make intelligent commitments concerning religion; but it is not within their province to encourage any particular kind of commitment—pro or con.

The second point is that public education has the responsiblity of cultivating intelligent tolerance toward the commitments of others. This is closely related to the first point, for both points involve the idea that public education should in general neither attack nor defend the religious beliefs students bring with them when they enter school. But this puts the point too negatively. It is not enough for students to learn merely to refrain from attacking beliefs which differ from their own. This is what I shall call *negative tolerance,* a tolerance which could be based upon ignorance; it is *positive tolerance* which is advocated here, and this is something which can only be based upon knowledge.

This does not entail an identification of the humanities with religion. It is agreed that there are dimensions of religion which may transcend the range of art, and that there is art which is not religious. But there is something poetic about religion and something religious about poetry. This does not mean merely that there is an overlap between the two areas with respect to subject matter: that there is religious poetry, for example, like the Psalms or the book of Job. There is, rather, an affinity between two spirits, the spirit of religion and the spirit of poetry. They may not be identical, but the one moves naturally toward the other, no matter which one one begins with.

Very sharp distinctions have been drawn between the humanities and religion. It has been maintained that there is literature which is really divine: the work of God; and it has been maintained that this divine literature is to be distinguished from human literature. (This view, in fact, is the basis of a long tradition in the use of the term humanities.) So sharp a distinction makes it difficult, perhaps impossible, to give any religious character to public education in a democracy such as ours. The distinction implies a view which would hold that the only truly religious literature was the Word of God, and it would not allow this divine work to be taught as one of the humanities. Other citizens, of course, who did not regard this literature as the Word of God would not tolerate its being taught as divine. The view proposed in this chapter recognizes a third kind of literature, literature which is not supposed to be the Word of God, but which nevertheless has religious subject matter and expresses religious aspirations of men. This view would allow literature which was in a sense religious to be taught, but it would not solve the problem completely. For these humanistic works, which would be adjectivally but not substantively religious, could be interpreted in only two possible ways, if one distinguished so sharply between religion and art: from the point of view of pertinent religious dogmas, or without reference to such dogmas. In the first case the dogma would have entered public education just as much as it would if a piece of literature were taught as the Word of God. In the second case the religious character of the literature would be left out. Consequences like these are inevitable if too sharp a distinction is drawn, for educational policy, between poetry and religion.

This chapter proposes to allow poetry to take on the adjective *religious,* but in something more than a merely adjectival sense. It bases the proposal upon a distinction between two kinds of intellectual activities. One kind is scientific, factual, cognitive, realistic, etc. The other is expressive, ideal, emotional, imaginative, etc. Religion and art are placed in the latter category. Neither is essentially concerned with positive inquiry into the nature of things, but rather with expressions of feelings, of ideal aspirations. Depending on how one evaluates these two sides of human activity, the scientific and the expressive, this view may seem to be favorable or unfavorable to religion.

It is likely to be repugnant to the man who thinks that religion is essentially distinct from poetry. He will think that it belittles religion to identify it as something made by man. Santayana is one thinker who illustrates the possibility of holding the view without disparaging religion: "This brings me to religion," he says in an autobiographical work, "which is the head and front of everything." And he adds: "I knew that my parents regarded all religion as a work of human imagination; and I agreed, and still agree with them there.

But this carried an implication in their minds against which every instinct in me rebelled, namely that the works of human imagination are bad. No, I said to myself even as a boy: they are good, they alone are good and the rest—the whole real world—is ashes in the mouth." And this high opinion of religion could harmonize, in Santayana's mind, with a statement like this: "Religions are the great fairy-tales of the conscience." (1)

The proposed view has many advantages in connection with the problem of religion and public education. The problem confronts us with terms which are hard to agree upon; but we must have working agreements on the meanings of these terms. On the one hand there is the term *religion,* defined very narrowly by some persons and very broadly by others. On the other hand there is the whole set of terms, *humanities, art, literature,* and *poetry,* which have always been defined in a rich variety of ways. Ideally, we should find meanings for all of these terms which would allow almost anyone to say, "the term certainly involves what your definition says it does," even if some persons would wish to add that the term involves something else as well.

The only definitions of religion which would really be adequate, for one group of persons or another, would be in essential respects doctrinaire definitions. If we are to solve the problem of religion and public education—i.e., if we are to find a *practical* solution for the problem—we must avoid doctrinaire definitions. The proposed view does avoid them, and yet it points to something important which is a characteristic of religious experience. I believe also that a very wide and representative variety of views about the humanities would agree that they possess an expressive, emotional quality which one does not characteristically look for in scientific works. The view also has great practical utility in a culture which includes so many different kinds of religious institutions and beliefs. It accepts a great many religions (not necessarily all religions) on an equal basis. It can take them all seriously without insisting on a dogmatic choice among them. Many dogmatically religious people could agree that the view calls attention to something important which all of the great religions share: a concern (not a coldly intellectual understanding, but a strongly emotional attachment) for ultimate ideals. It even offers an attractive possibility of finding some rather definite ideals or values which many religions can agree are fundamental. With respect to the humanities it has a similar advantage. It makes available an extraordinarily wide range of works which can be treated humanistically; and the humanistic manner of treatment which it suggests is well calculated to bring out the religious character which any of these varied works may have.

THE RELATIONSHIP BETWEEN THE HUMANITIES AND RELIGION

An essential point must now be emphatically underlined, or this chapter will lose the sympathetic hearing of many readers. What is proposed should not be taken as advocating that the schools teach humanism as a religion. This would of course amount to nothing better than a disguised form of dogmatism. It would make available to the religious humanist all of the resources of public education, for the end of subverting theistic religions. This is not what is proposed. It is not proposed that teachers teach that the correct view of religion is a humanistic view. Rather, it is proposed that the non-doctrinare attitude which the law requires teachers to take, when they deal with religious matters in public schools, is indistinguishable *in practice* from the humanistic attitude.

The dogmatic and the humanistic views of religion can be contrasted with reference to the different kinds of materials which they might admit into or rule out of public education. The dogmatic view would be most likely to rule out the use of material believed, by some people, to be truly sacred. They would admit its use only if it were not taught dogmatically, that is to say, if it were taught humanistically. There is no great harm in this. A good case cannot be made for insisting that the Bible, for example, must be taught in public education. There are other religious materials which could be taught, although this might give the dogmatist little consolation. He could still complain that the truly religious material is still outside of education. We could offer him little sympathy; we cannot allow him to teach religion in the schools dogmatically, even if he wishes to.

The humanistic view need not require the exclusion of dogmatic religious material. But it could nevertheless result in its actual exclusion, as well as in the expulsion of a great deal more. Here lies one of the dangers of this view. The humanistic position could omit anything it liked, and still maintain that its materials were thoroughly religious. It would be in possession of a blank check signed by the name of religion, and it could fill it out with almost any content. It could deny our problem by saying, "Teach the humanities, any humanities, and you will have dealt with religion." It follows that the use of the humanistic position requires the retention of some clear distinction between works of art which have emphatically religious dimensions, and works of art which do not. There is no difficulty here; common sense gives us the distinction. Only special theories obliterate it.

One advantage which results from treating religious materials humanistically lies in the fact that it opens the way for the humanities to venture into areas which are closed to the natural or social scientist. Dogmatic religious literature could have no place in natural science. If its teachings agreed with those of science, the basis of the agreement would not be scientific, so science would have no interest in the agreement —it would be mere coincidence. If science and religion disagreed, science would listen to no reasons but its own, and the disagreement could not be resolved. Nor would there be any real difference if it appeared that religious dogma was making statements about some aspect of the nature of things which science is as yet unable to speak about. If it is still impossible to speak scientifically, on some given question, science will not listen to an unscientific voice. There are persons who believe that there is some knowledge about the world which only religion can give us; but few scientists are willing to recognize rigid boundaries to what science can ultimately discover.

The social scientist too will not allow dogmatic religion to teach him anything about his own subject. He may study religion as a social institution, or as a force which influences individual behavior. When he does so, he is studying facts about human behavior, as these facts are relevant to the study of society. He is certainly interested in the fact that people believe certain things; he is in principle indifferent to none of these beliefs. But he is not primarily concerned, as a social scientist, with determining whether or not these beliefs are true. At most one might argue that, as a social scientist he does want to know whether or not it is good for men to believe whatever they do believe; he may follow out the consequences of beliefs, and this may lead him to pass judgment upon various beliefs with reference to their consequences. But any conclusions he might come to on these matters must be based on principles of social science, and it would be mere coincidence if these principles happened also to be matters of some religious doctrine.

Even if such material as dogmatic religious literature needs to be excluded from the natural or social sciences, it could be welcomed in the area of the humanities. For if this material is treated as poetry, it need not be argued with, nor looked at clinically.

There are, after all, many literary works which find asylum in the humanities, when they are not admitted, or not allowed to remain in the other great areas. The reasons for this could also apply to such material as dogmatic religious literature. The idea of the humanities as expressions of human values or ideals allows us to include many works which appear, *prima facie,* to belong elsewhere. Herodotus, Thucydides, Harvey, Lavoisier, Darwin, Adam Smith, and Ricardo have been regarded as historians, natural scientists, and social scientists. But they were also artists. Their work continued to be interesting and important examples of artistry, even after they began to lose their importance within the disciplines to which they originally contributed knowledge. To pay particular attention to their artistry is to treat them humanistically. This treatment may, at the hands of one teacher or another, include many things. All teachers could recognize that the writings of such men express, as poems do, the values or ideals of their authors, and it is these which can be the objects of the humanist's inquiry, according to the idea here proposed. Even scientific writings which seem most thoroughly devoted to the pursuit of truth for its own sake express, as an ideal, objective devotion to the truth. Anyone who reads Darwin adequately will get much more from his writings than his opinions about such things as the origin of species. He will also feel, in Darwin's style, the inquiring spirit of the man, and the strength of this spirit will not seem any the less for the fact that later research has in some things moved in non-Darwinian directions.

Works which were written primarily as historical or scientific works may, then, have poetic dimensions; but they should nevertheless be distinguished from more emphatically poetic works like plays, novels, or poems. But the line distinguishing these things is not sharp. It can hardly be denied that poetry and art tend at times to enter the areas of natural and social science. Not infrequently works written primarily for scientific purposes are more successful as works of art than as works of science; or, after their scientific value has begun to wear out, with the progress of science, we see better than men saw before how good they are as works of art.

THE LIBERALIZING INFLUENCE OF THE HUMANITIES

These reflections are intended to support the idea of treating certain pieces of literature humanistically, even if they are not *prima facie* fine art. They also suggest how the humanities can find importance in works, independently of the literal truth or falsity of the statements they contain. And they encourage us to think of the very distinction between humanistic and non-humanistic works as a flexible one. It is useful to treat the distinction flexibly, not only with reference to religion and poetry, but with reference to an even more general appraisal of what is done in the teaching of the humanities, in one educational program or another. The idea of extending our humanistic consideration over a broad range of things is harmonious with the broadness of interest which has been characteristic of great artists; and it is in harmony with the central importance the humanities have traditionally had in liberal education. The power of the humanities to develop liberal attitudes is fundamental to the role they can play with respect to religion. It will therefore be useful to undertake some reflections about this power. What sorts of liberal attitudes do literature, music, and art cultivate, and how do they cultivate them?

The liberal attitudes cultivated by the humanities must be distinguished from mere tolerance, tolerance which I shall call *negative*. Negative tolerance is the sort of thing that manifests itself in polite avoidance of certain topics of conversation. It may seek to steer clear of political discussion, in circumstances where people hold their political convictions very firmly. It is likely to avoid religious topics even more carefully. The reasons are not altogether the same in the two cases, but in both the tolerant man feels that no real possibility of communication exists, and that it would be bad manners to attempt communication.

There are indeed times when communication ought not to be attempted—when people should be let alone. But there is something wrong in acting as though communication is permanently impossible on any subject, like politics or religion. If we persistently say of the other fellow only that he is entitled to his opinion, we imply that he is really beyond the reach of reason, and that the best thing we can do is to tolerate him. If it is really impossible to communicate with him it is best to leave him alone. For to do anything else might only result in an outbreak of positive intolerance: one opinion would attempt to annihilate others by resorting to violence. So negative tolerance can indeed be good manners. It can smooth personal relationships in the parlor, and prevent bloodshed in the streets. But there is no sure guarantee that it will really prevent conflicts—it may only postpone them.

But perhaps overt intolerance and negative tolerance are not the only alternatives. Perhaps men can achieve a significant measure of true mutual understanding, even if their respective opinions cannot be brought into complete agreement. The world needs bases on which groups of men can work together regardless of disagreements. It is hopeless if we must either agree or fight. If men could agree to disagree there would be much more hope. If men could frankly recognize the disagreements which make them differ from one another, they could develop a liberal attitude which would respect the differences among men, and would at the same time make cooperative living truly possible. Such a liberal attitude can be cultivated through study of the humanities.

In addition to the study of the humanities there are other forms of education which may at first glance appear to aim at the same liberal attitude. There are courses in comparative religion, at the level of higher education, and what corresponds to them at the level of the Sunday school. These things may be well done, and if they are they may encourage the attitude I speak of. But it is easy for this kind of thing to result in nothing better than negative tolerance. If it does, the result may be ineffective in the development of the truly liberal attitude; or, much worse, it may produce a truly illiberal and pernicious attitude. Some Sunday schools, for example, introduce young children in a very superficial way to a wide variety of religious customs which they, being children, are quite incapable of comprehending; rituals, for example, of Roman or Greek Catholicism, of Buddhism, or of Islam. If the solemnity and beauty of these rituals do not strike home in these young hearts (and they are very unlikely to do so in superficial presentations), it is more than likely that the children will come to believe that the strangest things about men are their religious beliefs, since men go through so many senseless—or even ridiculous—motions in the name of religion. The things the children see may not appear important to them, but merely quaint. The immediate result may be better than active intolerance. But to nourish the feeling that unfamiliar ways of behaving are quaint or amusing is not to provide an enduring basis for the sort of tolerance which will stand up under real stresses. This is all the more likely if the children in question have never learned to take any rituals of their own seriously; and this may well be the case in such Sunday schools, for elementary studies in comparative religion are frequently found in Sunday schools where doctrine and ritual are really unimportant. The teacher of a collegiate course in comparative religion may think his situation is essentially different because he is not dealing with children. But his students too can leave his course with a negatively tolerant attitude toward other religions (or all religions), unless they have developed positive sympathy for the sincerity of the human feelings which are embodied in religious rituals and works of art.

The truly liberal attitude is built upon positive sympathy with the ideas and goals which men value. We acquire the deepest sympathy with an ideal when it takes definite hold upon our hearts, not when we merely contemplate it, in however friendly a manner, from the outside. Whenever we are really moved by a poetic piece of literature something does take hold of our hearts. Assuming that all one's aesthetic experience is genuine, the more catholic one's taste is the more liberal one is. It is not correct to speak of a person as merely tolerant of many different kinds of art, if his taste is well developed and catholic. Tolerance implies a willingness to endure things which are not altogether agreeable. The person we are considering has reached the point where the things he appreciates, in all their wide variety, are truly enjoyed by him—not simply tolerated. (For him the word *tolerance* is best applied in connection with his attitude upon approaching art which he has not yet learned to understand. Even here he is not negatively tolerant; he is determined to understand this new thing, if he can. This determination is based on faith in the goodness and reasonableness of expressions which are sincere, and this faith is based on actual experience of many good and reasonable expressions.)

The humanities are capable of liberalizing the mind by making it sympathetic, intelligently and positively sympathetic, to any human aspiration which is sincerely and intelligently expressed. The sort of sympathy it cultivates amounts to an active sharing of the ideals which are expressed. This use of the term *sympathy* requires some special elaboration. We tend to be sympathetic with any human joys or sorrows, and with their corresponding expressions. Childish laughter or tears tend to make us feel happy or sad; but these are natural rather than artistic expressions, and there is seldom much difficulty in understanding them. When the developed experience and wisdom of individual men or of peoples become embodied in artistic expressions, the problem is much more complicated, particularly if the forms of these expressions are comparatively unfamiliar. Consider an extreme case: the ravings of a madman. It may be said that we cannot really understand these ravings. Our sympathy with his expressions is more nearly like our sympathy with the natural expressions of children than our sympathy with the great artistic expressions which we adequately understand. We are sorry for the madman as a suffering fellow human being. Our interest in him may also extend to another level if, as scientists studying insanity, we take a clinical interest in him. But this cannot give us the kind of sympathy which is under consideration. A sane man is unable to understand the ravings of a madman—that is to say, he cannot share them as he would share the expressions of successful artists. (These comparisons are complex, and it is hard to be confident that one understands them correctly. It may rather be the case that the expressions of the madman offer us our best opportunity to get at—i.e., to communicate with—that which is still rational in him; he is after all still a man. It seems clear that a great deal of mental therapy depends upon getting the patient to express himself. This, however, would only reinforce the point intended by these comparisons: that the means by which other human beings express their feelings may present us with ways of understanding them, even if all other ways are closed. And anyone who achieved this kind of communication with the insane would surely be deeply moved by the experience—he would do much more than merely tolerate the madman.)

There are two closely related features of poetic expressions which are bases of their liberalizing power. First, they are so obviously non-scientific in character. Second, they give concrete representations of abstract ideas and values.

Sophisticated persons debate the cognitive character of art; some argue that it is, and some that it is not really distinct from science. Without really entering this debate we may notice that little children and unsophisticated adults recognize an obvious difference between fact and fiction, and that sophisticated people do too, in their hearts. Moreover, this recognition does not lead people to conclude that art is unimportant, merely because it differs from science. It would be illiberal to draw that conclusion. It is the mark of a narrow mind to believe that only facts are important, and that the only literature which really matters is factual literature. The more that children and adults are made to feel that imaginative expressions are important, and the more they come to realize that these expressions are different from statements of fact, the more they will be encouraged to believe that importance is not confined to the realm of fact. This is a liberal attitude; it can make us sympathetic with the opinions men hold, even if we believe that these opinions are false.

Can it not be suggested in this connection, at the risk of offending social scientists, that this same feature of the humanities encourages some students to regard the social sciences as important? However much the social sciences may aspire to the condition of natural science, they are not able to attain the same degree of precision. This is not simply because their subject matter, society, is so extraordinarily complex, but because this subject matter is so inextricably bound up with non-factual things—values and ideals (it is no doubt these things which make the subject matter of social science so complex). The same reflection affords a means of transition to the second of the two features just mentioned: poetry's concrete representation of abstract ideas and values. It is in the effort to attain abstract and general formulations of their problems and solutions that the social sciences are most like the natural sciences. But the problems of society resist abstract formulation. The full significance of the problems of society cannot be grasped by anyone who is unable to feel their force in the concrete particularizations in which they really exist. It is not that something like the issue of slavery cannot be scientifically understood without the help of a book like *Uncle Tom's Cabin;* but even a scientific understanding of this issue requires us to share the actual feelings of concrete individuals whose lives actually constitute the issue.

Works of art are not abstract statements; nor do they

consist of them. It is, on the contrary, characteristic of art to "give to airy nothingness a habitation and a name." This is the basis of poetry's strong appeal to our feelings. Its non-factual character nourishes our interest in and respect for those aspects of human experience which are somehow independent of the facts about the universe we live in. The strength of their appeal can be utilized, as it has been perennially, to deepen men's interests in the things valued by religion. In general we love concrete individuals more intensely than we love general types. We become more excited or distressed about particular concrete problems than about general kinds of problems. Furthermore, the best way to increase interest in a general problem is to bring men to see what it means in concrete terms. It is possible to remain comparatively indifferent to statistics on human suffering, but not so easy to be indifferent to the actual sight of suffering, or to a moving artistic representation of it. And it is not merely the concreteness itself which moves us in poetry; great artistry can make us see things vividly which we might actually overlook in real life.

The non-factual character of art has direct importance for our problem. Men are coming to recognize more and more that there is no competition between religion and science. The reason is not that one is thought to give knowledge of one sphere of things, while the other gives knowledge of another sphere. It is that religion is not expected to give us knowledge about the nature of things, but to express and to develop our aspirations toward what is ultimate in life. (This does not mean, however, that religion and art are indifferent to the nature of things.) There are thinkers who identify, or come close to identifying, religion and art. Whether they are right or wrong there must be close similarities between art and religion. He who develops a deep interest in art, literature, and poetry is cultivating that side of himself which is also involved in a willingness to take religion seriously.

THE EFFECTS OF LIBERAL EDUCATION ON RELIGIOUS ATTITUDES AND BELIEFS

If the development of our capacity to understand the humanities extends our capacity for sharing an ever-increasing range of human expressions, it should also extend our capacity to acquire a positive sympathy, not merely a negative tolerance, for the expressions of religious literature and art. The humanities, then, can help men to appreciate the civilizing power of religions, all great religions. But if we must in some way share a belief in order to have positive sympathy for it, is it not possible that sharing may lead us to abandon beliefs we had orginally? This question may not bother us if we have any missionary zeal for changing men's beliefs; for this zeal would require us to undermine the beliefs they already have. But the question is an important one for a problem which, like ours, is largely political. If we advocate a kind of education which questions and tests the beliefs and standards which men receive from tradition, we must expect to hear some protests from one part or another of our society. But the educator must not simply seek the safest course, the one least likely to arouse protests. Whenever education advances earlier beliefs or attitudes are bound to be put under new stress. Some of these beliefs or attitudes withstand the stress; others do not. But the educator must in any case move toward the goals he believes in.

Let us consider how a humanistic development of the liberal mind may affect existing religious convictions. First, in a person whose religious beliefs are not very strong, experience in the arts can broaden his sensitivity to the expressions of ideals and values which are so profoundly developed in any one of the great religions. So, genuine aesthetic experience can lead men toward religious conviction, or can strengthen convictions which already exist. Second, however, the person whose religious convictions are already clear and strong will be encouraged, by his aesthetic experience, to open his mind in some positive way to convictions which differ from his own. The two steps are to a certain extent incompatible. If we first come to conviction about one set of beliefs, and then develop a positively sympathetic attitude toward a different set, the later attitude seems to undermine the first.

There are, however, some reassuring considerations on this score. We should realize that negative tolerance may move in a similar direction, but without benefit of the counteracting forces I shall discuss below. The man who is negatively tolerant of convictions with which he has no sympathy regards these convictions as somehow unreasonable. He may even be led to abandon his own religious convictions because, impressed by disagreements about religion and by what he regards as widespread irrationality on the subject, he concludes that rational beliefs are impossible here. He leaves doctrine out of religion and tries to find in the great doctrinaire religions something he can approve of outside of their doctrines. He wants to love the believer without paying any attention to his beliefs, because these beliefs annoy him. This could be overstated by saying that the negatively tolerant man believes all doctrines are false, so he concludes that it does not matter what doctrine one holds—and that it would be even better to hold none. The positively tolerant man believes that there are fundamental truths in all the great doctrines, so that it does not matter too much which one of them one holds—although it is good to hold one of them. (2)

I have been trying to show that the liberal attitude of mind encouraged by wide and intelligent experience with the humanities is not the only attitude which may undermine existing religious convictions. It may now be added that art, though very powerful in its influences upon human attitudes, is not necessarily destructive of particular beliefs. Many thinkers, notably Plato and Augustine, have respected and even feared the power that art has over human feelings and actions. The arguments they use, however, are not favorable to some sets of religious beliefs and unfavorable to others. There are Catholics, Protestants, and Jews who are sympathetic to these arguments; there are Catholics, Protestants and Jews who oppose these arguments. Authorities of the Roman Catholic Church have made many pronouncements about religious music; there are many Protestants who agree strongly with the purport of these pronouncements.

Actual works of art may seem at first glance to be particularly favorable to particular sets of beliefs. After all, they were made by men who held particular beliefs. Still, it is striking that works of art intended as expressions of the beliefs and attitudes of Roman Catholics have been widely used in the services of other churches. So common is this sort of thing that it strikes one as tragic that different groups of people have shared so much appreciation of artistic expressions of religious attitudes, and yet have been indifferent or hostile to one another. How sad it is to reflect that Jews and Christians have both found the Old Testament a rich source of inspiration for many centuries, and that bitter enmities have nevertheless separated the two groups so often!

Is it not clear that art is capable of expressing profoundly felt values which appeal to many different faiths? To feel the expressive power of these things we need not, therefore, turn in the direction of one particular creed, and against others. The point is confirmed by the existence of many literary masterpieces which have been comparatively independent of use in organized religious institutions, but which are nevertheless strongly religious in subject matter. These too appeal strongly to men of very different faiths. Poems like Milton's *Paradise Lost* interest many persons who do not share much if any of the dogma to which Milton seems to have been committed. The same thing is true of Dante's *Divine Comedy*. The idea comes to mind that the dogmas in these poems have nothing to do with their poetic beauty; that one can ignore the dogmas and admire the poetry. This is too simple an explanation. There must indeed be something about the dogmatic material which can in some respect be ignored. But we must not go too far in this direction, or we may conclude that poetic expression is achieved in some mystical way, independently of the words and ideas which serve as vehicles of expression. Religious feeling is an essential part of such masterpieces as the *Divine Comedy, Paradise Lost, The Brothers Karamazov,* or *The Wasteland,* and those who feel the beauty of these works must share their religious feelings in some positive way. This difficulty can be solved by regarding the poet's feeling about the dogma, not the dogma itself, as the important thing, from the point of view of poetry.

Many of the particular features of the subject matter of great works of literature are looked upon very differently by the artists and by their readers. What does a reader find in a poem if he disagrees with the poet about some of the poem's details, and yet shares the expression of the whole? The reader may be indifferent or hostile to the poet's intellectual convictions about those details. But the sensitive reader cannot be indifferent to sincere poetic feeling. The way he takes the poet's feeling has some similarity to the way in which the scientist may take an hypothesis; like the scientist he follows it wherever it may lead. The parallel is not perfect, for the scientist's provisional acceptance of an hypothesis is colored by what we call detachment. Even if the reader of the poem disagrees with that which he is willing provisionally to accept, he cannot really go along with the poet in a spirit of detachment, so far as the poet's dominant feeling is concerned. The *Iliad* cannot be fully appreciated by a reader who does not in a significant sense share the wrath of Achilles; but this does not require that he really accept the moral standards Homer gives to Achilles. Real life offers clues to what is meant here, in the field of emotion. We may think that the child's hopes and fears are foolish; but if we love her we cannot be detached about her hopes and fears. The lost doll is a trifle, in adult eyes; but the loving parent appreciates the crisis this causes in the child's life. On the adult level, too, we may not be able to understand very well why our friend loves some of the things he loves—a dog, a book, a friend, or his wife. But if we know anything of love we do far more than tolerate these objects of our friend's affection, even if the objects themselves repel us. We sympathize positively with his attitudes toward the things he loves; but we do not try to take these things for ourselves. We can also sympathize with many religious beliefs, but this does not mean that we have to make these beliefs our own.

It is not maintained here that religious art is not at all likely to change convictions. On the contrary, it very well may—it would certainly dismay the artists if they thought it could not. But this is a risk education must be willing to take. When education changes people (and it is not education if it does not) it makes them hold their convictions, whatever they may be, more sincerely and more intelligently. If a broadening of our range of sympathies makes us seek new foundations for our lives we must have needed new foundations. The new foundations must be there to find. They may or may not be appropriate for our traditional beliefs. But no belief can be damaged by being placed on a firmer foundation.

HUMANISTIC EDUCATION FOR PROSPECTIVE TEACHERS

Let us now consider in a more concrete way the humanistic education needed by prospective teachers, whether teachers of the humanities or of other subjects. First it should be clear that we are not asking how we should begin the higher education of the professional humanistic scholar. We must not presume that his higher education should begin in the same way as that of the prospective teacher, and it is the latter that we are considering. (3)

Let us begin with the person who expects to teach the humanities. What relationship with the humanities will peculiarly characterize his work? The teacher of humanities will continually be endeavoring to lead his students to genuine aesthetic experiences. His activity is one of those activities which must continually keep its goal directly in view. This is not true of all activities. The general practitioner and the medical research scientist both have health as their goal. The former must keep this goal constantly in mind. The people he works with are sick people whose health he tries to restore if he can. His activity is therapy, and his work is directly therapeutical. If he cannot cure a patient, he will refer him to someone who he hopes can cure him. So different is the work of the research scientist that we can easily imagine him making persons sick on purpose. When he performs experiments along this line he ordinarily uses animals as his subjects, not human beings; but the principle of the difference is not affected by this. He may take his eye off the ultimate goal of health; his work not only allows him to do this, it may require it. There is a similar difference between the teacher of humanities and the humanistic research scholar. The former always has human "patients" before him; his interest in producing health. There may, on the other hand, be a considerable distance between the work of the humanistic scholar and the appreciation of art which lives only in the experiencing of art. If it is good scholarly work, it should ultimately enrich those experiences, but seldom directly. The humanistic scholar can and does separate himself for long intervals of time from actual contact with the struggles of the humanistically ignorant. The teacher of the humanities lives with and struggles against their ignorance.

If the work of the good teacher of humanities is particularly characterized by his continual contact with the development of living appreciations, in this mind and that, of this work and that, a very great proportion of his humanistic education should be devoted to the acquisition of a very broad range of aesthetic experiences. He will have less time than his more scholarly colleagues to devote to the "scholarly literature" in his field. He should read, look at, and listen to very many works of art; he will not need to read much *about* them. Sharp lines between teaching and research do not exist, and the teacher must learn to follow some of the bypaths of humanistic research because these bypaths may disclose to him means which he may find useful in bringing genuine appreciation to life in his students—just as the general practitioner can make his therapy more effective by keeping up, so far as he can, with the latest research.

Having emphasized the broad range of aesthetic experiences which our prospective teacher should achieve, I must qualify this emphasis. I do not mean that he should read, listen to, and look at as many works of art, of as great a variety, as he possibly can. If he does, he may indeed acquire an acquaintance with many things; but acquaintance is not enough for the liberal humane attitude. He who tries to get too much will get nothing. Too high a price could be paid for broad acquaintance: one might fail to understand any one of the works he became acquainted with. The consequence of this would be nothing more than the negative liberal attitude. If no expressions of great value have really been communicated to him, our student would have achieved no positive foundation for his teaching.

There is no simple rule of thumb which can tell what the best education should be for such a student. In general he must be brought to some minimum variety of genuine aesthetic appreciations. The appreciation must be genuine, and it should also have some minimum variety. Theoretically the germinal forces capable of spreading toward catholicity, i.e., toward liberality, could be firmly established in *one* kind of genuine aesthetic experience; but sound pedagogy requires us to go at least one more step. The humanistic liberal spirit which we wish to make viable will need to be nourished by experience in several strikingly different kinds of art. At the very least this means that, for each prospective teacher of, say, English literature, some real variety of English literature should be studied to the point of real understanding. I should not go so far as to say that this student should not allow himself to become expert in any one phase of English literature. Nor should I say that he cannot afford to be comparatively ignorant of one or more phases. He should have the rewards which come through expertness, and he should be allowed to pay the price of expertness: comparative ignorance of some things. But he should be primarily concerned with having a good grasp, even if not an expert's grasp of several phases. Men are seldom truly expert in more than one phase of their subject, although they can develop a high degree of intelligence about several phases. It is the latter which should be the primary object of the prospective teacher of the humanities.

This same person should also attain intelligent understanding of literature outside the English-speaking culture. How far should this go? To non-Western literature? The general answer should be yes. One should hesitate only in situations where there is not adequate professional guidance for leading students to sound understanding of works significantly foreign to those of our own culture. (4) And the student should not be allowed so to dissipate his energies, in exploring many more or less exotic fields, that he never really arrives at a true appreciation of anything. Exotic works are, generally speaking, more difficult to understand than works from our own culture. One should learn to read and write one's own language first. The study of exotic works, therefore, should be postponed until the later years of education. May I note here that this assertion seems to imply a general principle: that one should always begin with the familiar, and postpone study of the unfamiliar. This cannot be made a general principle, as will appear from what follows.

How do these considerations, about the range of materials

appropriate for humanistic study, and particularly about the role of exotic literature, apply to art and religion? The first point to notice is that our culture, although it has many single strands running through it, is very heterogeneous with respect to religion. The situation is of course different in different American communities, for some are less heterogeneous than others in this respect. But there are very many communities where it is simply impossible to point to one religion and to say, "This is the religion which is familiar to our students; the others are unfamiliar." There are also two other features of the humanities which qualify what I have already said about art in general, and which are of special importance in application to religion. First, much of the appeal which art makes to men is founded on their interest in the unfamiliar. Second, art has extraordinary power to break down the walls which separate one kind of life from another.

Interest in the unfamiliar is congenital and universal. One of the major sources for satisfying this interest has always been art. We think of the tale which holds children from play and old men from the chimney corner as a tale of wonder. The perennial vigor of what has been called "romantic art" (which was never confined to the historical movement known as "Romanticism") is based upon this: the appeal of unfamiliar far-off things, of "magic casements." This fondness for the remote manifests a desire for vicarious experience of many things which are not, and perhaps never will be available in real life. It is not merely a desire for a clearly better life than fortune has given us. It is not only the case that the kitchen maid likes to read stories placed in circumstances of wealth and high social position. The aristocrat also likes to read about the virtues of poverty and the simple life. The ideas of chivalry and of the noble savage are very different, and both now belong—and perhaps always did—to a world at some distance from reality; and both have worked a perennial fascination over the minds of men.

The other feature, art's power to break down the walls of prejudice, is the basis of its importance for our problem. The liberalizing effects of art are so great that they should not be delayed if they do not need to be. The feature dealt with in the preceding paragraph indicates that little delay is necessary. The teacher should exploit this fact. He does not need to push very hard to get his students under the power of works of art which express ideals and values very different from his own. The student walks willingly, nay eagerly into the trap. Why keep him out?

Nevertheless, it is not altogether easy to reconcile these reflections with the idea that the familiar is easier to learn than the exotic. The two things must be harmonized, but they can be harmonized only in practice. Some humanistic education should go rather far from the ideas and values which are close to the traditions of our students. How far is a question only the teacher can decide, in the light of the circumstances he works in and of the successes or failures of his experiments. We do not really know how difficult it may be for students to understand, say, works of Oriental art; we simply have not had enough experience in teaching such things. Experimentation is called for, and there are already signs which should encourage us. We do know now that the kind of perspective which characterizes Oriental drawings, and which is so different from techniques of perspective in Western art, presents no serious stumbling block to the Western student. Moreover, many teachers of art find that it is very fruitful to get students to think about such drawings very early in their experience. It not only opens their minds to an appreciation of the characteristics special to Oriental art; it also provokes interesting reflections about art characteristics which are more familiar. In summary, it is foolish to try to say that humanistic teaching can go so far, but no farther, at this point or that in a student's education, in introducing him to works which are in some degree foreign to his own culture. Experiments should be tried, and those who try them should come to their own conclusions, and publish them.

Something more definite can be said about the kinds of works which we ordinarily think of as belonging to our culture. But very little actually needs to be said. I have considered a considerable quantity of course materials in the form of reading lists and schedules, and many anthologies and publishers' lists of humanistic material. In general these materials leave very little to be desired. The humanities may be significantly different in this respect from the other areas dealt with in other chapters of this book. Humanistic works of various sorts which have significant religious dimensions are ubiquitous; and humanities teachers and staffs are using them. One could compile a composite list of works which receive continual attention in very many good colleges, and one could mark with an asterisk those works which have interesting and significant religious dimensions; the number of such works would be large. But such a list would not be very illuminating for many teachers. Teachers know these things already. Perhaps the reading lists of individual teachers would not always stand up well when compared to such a master list; but the reason for this would not be that the teacher did not know the works on the master list, nor which ones were significantly religious. Narrowness in the materials used by this teacher or that is usually the consequence of the teacher's personal narrowness, a narrowness of his own taste, not of knowledge of what the great works are generally acknowledged to be.

Consider how common it is for humanities courses to make use of works produced centuries ago, and to do this very early in the course. And these works are used by courses which are very different in their plans. A course may, for example, treat art chronologically, against an historical background; or in terms of standard types of literature; or in connection with some pattern of ideas; etc., etc. Regardless of the manner followed by teachers or anthologists, works from the ancient world, from the sixteenth century, and from more modern times are usually included (some periods are neglected, to be sure, but this does not matter too much for our present problem). Some form or other of historical presentation is generally followed, even if the principle of organization is types, rather than periods of literature. We begin with something like the Old Testament, *The Iliad*, or plays of Sophocles, move on to Shakespeare, and only at the end deal with works of our own particular culture. This, incidentally, is good enough from the point of view of one of my principles. It confronts the student very early with something very remote from his own experience, at least superficially remote. But it has the odd consequence of seeming to treat modern art and literature as more strange than any other. (No doubt this is not always accidental, for many teachers, like many laymen, probably feel in their hearts that modern art, music, and literature are very strange indeed!)

I have been speaking of degrees of broadness or narrowness. Actually, the number of instances in which individual teachers use too narrow a range of materials is small, and the reasons for this follow from the general character of the humanities, as I have been viewing them. If the study of the humanities is broadening and liberalizing, those who teach them are likely to have been liberalized by them, or they would not be teachers of the humanities. Still, it may be worthwhile to add a few words calculated to reduce the amount of narrowness which may actually exist.

First, one of the great advantages possessed by courses or sequences of courses taught by staffs, rather than by individuals, appears in this connection. Be the humanities ever so liberalizing, peculiarities of individual taste will always exist. But the larger the number of persons engaged in a common enterprise of planning and teaching a humanities course or sequence, the more these peculiarities of taste are likely to be balanced. This advantage is of course easier to obtain in a large college or university than in a small one. But it is not always as fully exploited as it could be.

Second, where the broadening influence of staff planning and teaching is not practicable we can at least exhort the individual teacher to be aware of the dangers of narrowness. It is easy to find out what colleagues are doing, within or outside of one's own college, and it is the duty of individual teachers, particularly those who have the most freedom in the planning and teaching of their courses, continually to compare their work with the work of their colleagues, and to be candid in judging themselves. This applies to all the kinds of material which might be utilized in the teaching of the humanities. It is not specially applicable to religious materials. Still, the question of religion provides a good touchstone for examining one's own work. One need not try to "bring religion into" one's teaching, but one can nevertheless ask what religious dimensions are in fact included in the materials we now in fact use. If these dimensions are liberally represented we have a sign of health; if not, something is likely to be wrong. For religion has been and continues to be so powerful a force in life that no broad range of humanistic materials could leave religion out, by sheer accident, for the humanities have always expressed the things which men have found important.

Turning now to prospective teachers of subjects other than the humanities, we must ask what their own humanistic education should be. The amount of time they have available for the humanities will be comparatively limited; nevertheless, I hope that what I have been saying applies also to them. I should at the very least plead for as much humanistic education as the other needs of these prospective teachers would allow. It is perhaps my prejudice that all teachers, regardless of the subjects they teach, would be better teachers if they received far more education in the humanities than they now do. Aside from differences in quantity, and from factors that follow from them, I do not see that the humanistic education of prospective teachers should be essentially different just because they are to teach different subjects. If I were planning the humanistic study for a teacher of science, say, I would take as my model what I have proposed for the teacher of the humanities, and approximate it as closely as possible. The same principles would apply: 1. to endeavor to develop a genuine appreciation of each work studied (in a genuine appreciation a person grasps a work *intellectually,* and is *moved* by it), and 2. to make certain that the works thus appreciated include some which are very different from one another, and some which the student is likely to regard, from the point of view of the traditions most familiar to him, as strange.

4

Teaching About Religion in the Social Sciences *

Nearly a century ago the French historian, N. D. Fustel de Coulanges, took the occasion of his inaugural lecture on Greek and Roman history (1) to comment upon some defects in his own education. Fustel told his listeners that he, like most men of his generation, had been raised on the history of ancient Greece and Rome, yet, when he left school and tried to reflect seriously upon the ancients, he discovered, "At each step I was hampered by facts which struck me as odd, which upset my ideas, and which I could not make clear to myself." (2)

Disturbed and fascinated by his own lack of understanding Fustel decided to disregard what he had been taught about the ancients and turned instead to what they had written; he would "have no other teachers on Greece than Greeks, nor on Rome than Romans." (3) In the study of the sources Fustel thought he discovered the reason for his own defective historical education. His teachers had described the deeds and institutions of the ancients without realizing how greatly their own

* This chapter prepared by Dr. Kenneth S. Cooper, Professor of History, George Peabody College for Teachers, Nashville, Tennessee.

beliefs about man, the soul, and life after death differed from those of the ancients. They tried to view the Greeks and Romans "through the opinions and facts of our own times." (4) Failing to understand ancient beliefs, modern historians failed to understand ancient institutions because "between beliefs and institutions there is such a close bond that one explains the other." (5) If a student approached Greek institutions without understanding Greek religions, Fustel argued, he found them "obscure, whimsical, and inexplicable." (6) What men had thought of their own nature and destiny was essential to understanding their politics; "the opinion that a man forms of human nature must in every society have a great influence on the manner in which he lives and governs himself." (7)

Like many men intent upon pushing a particular approach to history, Fustel stated his position in an extreme form, but it is not necessary to agree without qualification that beliefs explain institutions to recognize that we must understand beliefs in order to understand societies. We need not, for example, assert that the Hindu religion is the cause of the caste system in order to agree that religious beliefs help justify this social institution to those who live under it.

This chapter is based on the assumption that knowledge about religion is an important aspect of the scholarly study of human society, and it is particularly concerned with the place of such knowledge in the education of teachers. Such interest in religious beliefs may be misunderstood as an effort to promote religion. Many of Fustel's contemporaries assumed that he sympathized with the Church in French politics since he emphasized the importance of studying religious beliefs. The clericals who publicly approved his work actually embarrassed him because, of course, they missed the point. He was not trying to advance the cause of institutional religion; he was simply seeking to understand history better. (8)

It should also be noted that some who have written about the role of religion in higher education want a great deal more than Fustel. Some Christian scholars, for example, have called for the teaching of history of political science from a Christian point of view. (9) They believe that only Christianity illuminates the truth which the college or university seeks.

Arguments for Christian approaches to the study of man deserve a hearing, just as do arguments for a materialist approach or any others, but this is not the position taken in this chapter. This is not a plea for teaching the social sciences from either a Christian or a religious perspective. This chapter seeks to discuss the place which knowledge about religion should have in the social sciences in order that they may realize their own purposes as scholarly disciplines.

Some readers may think this too limited a view; they may even think it a shallow one. They may believe that such a restricted approach leaves out the heart of the matter. They may feel that this is like going to a football game merely to watch the spectators instead of the players. Some Christians and Jews believe that education should do more than teach knowledge about religion because their own faiths are the foundation on which they base their whole view of the world, and they cannot regard any education as complete which leaves out what they believe is the central truth of life. Although public and non-denominational teacher education institutions may recognize the importance of such convictions, they cannot base education upon religious truth for the time-honored and practical reason that men in our society have such diverse and contradictory ideas about truth. Such institutions can hardly do more than teach students about religion in society, which practice at least provides an intellectual setting for whatever beliefs they hold.

Some readers will, no doubt, note that the point of view taken here is based upon certain beliefs; some may call it a religion of sorts. It is assumed, for example, that knowledge is good, that men benefit from a fuller understanding of their own and other societies. Far from denying the assumptions, we will devote a later part of this chapter to pointing out that all of the social sciences make such assumptions and that many of them inescapably have religious implications.

RELIGION AND SOCIAL SCIENCES IN GENERAL

Fields Considered as Social Sciences in This Chapter

The term social science is used in several different ways in spite of repeated efforts to frame some standard definitions, and no attempt is made in this chapter to frame yet another one. In practice, American teacher education institutions commonly class together as social sciences those disciplines or studies which treat of human society both in the past and present, although the methods and even the purposes of these fields may differ somewhat. In such institutions the social sciences generally include history, political science, economics, sociology, anthropology, and human geography. Certain of these disciplines may well be classed with other divisions of knowledge; history, for example, may also be considered as one of the humanities. There are also other fields of learning which may belong, or should belong, among the social sciences. However, no division of human learning is completely satisfactory, and custom determines the division used here since the partition of learning is not the main business of this chapter.

Religion Not Defined

Definitions of religion are about as numerous and varied as its forms, and there is no effort in this chapter to propose another. Definitions in the social sciences are tools, (10) and scholars in the different disciplines may find it useful to define religion in different ways. A historian may well regard religions as systems of belief in the supernatural, divine, or spiritual, since such a definition describes the historic religions of

Christianity, Buddhism, Judaism, Hinduism, and Islam. A sociologist, on the other hand, may find it useful to define religion in terms of function and so class such secular movements as nationalism, socialism, fascism, and communism as "secular religions." (11) The definition used will depend upon the purpose sought.

Two Aspects of the Scholar's Task

The person who teaches or writes about human society does two kinds of things; he ascertains and presents facts, and he reflects upon them or interprets them. The factual and reflective aspects of the scholar's work can be seen in almost any class lecture or any book. In a solid work of history such as Steven Runciman's *A History of the Crusades,* (12) the reader finds an impressive number of facts about the Fourth Crusade as to dates, persons, and events. But in addition to describing an event such as the Crusader's attack upon the Christian city of Constantinople, Runciman's book also includes passages like this:

> There was never a greater crime against humanity than the Fourth Crusade. Not only did it cause the destruction or dispersal of all the treasures of the past that Byzantium had devotedly stored, and the mortal wounding of a civilization that was still active and great; but it was also an act of gigantic political folly. It brought no help to the Christians in Palestine. Instead it robbed them of potential helpers. And it upset the whole defense of Christendom . . .
>
> In the wide sweep of world history the effects were wholly disastrous. Since the inception of its Empire Byzantium had been the guardian of Europe against the infidel East and the barbarian North. She had opposed them with her armies and tamed them with her civilization. (13)

Here is history in both its factual and reflective aspects. The fact that the Crusaders sacked Constantinople cannot be doubted, but as to whether "there was never a greater crime against humanity than the Fourth Crusade," this is a reflective judgment of the historian. Such reflections are properly a part of the scholar's task because without them the facts have little meaning. To be told that the Crusaders sacked Constantinople means little. It is only as the historian judges the effects that the conquest has significance.

The Factual Aspect and Religion

Religion, directly or indirectly, concerns both aspects of the scholar's task, the factual as well as the reflective. The historian, for example, may broadly define his field as the study of what man has thought and done, yet in practice he can study only a tiny proportion of the facts about human history in his whole lifetime. No class which he teaches, no book which he writes could ever contain all the facts about human thoughts and deeds. The historian has to choose which facts he will use, and he selects those which he, or society, judge interesting or important. He selects the facts which he studies and presents upon the basis of a system of values. For example, he chooses to tell the history of technical change and representative government, and so makes a judgment that inventions and governments are important human achievements. The historian may not think that he has made a religious judgment, yet his decision clearly implies certain beliefs about man's nature and destiny which are concerns of religion. A man with other beliefs might think other facts about man's history more significant. A religious mystic, for example, might think that concern with inventions distracted men from their real purpose of seeking communion with God. To him the story of mysticism would supply the significant facts of human history.

There are even religious implications in the approaches of the various disciplines to the study of human society. An economist chooses to study the material means by which men satisfy their wants. This implies a certain view of man's nature —a view which the ascetic Simeon Stylites probably did not share. The concern of the economist with the production and distribution of goods seems to indicate a belief that man's ends are better served by plenty rather than poverty. An ascetic would likely hold the opposite view. Thoreau probably would never have chosen to specialize in economics. In fact, it is hard to imagine any civilization which greatly valued ascetic poverty giving rise to a study like economics.

The Reflective Aspect and Religion

When the teacher or writer treats religious events or institutions directly, he must interpret his material, and his interpretation almost inescapably has religious implications. Here, for example, are the reflections of one historian on the Protestant Reformation.

> As a result of a prolonged and almost morbid religious experience, he (Luther) became convinced that the Catholic Church was wrong in its emphasis upon the possibility of achieving salvation through good works. (14)
>
> . . . . . .
>
> One might well ask why Luther succeeded where Huss had failed a century earlier. The answer is to be found in the changed conditions of the first quarter of the sixteenth century. The abuses of the Church had become more apparent in the century since Huss, and the financial burdens imposed by the Church had become heavier. Likewise, the forces and tendencies likely to find the Lutheran movement congenial to their personal tastes or material interests had become far more prominent and better integrated. German nationalism had become more pronounced and this encouraged the German princes to seek relief from the financial exploitation of the great international ecclesiastical state, the Roman Catholic Church. Moreover, the middle-class merchants and business men had become more numerous and powerful and their policies were more articulate. They welcomed anything that promised relief from the restrictions and limitations imposed upon their practices by the more social-minded Catholic economic doctrines. Especially did they approve of an opportunity to cloak their economic aspirations under the guise of a great moral and religious revolt. (15)

This passage makes it plain how the beliefs of the historian enter into the history. To describe Luther's religious experience as "almost morbid" (16) and to assert that the middle-class merchants welcomed the chance "to cloak their economic aspirations under the guise of a great moral and religious revolt" indicates much concerning the historian's beliefs about men's nature. Plainly he takes their economic desires more seriously than their religious aspirations. When the scholar studies religious events, he obviously must take into account his own beliefs about religion.

But the religious aspects of reflective scholarship are not confined to the direct study of religious institutions. There may be important religious implications in almost any reflective thought even though none is intended. Consider the following declaration of faith written by the anthropologist Margaret Mead in *New Lives For Old*.

> For what we need today is imagination, imagination free from sickly nostalgia, free from the terror of machines bred of medieval fantasies or from the blind weather-bound dependence of the peasant or the fisherman. And yet that imagination must not be empty, for an empty imagination and a free imagination are not the same thing. . . . To be really free one must have good fare to eat, adequate for flesh and bone, one must have tools that one can trust, a horse or a ship or a car or a plane with which to travel swift and far as need be; one must have companions for the task in hand, elders whom one can trust and youngsters for whom the effort is worth the making.
>
> There are a host of voices raised today to say that one or another or all of these conditions cannot be met, that there are no good fares, no tools that can be trusted, no steed to be safely mounted, no companions for the task, that we are hopelessly alienated from the old and only fearful of the fate of the young, and so without fate.
>
> This book is set firmly against such pessimism. It is based on the belief that American civilization is not simply the last flower to bloom on the outmoded tree of European history, doomed to perish in a common totalitarian holocaust, but something new and different. . . .
>
> This precious quality which Americans have developed, through three and a half centuries of beginning life, over and over, in a virgin land, is a belief that men can learn and change—quickly, happily, without violence, without madness, without coercion, and of their own free will . . . we believe that others can change also, and we believe that they will want to change, that men have only to see a better way of life to reach out for it spontaneously. . . .(17)

In this passage Mead gives her answer to the Psalmist's ancient question, "What is man?" All writers do not answer the question so frankly and directly, but they do answer it—at least implicitly. Herbert Butterfield, the historian, has pointed out that it is impossible for a scholar to avoid having a "doctrine on the subject of human beings as they are in the first place,"(18) and that this doctrine determines to a large extent the consequences of his work.

Butterfield noted after the Second World War, that "many people, as they face the developments that are taking place in the world, feel that their expectations have been cheated—feel that the future is not what they thought they had a right to hope for."(19) Their false expectations, Butterfield believed, resulted directly from the kind of history which they had been taught. They had, for the most part, learned a version of history selected and interpreted by historians who thought that man was naturally rational and humane, and that wickedness was due to ignorance and poverty. Since Butterfield believed that "what history does is rather to uncover man's universal sin," he could only regard the optimistic historians as "False prophets who flourished by flattering and bribing human nature, telling it to be comfortable about itself in general, and playing up to its self-righteousness in times of crisis."(20) To Butterfield as a Christian there were important religious implications in the optimistic belief in man's reason and goodness, even if those who held this belief did not realize it.

The social sciences cannot avoid religion. In certain disciplines, as noted later, it forms part of the subject matter which must be directly presented and interpreted. But the concern with religion does not stop here. There are religious implications in the selection of other facts and in the making of other interpretations. The teacher who would avoid all religious matter would, in fact, have to give up teaching about man in society.

The Religious Consequences of the Study of Religion in the Social Sciences

What effect does direct study about religion in the social sciences have upon religious faith? There is no single answer to the question because it obviously depends upon the faith. Scientific learning does not necessarily conflict with religious faith, but *some* learning undoubtedly conflicts with *some* faiths. A group which holds as a fundamental belief that the earth is flat finds conflict between their faith and elementary school geography. The scientific history of languages conflicts directly with the faith of those who believe that the Tower of Babel literally explains the origins of the world's different tongues.

Some people find conflict between their faith and teaching in the social sciences. We should not blink at the fact that a student whose faith depends upon a very restricted view of either nature or human history almost surely faces spiritual problems in higher education. The college or university does not require him to give up his faith, but it does confront him with a scientific view of nature and a larger view of history so that he necessarily sees his faith in a new perspective. He may, for example, continue to believe that the world is flat, but he does so with the knowledge that geographers have what they regard as conclusive evidence that it is round. He may continue to believe a version of history held by none but the members of his own religious group, but he will have to take into account the unusual nature of his belief and realize that it is such a belief which helps explain the group's existence.

It is assumed here that it is good for men to know and that education should seek to give the student a broader view of man and the universe. These assumptions in themselves have religious implications.

Although teaching about religion in the social sciences may affect religious beliefs, a college which tried to avoid direct teaching on this subject would by no means avoid religious concerns. Teaching which ignored religion, which took no account of man's great concern with such things as salvation, righteousness, and God's law, would have very great religious implications, for it would seem to indicate that religion is not real as disease, political power, and economic wants are real. Since those who teach the social sciences cannot avoid religion, at least by implication, it seems desirable that they should be conscious of what they do in this regard.

But along with the obligation to study religion as an aspect of human society, the scholar also has an obligation to make the limits of his study perfectly clear. As a student of the social sciences, he is not seeking to judge the theological truth of religion. The sociologist studies religion as a social institution, not as a system of metaphysics. He may be concerned with the fact that certain religious groups have particular views on such matters as bearing arms or birth control, and he may legitimately reflect upon the social consequences of these beliefs. But as a sociologist he should not try to judge the religious truths or validity of these beliefs. This is a matter beyond the limits of his study, and he should keep these limits clear both to himself and his students.

Recognizing the Importance of Religious Diversity

When teaching directly about religion, the teacher or writer must subject his own beliefs to searching examination and criticism. A person's most lofty desires may produce curious distortions of what is taught. For example, a teacher, eager to promote mutual understanding among peoples may place an unrealistic emphasis upon the similarities of religious faiths and ignore the differences. In an extreme form, he may hold that all religious faiths are fundamentally the same.

It is true that from the sociologist's point of view religions do have some common characteristics. It is also true that men of different faiths may agree about important substantive matters, but they also disagree, and the disagreements are important in understanding the faiths. Buddhist and Christian, Christian and Jew, Protestant and Catholic, all have some of the same beliefs, but they also have some basic differences, and to the devout men of these faiths, these differences are supremely important.

The job of education is to promote understanding of what the social realities are so that students may live more intelligently with them. A teacher or writer may feel that the differences in beliefs are trivial, but he cannot as a scholar judge these matters for other men. Above all, he must not mistake his own views for mankind's. To ignore the fact of religious differences is unscholarly and, incidentally, does organized religion no service.

THE APPROACHES OF DIFFERENT DISCIPLINES

The disciplines classed together in this chapter as social sciences differ in a number of ways. All study human society but with different approaches and emphases. Anthropology, sociology, and history take *whole approaches* to the study of a society or a period of the past, although within each of these disciplines, there may be specialized divisions, such as a history of arts or a sociology of religion. On the other hand, economics, human geography, and political science by their very nature take *special approaches* which emphasize particular aspects in the study of society.

The attention given to religion varies according to the nature of the discipline. The whole approaches can scarcely escape the study of religion. If anthropology is "the study of man and all his works, in time and space," (21) it obviously includes religion. If sociology is "the general analysis of the basic nature of human groups and institutions,"(22) it certainly must include the analysis of religious institutions. If history is "the memory of things said and done" (23) men's religious activities certainly fall within its scope.

Religion is so obviously an object of study in these whole approach disciplines that there is no real question of excluding it. Judging by the widely used textbooks, history courses teach something about Christianity, and sociology courses study the church as a social institution. The only real question concerning religion and the whole approach disciplines in teacher education is: are the treatments of religion adequate and appropriate for those preparing to teach?

The special approach disciplines may also treat aspects of religion. A political scientist, for example, ordinarily considers church and state relations. But in some fields, such as economics, religion receives little or no direct attention, although this does not mean that there are no religious implications.

In discussing religion's relationship to the particular fields, we will consider primarily the general courses taken by large numbers of students rather than the more specialized courses taken by relatively few future teachers. We will, for example, pay more attention to general sociology courses rather than the sociology of religion.

Teaching About Religion in History

The historian is obliged to take religion into account, and this obligation also affords an excellent opportunity to demonstrate the usefulness of history. There is, perhaps, no better way to show how understanding what *was* helps to make plain what *is*. To understand the differences between Protestant and Catholic, or to explain the great variety of religious bodies in the United States, it is necessary to use a knowledge of history.

Most college history teachers make some use of this opportunity. A general history course which completely ignores the history of religion is rather rare in American colleges. Histories of civilization or general histories of Europe pay some attention to the ancient Hebrews, the origins and spread of Christianity, the Medieval church, and Protestantism. If the courses include the civilizations of non-Western peoples as well, students learn something of the origins of Hinduism, Buddhism, Confucianism, and Islam. Most courses at least touch on the issues involving religion and science in the eighteenth and nineteenth centuries, and they probably treat the role of religion in nineteenth century European politics and imperialism. In the usual course in the history of civilization the student will encounter the names of Moses, Jesus, Paul, Augustine, Jerome, Thomas Aquinas, Luther, Calvin, Wesley, and a number of others.

In American history courses students from elementary years on learn of the role of religion in the settlement of the American colonies. They also study something about the place of religion in the life of the new nation, particularly noting such things as the revivalism of the frontier. Almost all American histories describe the importance of religion in promoting social reform in the nineteenth century, and they also note the conflict of science with some aspects of religion, usually bringing in some account of the Scopes trial in Tennessee.

In both histories of civilization and histories of the United States, there is, of course, considerable variation among individual teachers and books with regard to the attention devoted to topics about religion. Some courses will include a number of matters not listed above.

The extent to which this kind of material about religion is included in history courses can be judged by an examination of general textbooks.(24) In addition, other standard materials give some attention to religion. One widely used series of source problem pamphlets includes among its titles: *Puritanism in Early America,*(25) *The Transcendentalist Revolt Against Materialism,*(26) *Pragmatism and American Culture,*(27) and *Evolution and Religion.*(28)

Special courses in history, such as those which treat the

history of thought or that of some particular period, such as the Reformation, naturally give considerable attention to religious topics.

Although history courses include material about religion, the selection is not altogether satisfactory. The typical course in the history of civilization gives much more attention to religion in remote times than in recent times. A student learns about Judaism prior to the Christian era, but he learns almost nothing of the later history of the Jewish faith. A student reads about the structure and teachings of the church during the Middle Ages, but he finds little in his course about Roman Catholicism after the sixteenth century. American histories describe in some detail the role of religion in colonial times, but they say much less about American religion during the past half century.

To treat religion primarily in remote times omits important information about the world as it really is. The story of Prince Gautama is properly a part of Buddhism's history, but it does only a little toward helping a student understand modern Burma or the forms of Buddhism found in Japan and China.

No one would seriously suggest that we omit the history of the ancient Jews in the history of civilization, but should the student also not learn something about the more recent history of the Jews, including the story of Judaism in the United States? Should a student's knowledge of religious leaders stop with John Wesley? If we taught the history of technology as we often teach the history of religion, we would end our account with the invention of the steam engine.

To emphasize religion in remote times and neglect it in recent times may suggest to students that religious faith is outmoded, that it is something which mankind has "outgrown." An individual teacher may, of course, believe that this is true, but he can hardly permit his belief to so limit his course. Those who feel this way may consider the observation with which Will Durant, at the age of seventy-two, begins the sixth volume in his *Story of Civilization.*

> In our youth we may have resented, with proud superiority, its (religion's) cherished incredibilities; in our less confident years we marvel at its prosperous survival in a secular and scientific age, its patient resurrections after whatever deadly blows by Epicurus, or Lucretius, or Lucian, or Machiavelli, or Hume, or Voltaire. (29)

Some teaching about religion proves inadequate because it emphasizes the unusual and colorful incidents rather than the important and representative events. Nearly a half century ago James Harvey Robinson complained of the "kind of history which does not concern itself with the normal conduct and serious achievements of mankind in the past, but, like melodrama, purposely selects the picturesque and lurid as its theme." Such emphasis on the sensational, Robinson declared, was hardly worthy of a serious academic discipline. "In every study except history the teacher seeks to make the important and normal clear at any cost." As an example, Robinson pointed out that, "The teacher of chemistry does not confine himself to pretty experiments, but conscientiously chooses those that are most typical and instructive." (30)

Although James Harvey Robinson was not writing about religion, his criticism may justly be applied to teaching about that subject in many history courses. One might conclude from some American histories that the most important facts about twentieth century American Protestantism were the Scopes trial at Dayton, Tennessee and the revival of the Ku Klux Klan in the 1920's. Even if we grant that these are facts of history, do they "make the important and normal clear"?

History inescapably teaches about religion, but in judging what it teaches, we must ask two questions: 1. Does history represent religion as an aspect of modern as well as ancient life? 2. Does history select facts which meet Robinson's standard of "the most typical and instructive"? Unless history does do both of these things, it falls short of its own purpose as a scholarly discipline.

Teaching About Religion in Anthropology and Sociology

Anthropology and sociology are treated together in this chapter because in the study of religion these two fields become so intermixed. General sociology courses, for example, draw much from anthropology in the treatment of this topic. One recent writer on the sociology of religion, J. Milton Yinger, explains his failure to distinguish between the fields in this way:

> In using the term "sociology," therefore, we have adopted a shorthand way of writing "anthropology-social psychology-sociology," in the conviction that these three fields so thoroughly interpenetrate that a theory based on one of them alone, even if it could be worked out, would be too abstract to be of value. (31)

From their very beginnings as scholarly disciplines both anthropology and sociology have studied religion. Edward B. Tylor's pioneering introduction to anthropology published in 1881 devoted one of its sixteen chapters to religion, for Tylor assumed that the anthropologist had "to look at the religion of nations as a main part of their life." (32) As with other aspects of man's culture, Tylor believed that the scientist could "best become acquainted with their (religions') general principles by beginning with the simple notions of the lower races as to the spirit world." (33)

Herbert Spencer's *The Study of Sociology,* published in 1874, certainly did not ignore religion, although some present-day sociologists might question his conclusion: "Speaking generally, then, each system of dogmatic theology, with the sentiments that gather round it, becomes an impediment in the way of Social Science." (34)

In the usual college course in general sociology, the student studies among other things the following matters:

1. How the anthropologists and sociologists define religion;
2. Theories concerning the origin of religion;
3. The functions of religion—a matter which has received considerable attention in recent years;
4. The nature of religious practices;
5. The ways that society and culture influence religion;
6. The ways that religion influences society and culture; (35)
7. The variety of religious bodies within the United States.

In teaching this kind of material, there are several matters which the college teacher of sociology or anthropology should consider. He should, first of all, keep in mind that his approach, although important, may not necessarily treat all that is important in religion. Professor Yinger firmly believes in the value of a sociology of religion, yet he acknowledges that it does not exhaust the meaning of religion any more than "the analysis of paint, painter, and patron exhausts the meaning of art." (36)

As an educator the teacher of sociology also needs to consider the implications of his teaching. At least one sociologist, William L. Kolb, believes that the objective study of religion confronts scholars in his field with a serious moral dilemma. (37) On the one hand, the functional theory of religion leads to the conclusion that most men in a society must share values and that to do this they "must believe in the validity of values" (38)—they must believe that they are really "true." On the other hand, the knowledge of comparative cultures may lead to the conclusion that there is no way to establish the ultimate validity, or truth, of any values. Kolb believes that the sociologist here faces an unhappy choice. He "must either deceive his public or help in dissolving the forces which hold society together," (39) because "men cannot know to be false what they must believe to be true." (40)

If this were, in fact, the undoubted consequences of the study of religion in sociology and anthropology, many religious groups might understandably view these disciplines with misgivings. But other scholars find other implications. Yinger, also a sociologist, points out that the functional study of religion may lead the student to understand "that religion is a permanent, necessary, and inevitable part of human life."(41) Conceivably such an understanding could provide an intellectual support for religious faith.

Two anthropologists, A. L. Kroeber and Clyde Kluckhohn, have also pointed out that social science does not necessarily destroy a belief in the validity of all values, and they are willing to write of "universals or virtual universals in the realm of values."(42) Although these two anthropologists regard cultural relativism as an "inescapable fact," they do not believe that it justifies "the conclusion that cultures are in all respects utterly disparate monads."(43) Concerning men's value systems, they write:

> There are at least some broad resemblances in content and specifically in value content. Considering the exuberant variation of cultures in most respects, the circumstance that in some particulars almost identical values prevail throughout mankind is most arresting. No culture tolerates indiscriminate lying, stealing, or violence, within the in-group. The essential universality of the incest taboo is well known . . . We know of no culture in either space or time, including the Soviet Russian, where the official ideology denies an after-life, where the fact of death is not ceremonialized.(44)

It should be made clear here that this is not an attempt to prove the truth of traditional religious values. In fact, Professors Kroeber and Kluckhohn see "nothing supernatural or even mysterious about the existence of these universalities in the culture content." They stem from the fact that "Human life is—and has to be—a moral life (up to a point) because it is a social life." If there have been groups which did not hold these social values, they, presumably, "dissolved as societies or perished without record."(45)

As anthropologists, Kroeber and Kluckhohn seek to explain man's values in terms of his biological and social nature. Such a natural explanation illustrates admirably how inescapable are the religious implications of social science, for in dealing with values, the sociologist or anthropologist concerns himself with matters which the theologian also regards as theological. This is also strikingly illustrated in a recent book by the anthropologist Ashley Montagu in which he quite frankly declares:

> Anthropology, the science of man, is just about the youngest of the sciences, and it is, without any doubt, the most important—the most important because it deals with humanity itself, with the great questions of life and of death. What is man? What is he born as? What is he born for? Where did he come from? Whither has he been going? (46)

It may remind us of how largely the anthropologist is dealing with matters also regarded as religious to note that answers to several of these questions could be found in various catechisms.

Nor does the matter stop with these questions. The same author in another work indicates his belief that science and religion give some of the same answers to their common questions.

> The dominant principle which informs all behavior which is biologically healthy is love. Love, social behavior, cooperation, and security mean very much the same thing. Without love the other three cannot exist. To love thy neighbor as thyself is not simply good text material for Sunday morning sermons, but perfectly sound biology. (47)

Professor Montagu does not hesitate to tackle so thorny a matter as the nature of man, a question fraught with theological significance, to put it mildly. In a section entitled, "The Child is Born Good," he sharply criticizes the traditional view of man based upon the idea of "original sin" and reinforced by nineteenth century biology and early psychoanalytic theory. Recent studies, he argues, have "happily" shown that the traditional view is both "unsound, and, what is worse, capable of being profoundly damaging to human beings and to their societies." According to this particular social scientist, "human beings are born good—'good' in the sense that there is no evil or hostility in them."(48)

Professor Montagu recognizes the religious implications of what he writes. He believes that "Our revised conception of human nature . . . should have the profoundest influence upon religion and ethics."(49) To make his meaning clear, he writes:

> Christians believe that God is Love. Our inquiry in this book has amounted to the conclusion that Love is God. It is a distinction with a significance, the difference being that while most Christians accept the view that God is Love, and let it go at that Jesus himself felt also that Love is God, that love of God was essential, but equally essential was the love of man for man.(50)

Regardless of whether this is sound anthropology or theology, it certainly illustrates the important religious implications of an interpretation in social science.

Altogether it would seem that in no other fields of the social sciences would it be more difficult to eliminate all study of religion than in anthropology and sociology. Scholars in these fields must both study religion directly, and, just as important, their interpretations frequently have significant religious implications.

Religion and the Study of Economics

Economics is one of the social sciences which takes a special approach to the study of society. A number of years ago F. R. Fairchild indicated the nature of this special approach when he defined economics as the study of "man's activities devoted to obtaining the material means for the satisfaction of his wants."(51)

Most contemporary economists, judging by the books they write for college classes, seem to believe that economics so limited does not include the study of religion or of even ethical values. They may study the factors which produce inflation and describe its results, but as economists, they *supposedly* make no judgments as to whether inflation is good or bad. Except in economic history, religion receives almost no attention.

The limits of a special approach may be most useful, but those who teach from a particular point of view may well consider several matters. They need to remind themselves that the wants of men mentioned in Fairchild's definition are frequently affected by religion. Men decide according to their beliefs whether to use their resources and labor to build a workshop or a temple, a highway or a monastery. Religion also affects the ways men go about satisfying their wants. Social scientists have long discussed the relationship between religion and the rise of capitalism.

Economists, of course, readily acknowledge the interrelations of religion and economic affairs, but they generally pay attention to these interrelations only in economic history. They generally ignore the matter when they turn to their main concern, the study of the contemporary economic order.

Perhaps, the separation of economics, religion, and ethics may be useful for purposes of analysis, but the separation exists—if it does exist—within the economist's mind, not in society itself. Even if men are able to think about economic processes without reference to ethical judgments, they rarely can act upon their knowledge without reference to some ideas of good or bad. The economic theorist may show a government how it can regulate the flow of money to produce various effects, but when those who govern decide to limit inflation, they make a value judgment. They decide to act because they believe inflation is bad. In actual fact, a wholly economic act probably does not exist any more than a wholly economic man.

Most economists in reality do not refrain from making value judgments. As one of their number, Howard R. Bowen, has pointed out, "few economists, however devoted to scientific purity, have been able to resist converting their abstractions into proposals."(52)

Even in theory economists probably never completely succeed in freeing themselves wholly from value judgments. Shorey Peterson points out in a general work on economics:

> As much as it can, economics tries to avoid rendering ethical judgments, but one basic ethical assumption, nevertheless, is present. It is the assumption that more goods are preferable to fewer goods; that when labor is expended and materials are used, it is better to have a large product than a small one. The very word *economy* implies a primary concern over the ratio of output to input. The word progress is applied to an expanding production and a higher level of living resting on economic goods. Business methods, labor practices, public policies are criticized when they obstruct the flow of goods and approved when they further it.(53)

Since those who teach economics do take a special approach, they should make sure that those who study within the limits never forget that they are there. When looking at one part, they must not assume that they are seeing the whole.

The economist should also never assume that he has escaped all religious concerns merely because he does not study religion directly, outside of economic history. There are also religious implications to his study—implications in his very selection of the special approach, as pointed out in the first section of this chapter. Like the other social scientists, the economists, too make assumptions about what man is and what he is born for, and to the theologian and many others these are religious questions.

Geography and Study About Religion

Insofar as geography is one of the social sciences, it too takes a special approach to the study of society. Isaiah Bowman is said to have once explained its special approach by saying that "geography tells what is where, why, and what of it."(54) More recently, Richard Hartshorne described geography as "the study that seeks to provide scientific description of the earth as the world of man."(55)

These definitions make it clear that, although geography is a special approach, it is also an inclusive study, broad enough to include at least some aspects of religion. Geographic determinists of an earlier day, such as Ellen Churchill Semple, did not hesitate to include religion among the matters they considered. In one famous passage Semple even suggested a causal relationship between monotheism and certain geographical environments.

> Up on the wind-swept plateaus, in the boundless stretch of the grasslands and the waterless tracts of the desert, where he (the pastoral nomad) roams with his flocks from pasture to pasture and oasis to oasis, where life knows much hardship but escapes the grind of drudgery, where the watching of grazing herd gives him leisure for contemplation, and the wide-ranging life a big horizon, his ideas take on a certain gigantic simplicity; religion becomes monotheism, God becomes one, unrivalled like the sand of the desert and the grass of the steppe, stretching on and on without break or change. Chewing over and over the cud of his simple belief as the one food of his unfed mind, his faith becomes fanaticism.(56)

Very few contemporary geographers would accept this kind of relationship between environment and religion, but a number would agree that all factors relevant to the study of man's relationship to a particular environment may be studied geographically, including religion.(57) A geographer could hardly explain the "why" or the "what of it" of Bowman's definition unless he did accept broad limits upon his study.

The influence of religion as one aspect of culture upon men's relationship to their environments can be illustrated readily. People in Moslem lands do not raise swine because of their religion. Hindus in India do raise many cattle, but they do not slaughter them for food because of their religious beliefs. It has been observed that changes in religious beliefs may directly affect the landscape. In some districts of India the people had for centuries preserved groves of trees which they regarded as sacred. The spread of Christianity in certain places destroyed the belief in the sacredness of trees and, indirectly, destroyed the groves as well. One observer has said, "thus the traditional conservation was negated by the advance of civilization." (58)

Although a number of geographers might admit that religion may be relevant to their study, they have not usually given the matter much attention. A general college textbook may state that India has many cattle which are not eaten because they are held sacred, but it gives no further explanation. (59) It is, perhaps, significant that two recent efforts to sum up achievements in the field of geography include chapters on the geography of medicine, manufacturing, race, and military affairs, but they contain none on the geography of religion. (60)

As an instance of what might concern geographers in the study of religion, we cite the suggestion of F. Fraser Darling, a British ecologist, who has pointed out that differences among religions have affected the ways men have changed the face of the earth.

> Western civilization has been markedly influenced by the idea of man's domination over the earth put to him in Genesis. Western man has tended to set himself apart from the rest of animate nature, while other and older civilizations and systems of religion have regarded man as being a part of nature.
>
> . . . . .
>
> Respect for habitat is fundamental in some of the other past and present religions of the world, but in our own it has been foreign to our idea that we have dominion over the earth. (61)

This is the sort of relationship between man's religion and his environment which concerns the geographer as a geographer. Understanding religion becomes clearly relevant to understanding "what is where, why, and what of it."

Teaching About Religion in Political Science

Definitions of political science usually emphasize that it is a discipline which specializes in the study of one aspect of human affairs. Political science is the "scientific method applied to political events"; (62) it is "that science which treats of the organization known as the state." (63) Put most simply, "political science deals with government." (64)

We can expect the political scientist to be concerned with religion only when it affects or is affected by government, but in this regard he has a special responsibility, particularly in teacher education programs. Most students preparing to teach will teach in public schools, and it is essential that they understand the relationship between religion and such public institutions.

It is not enough for students to know that "Congress shall make no law respecting an establishment of religion, or prohibiting the free exercise thereof." An adequate political science will not stop with a mere statement of the constitutional provision; it will make plain the reasons why this provision was added to the Constitution. In addition, political science must teach what this part of the first amendment has come to mean in the course of time.

The field of education is one in which both the states and the churches have had an interest. Regardless of whether a student will teach in a public or a private school, he needs to understand the different points of view which exist regarding religion and education. It may well be that students have too often heard only one side of this matter. Both public teachers colleges and certain church schools have had so great an interest in this issue that objective teaching about it may have suffered. Political scientists in both kinds of institutions should seriously examine their teachings on this point in order to see if they have truly sought to approach objectivity.

Courses in the history of political theory have the same obligation to treat relevant religious material as any other sort of intellectual history. Such courses not only must treat such men as Augustine, Thomas Aquinas, and Bodin; they must also consider the moral judgments present in the thought of almost every political theorist from Plato to Harold Laski.

Teaching About Religion in General Social Science Courses

A number of teacher education institutions have general courses in social science which draw material from the different social science fields. Some of these general courses include material about religion.

The approaches to religion used in these courses vary greatly, but, in general, they use either historical, sociological, or anthropological materials. In some courses students study religious groups as one kind of contemporary social institution, and the treatment generally resembles that of sociology. Other courses offer the student a look at comparative religions, much of the material being historical. Another approach emphasizes the history of the Western religious heritage.

Aside from organization, the general courses have few problems in teaching about religion which are not encountered in the separate disciplines from which they draw material.

ON DOING THE JOB

Good teaching about religion in the social sciences differs little in method from good teaching about any subject. But, although there is no special method for teaching about religion, there are several special things to consider about doing this job.

The Competency of Teachers

When teaching about religion in the colleges is discussed, some people, who willingly admit the importance of religion in human affairs, raise the question: can ordinary social science teachers teach about religious matters in a competent fashion? They point out that religion has its own body of systematic knowledge, its theology, and the mastery of theology is a specialty in its own right. Granted the importance of religion, should anyone teach about it except a theologian?

If a college offers courses in theology, they should certainly be taught by a theologian, however, this chapter is not concerned with courses in theology. This chapter is concerned with courses in sociology, anthropology, history, political science, and economics. It is not a question of the need for courses in theology, but rather the need for the social sciences to give a proper place to religion.

Teachers of the social sciences must teach about many subjects within the context of their fields without being specialists on these subjects. A historian must teach about Galileo, Newton, and Einstein although he is not competent to teach a course in physics. A sociologist must teach about the family in society although he is not an expert marriage counsellor. Certainly a political scientist, although not a lawyer, must discuss the decisions of the Courts.

In these instances the social scientist is not teaching the particular field of science or law; he is teaching about the relationship between science or law and the whole social order. This is his specialty. This is the job which he can do better than the ordinary scientist or lawyer. If social scientists lack the knowledge about religion necessary for teaching their own disciplines, it reveals a very serious shortcoming in the way universities prepare men for these fields.

Furthermore, if there is such a shortcoming, the solution is not to exclude from the social sciences a subject which properly belongs to them. The solution lies in improving the education of social science teachers so that they can teach competently what their disciplines require.

Practicing teachers can certainly "work up" knowledge on this subject just as they do on many others. It is not unreasonable to expect a history teacher to consult such a book as Kenneth S. Latourette's *A History of Christianity.*(65) He will find in it the same historical standards to which he is accustomed in the histories of other subjects, for, although Professor Latourette is a Baptist, a Jesuit reviewer said of this book:

> Here a well-informed outline of the history of Christianity by an eminent specialist who has no Catholic presuppositions and yet endeavors to render account of all the Christian past without any special pleading.(66)

A Methodist reviewer thought that Professor Latourette's style "has been tempered to the point of objectivity whence it is impossible sometimes to discover whether a Baptist or a Roman Catholic is writing."(67)

For what has been described as "a valuable statement of the Roman Catholic position,"(68) a teacher can consult Philip Hughes', *A Popular History of the Catholic Church.*(69) John Tracy Ellis' *American Catholicism*(70) is an excellent history of the Roman Catholic Church in the United States. We should not ask the historian to become a theologian, but we should insist that he teach a truly adequate history.

Some people look suspiciously upon teaching about religion in the usual course of study because they think that the personal beliefs of the teacher will obtrude into the class. They apparently think that a Catholic cannot treat Luther in a satisfactory way, or that a Protestant cannot teach about the role of the Papacy without offending Catholics. The beliefs of the historian are important, as has been discussed elsewhere, but it is well to note that many Protestant denominational colleges over the years have used the European histories by the Catholic historian, C. J. H. Hayes.

It would also surely be a peculiar standard of academic competence to require that only teachers who agree with a position should explain it. If we applied this standard, no one could teach about the South but a Southerner, and no one could lecture on John Calhoun but a fervent believer in states' rights. History departments would always have to divide their labor so that only a Republican would teach about the administrations of Harding, Coolidge, Hoover, and Eisenhower while only a Democrat would deal with the times of Wilson, F. D. Roosevelt, and Truman.

Religion is admittedly a delicate subject so that when teaching about it, a teacher needs to cultivate the qualities of tact and knowledge, qualities important in all good teaching. Tact is a personality trait, the roots of which lie deep in our lives. Some people are undoubtedly more blessed than others with this trait. But the completely tactless teacher will not only have troubles in teaching about religion; he will have troubles teaching about many things.

Although people differ in their sensitivity to the feelings of others, ignorance is one of the causes of tactlessness. The worst blunders are usually those made by people who simply do not realize that their own point of view is not the universal one. The ordinary teacher will avoid stepping on sore toes if he knows where they are. More knowledge is about the only help for tactlessness. If teaching has been tactless, it simply shows the need for more education on this subject.

Clergymen as Sources of Information

A theologian or clergyman should not teach social science courses unless he is qualified in these fields, but he may quite properly be brought into the social science classroom. A teacher of sociology may find it desirable to have a Catholic priest, a Jewish rabbi, and a Protestant clergyman explain to his class the nature of their distinctive faiths. Classes sometimes find it helpful to visit churches and synagogues to learn of different religious practices.

Teachers may well encourage students to explore the periodical literature published by different religious groups. Where there are differences among points of view, such as in the interpretation of history, teachers should encourage students to read historians with different views. When this is done, the teacher should make the points of view of the authors he suggests very clear.

Teachers who have taken their classes to visit different churches almost always report that the procedure both arouses student interest and generally promotes tolerance and respect for the different groups. Incidentally, such visits do not seem to weaken the student's own faith according to the report on one sociology course which stated:

> Some comparative knowledge of religion does not seem to impair individual commitment. The individual who is well indoctrinated and closely identified with a religious system does not become less deeply involved or weakened in his commitment merely by learning about other concurrent and competing faiths. (71)

The respect and tolerance brought about by first hand experience with various groups and their literature will also have the advantage of not being based on a false idea that all groups are really alike. When each group is allowed to speak for itself, the student can see plainly that the differences among religious bodies are both real and important to those who belong to those bodies.

The use of clergymen and visits to churches and synagogues are valuable sources of information, but they do not relieve the teacher of the main responsibility for teaching about religion. The clergyman speaks as a clergyman. He does not come before a class as a sociologist or as a historian, and it must always be kept in mind that the class is studying social science—not theology. The task of interpreting the social science materials remains the specialist's job. The teacher should not abdicate his own special role when he uses sources of information from outside the classroom.

There are several practical matters about using clergymen as sources which a teacher must consider. First of all, the teacher must make the nature of the clergyman's role perfectly clear so that he understands that he comes to inform the class, not to preach to them.

A teacher must also realize that a local clergyman may not always be a particularly effective spokesman for his group on the matters which concern the class. A man may be a most effective local pastor or rabbi, and yet have a rather limited knowledge about the historical or sociological backgrounds of his group. The use of denominational literature is not quite so limited by the local situation, although here too, the teacher must help the student to put such literature in its setting.

A teacher who wishes to use clergymen in class faces a problem of deciding how many to use. Merely to have a Jew, a Catholic, and a Protestant will not be adequate, for American religious life is not simply a three-way division. There are, of course, the Eastern Orthodox Churches and the wide differences among Protestant bodies. There are even differences of opinion as to just which groups are Protestant. Can a Presbyterian clergyman speak for High Church Episcopalians, Nazarenes, and Lutherans, to say nothing of Christian Scientists, Mormons, and Jehovah's Witnesses? Yet, it is clearly impractical to have spokesmen from every group appear before a class. In practice a teacher must do much to present material about many of the groups through his lectures, class discussion, and assigned readings.

The Use of Discussions in Teaching

In teaching about religion teachers have found both lecture and discussion techniques useful. Under one plan which has been tried, a sociology class was divided into small discussion groups, each containing Protestants, Jews and Catholics. (72) Each member of the group explained what he knew about his own faith, and then the group drew up a list of questions about matters on which they wanted more information. These lists were passed on to the clergymen who were invited to lecture to the class. This technique caused students to think more clearly about their own faiths, and it also indicated to the lecturers what they were expected to talk about.

Discussions probably mean more to students when they deal with specific situations rather than generalities. The relationship of church and state in this country probably becomes clearer and more interesting when students discuss it in terms of the specific cases which have reached the courts. (73)

The Use of Questionnaires and Inventories

Some teachers in social science courses have found it useful to use questionnaires which seek to discover how much information students have about different religious groups. Such questionnaires give a teacher information about his group, and we need to know what our classes know in order to teach most effectively. A questionnaire may also be given to a class at the end of a period of study so that there can be some indication of whether any changes have occurred.

Some instructors have also used religious and value inventories. These too may help a teacher to know his class better. In addition, an inventory will help focus student attention upon the subject of religion. For example, when an inventory was given to one class, one member of the group later asked for an extra copy of the inventory so that she and the other girls in her dormitory could discuss it.

Such inventories must be administered with care, since a teacher's desire to stimulate interest in religion should not differ significantly from his desire to stimulate interest in any of the major topics studied. A teacher obviously should not make it appear that certain positions on an inventory scale are good or right and others wrong. This would not only defeat the purpose of making an inventory, but—even more important—it would violate the purposes of teaching about religion in the social sciences. In his methods as in every other part of his teaching about religion, the social scientist must remember that his purposes are those of describing and understanding human society more fully and adequately.

5

Teaching Reciprocal Relations Between Natural Science and Religion[*]

THE POINT OF VIEW

This chapter is about natural science, i.e. with the biological and physical sciences. Primarily, of course, it is about science teaching and the preparation of science teachers. It discusses religion also, but mainly to ascertain whether—and possibly how—knowledge and understanding of religion can contribute significantly to the realization of worthy objectives in science teaching. It is not concerned with religion for its own sake and does not propose that science be taught as an adjunct to religion. It takes for granted that the professional business of science teachers, especially in public education, is to teach science—not religion.

Admittedly this is not only an inquiry. It also presents a particular educational point of view and definite proposals as a basis for discussion and for attempts to solve an important problem. For one thing, it advocates that the expression "to teach science" must not be interpreted too narrowly. Indeed,

* This chapter prepared by Dr. Harold K. Schilling, Dean, Graduate School, The Pennsylvania State University, University Park.

it insists that both "to teach" and "science" have far-reaching connotations, even if the use of this term is restricted, as it is throughout this chapter, to the natural sciences. The argument rests on the following assumptions about science, about teaching, and therefore about science education:

1. Teaching should do more than transmit items of knowledge and develop a technical understanding of them.
2. Knowing science means far more than being able to recall an aggregate of either isolated or connected facts and ideas. It includes an understanding of their nature and interrelations, of how together they constitute useful conceptual systems, and how they depend upon a particular methodology.
3. Knowing science means also understanding how the kind of knowledge attainable through science is different from, or similar to, other kinds.
4. Science, like every other discipline, can be understood and appreciated adequately only when it is seen in broad perspective, as one of many components of the total intellectual enterprise and of life, each having reciprocal relations with all the others.
5. Science education should therefore not only present science in the details of its content but should also develop an understanding of its nature, its methods, its relation to and significance for other fields. Moreover it should stimulate the student to develop his own philosophy of the world and of life, and help him to see what unique contribution science and each of the other disciplines can make to it, and how within it they can be related to each other meaningfully.
6. A student's knowledge and philosophy affect his attitudes, motivations and actions, as well as his growth and maturation. They may generate intellectual, spiritual, social and professional desires, produce good or bad tensions, and strengthen or weaken his character. Science has such

effects, and it is proper for the science teacher to take such matters into account in designing his courses, especially those intended for general education.

Now it is maintained throughout this book that the study of religion in its various manifestations and aspects is a discipline, a field of learning (discipulus: learner) with its own body of knowledge and method, and that it is significantly related to other disciplines. If this premise be accepted, then in harmony with the foregoing assumptions there exists at least the possibility that a study of the interrelations and interactions between science and religion may contribute to the student's understanding of science and may therefore be a proper subject of study in science education—and in the education of science teachers. Whether this is more than a possibility depends, of course, on whether the relations in question are truly significant from the viewpoint of science itself and of the broader educational purposes expressed in the foregoing assumptions. My thesis is that the relations are indeed significant.

Before proceeding with this analysis I should state that, with the other authors of this book, I have deliberately chosen not herein to define either religion or science. Both have been defined elsewhere from many points of view. (1) Our position is that any religion, recognized as such by scholars, can be the subject of disciplined, intellectual inquiry, and therefore has significance relative to other studies including science. "Official" adoption for purposes of public education of any one definition of religion would, no doubt, at once invite criticism and protest from those employing other definitions, on the grounds that their own religion would thereby be discriminated against and thus be made to appear in the wrong light. As to theology, in harmony with one of the standard usages I regard it as being internal, not external, to religion. In this sense theology is the interpretational aspect of religion, and is related to experiential religion somewhat as theoretical physics is related to experimental physics.

This chapter is not intended to be a systematic discussion of *Science and Religion,* or *Science versus Religion.* I have tried not to "take sides" or espouse particular points of view regarding the many perplexing problems in this field, or suggest what conclusions teachers and their classes should reach in their studies and discussions. My purpose is, rather, to survey the field to identify reciprocal relations, problems and issues that are important and worthy of discussion, and to point out where pertinent material about them may be found in the literature.

SCIENCE EDUCATION AND RELIGIOUS THOUGHT

Let it be understood that I do not claim that religion, religious experience, religious phenomena and concepts constitute any of the "subject matter content" of the natural sciences. Obviously the situation here is distinctly different from that in some of the social sciences. Thus for anthropology, history and sociology religion is an object or phenomenon to be investigated as part of their business. For mechanics, optics and genetics, however, it is not. Therefore I can see no reason for introducing religious subjects into the traditional courses devoted exclusively to the exposition of the subject matter of natural science itself. Surely, when the purpose of a course is to portray only what is internal to a particular discipline, the study of its reciprocal relations with others is not pertinent.

On the other hand, many science teachers feel that the over-all purposes of science education cannot be achieved if they confine their efforts exclusively to teaching courses with such narrow purposes. Moreover, most of them would no doubt reserve, and vehemently defend, the right to philosophize in any of their courses, to look critically at scientific (2) methodology and to contrast it with other kinds, to compare the scope and range of competence of science with those of other disciplines, and to discuss its significance for culture and its contributions to technology. Indeed most, if not all, of them would assert that only thus can science really be taught—and learned—in all its aspects. If there must be courses, they would say, with as restricted purposes as those discussed in the preceding paragraph, there must also be others with broader purposes—and therefore more inclusive content.

The basic issue, however, is not one of attitudes of teachers, of their likes and dislikes, or their rights relative to the content of their courses. Nor is it even a question of how science courses can achieve worthy educational objectives. Rather, it involves the fundamental question of what science actually is. While it is often thought of narrowly, simply as the sum total of its conceptual content, its laws, principles and theories, many scientists take the position that actually it is much more, that it is method, a mode of thought, a point of view, and even in a sense a way of life. There are good reasons, many would say, for even regarding it as continuous with, and not sharply divided from, the arts and as having a rightful place among the humanities. Certainly it is a product of complex social and historical processes, and not a purely intellectual *tour-de-force* in the structuring of isolated knowledge for its own sake. When science is viewed in this light, an understanding of its many reciprocal relations with other disciplines, including religion, becomes requisite to the understanding of science itself.

Similar conclusions follow from consideration of the meaning of religion. While it, too, can be thought of narrowly in terms of only its own internal content, actually it, like science, is much more than that, namely method, a mode of thought, a way of life and a social phenomenon affected by historical forces and cultural influences. Its systematic study is a discipline with a vast literature, an appropriate methodology, a long history of scholarship, a huge accumulation of knowledge and insights, and impressive conceptual and theoretical structures. That it has influenced science in many ways, and has in turn been greatly affected by it, no one denies. He who is unaware of these interactions does not know all he should about either religion or *science.*

We now state some basic principles which we think should govern the introduction into science courses of non-science subjects, particularly religious subjects. It is desirable, in a highly controversial field like this, to formulate issues and fundamental principles explicitly, especially when there are serious questions of limitations imposed by common sense, professional ethics and legal restrictions. While we present these principles for their special relevance to religious subjects, we have so stated them as to suggest that the argument is general, and applies to those of all fields. Our contention is that in the curriculum the study of religion should be treated just like the other disciplines—with no less and no more rights and responsibilities than the others—and that this is defensible both ethically and legally.

Guiding principles: It is proper and desirable to include a non-science subject, such as some aspect of religion or religious thought, in a science course:

1. Whenever it is likely to produce more adequate understanding in science in any of its aspects;
2. Whenever it enhances an understanding and appreciation of the significance of science for another field;
3. When the objectives of the course in question call for comparative studies of the nature, the methodologies, scope and realm of competence of the various disciplines; or for a study of their mutual interdependence or interactions;
4. When those problems are being considered that science and other fields have in common, such as the philosophical ones of knowledge, truth, certainty and reality;
5. For the purpose of showing how science and other fields

may possibly be fitted together meaningfully in an over-all world view or philosophy of life;

6. In order to analyze and clarify misunderstandings and tensions that are known to exist between science and other disciplines and that cause undue perplexity, or tend to hinder the understanding of either science itself or of its relations to other fields;
7. For the consideration of the ethical and social implications, consequences and obligations of science;
8. When the purpose is to discuss the possible effects of science, and science education, upon the growth and development of character and personality.

In summary, we suggest that it is proper to consider religion, or any other non-science subject, in a science course whenever, but only when, this is logically or psychologically necessary or desirable from the viewpoint of the objectives of a course. In a course with restricted, specialistic purposes such necessity might never arise; in one intended for general education it might arise frequently. Never should the integrity of a course, as defined by its objectives, be violated by the "dragging in" of religion (or any other non-science material) where it is not pertinent. These principles do not apply, however, only to individual courses, but to the whole curriculum of science education. We would emphasize that they should not be thought of as merely permissive, but as having also a mandatory aspect. Clearly if science is to be taught adequately—in its deeper meanings and farther reaches—a curriculum designed for that purpose must include courses in which these principles can and do operate positively, i.e. in which non-science subjects, including some aspects of religious thought, are included systematically and by deliberate intent.

The basic positive goal of the science teacher should be, of course, to present his science so accurately and comprehensively that his students will, first, really understand its nature, content, methods, potentialities and limitations; second, will see it in true perspective relative to other disciplines, including *religion,* and appreciate how it differs from them in method and in the realms of experience and reality with which they are concerned; and, third, may be able to relate them all meaningfully in their thinking and philosophizing.

We urge that to achieve this will require careful planning not only of individual courses with such broad goals explicitly in mind, but also of entire programs of science study in order that the definite availability of such courses may be assured.

CERTAIN PRACTICAL DIFFICULTIES

Teachers wishing to put these educational principles into practice may encounter difficulties arising out of three unfortunate circumstances, which we must recognize, even though we cannot take time to analyze their underlying causes. First, the area of relationships between science and religion, and especially theology, is regarded by many people as one of warfare, or at least serious incompatibility. In it the tone of discussion is often determined more by deep emotion, fear, misunderstanding and suspicion than by fact and unbiased inquiry. Regarding it many men have strong, honest and widely differing convictions. For many it is sacred ground. Therefore the teacher will need much tact, sympathetic understanding and wisdom, as well as deep insight and more than ordinary knowledge of the subject matter of both science and religion. Moreover, this is a field in which too little knowledge, especially if it be inaccurate, can be very dangerous. He who is not willing to pay the price in serious and prolonged effort to achieve real mastery should not enter here.

Unfortunately—and this is the second misfortune to plague us—the knowledge needed in this connection is not easily come by. As far as religion is concerned, what the teacher needs especially to know for present purposes is its intellectual aspects, for those of its relations with science which fall within the purview of the science teacher are mostly conceptual in nature. They pertain to theology and the philosophy of religion more than to religious commitment and practice. But opportunities for gaining such knowledge are rare in public education today. Regarding science the situation is no doubt somewhat better. But while the opportunities are excellent for mastering the internal content of any given science, there are fewer opportunities in conventional teacher education programs, both at the undergraduate and graduate levels, for gaining adequate insights into the interdisciplinary relations of the various sciences. And very few science students, even those attaining the doctorate, carry on systematic studies, voluntary or required, in the philosophy of science.

Where, then, can teachers be found who are competent to teach from the viewpoint presented here? Even highly trained science teachers are likely to be uninformed in the very areas of science and religion where their relations and interactions are at once most perplexing and most significant in terms of educational goals. There can be only one answer. The present generation of science teachers, at least those who accept the challenge of this book, faces a formidable task of self-education—both in science and religion.(3) Those engaged in teacher preparation have the further responsibility of educating coming generations. This is why the American Association of Colleges for Teacher Education is vitally interested in these matters.

The third handicap is the strong opinion held by many scientists that religion is a field in which it is impossible to be scholarly, objective or logical, and that therefore to include it in science education, either directly or indirectly, would be to introduce an undesirable, alien influence. We have no disposition to deny that there is much justification for the prevalence of such views. We would plead, however, that fundamentally they are not sound. There is no field of study in which one cannot, and should not, be logical, unprejudiced and intellectually honest—and the study of religion is no exception in this regard. Religious thought *can* be governed by evidence. And the study of religion *can* be conducted with an open mind, and teaching in this field can be done with unadulterated devotion to scholarly ideals. We urge the study of the relations between science and religion as a legitimate component of science education only on the assumption that such integrity is indeed possible. When the teacher who enters this field encounters opposition he should recognize its legitimate elements and proceed with caution, realizing that it can be overcome in the long run only by demonstrating in actual teaching situations that this subject can be handled successfully without violating the canons of professional ethics and propriety.

APPROACHES IN THE TEACHING OF RELATIONS

We shall now suggest a few general methods that seem especially appropriate for the kind of teaching under discussion here. Much of the material presented hereafter will be more meaningful when seen against the background of purposes and goals toward which these approaches are directed.

Basic to all good teaching, and utterly indispensable for present purposes, is emphasis on meanings. Unfortunately, many a student can glibly recite laws stated in a textbook and yet be utterly unable to say what the word *law* really means in science. Many a student can assert with unhesitating facility that science is organized knowledge—without understanding what kind of knowledge it is, and in what sense it is organized. Even less may he be able to say just when or why he is justified in claiming that he does or does not "know" something. He may assert positively that science "discovers," while the arts "create"—but be pathetically inarticulate when asked what meanings these terms have, whether they are mutually exclusive or not, and what the evidence for such an assertion might be.

Analysis of Similarities and Differences

One effective approach in teaching for meaning is analysis of similarities and differences. To illustrate, the purposes and tasks of science are seen more clearly when it is pointed out explicitly what science does or does not try to do in contrast to the arts, philosophy and religion. The meaning of "law" in science may be clarified by contrasting it with what it does *not* mean, and with what it means in jurisprudence, economics and theology. The understanding of "knowledge" in science is enhanced when contrasted with that of the arts and religion. A discussion of the question, When in science, in art and in religion may we legitimately claim "certainty"? yields more adequate understanding of science itself than one directed to science only. Moreover, teaching by negatives, comparisons and contrasts is a powerful aid in developing awareness of relatedness and an over-all perspective. It also encourages discriminating and critical thinking. (4)

To point up the possibilities of this approach we present the following few questions as illustrations of topics suitable for classroom discussion or term papers. We shall not attempt to answer them—since our purpose is simply to suggest ways of employing this method. Admittedly these are not "easy" questions. Each of them opens up a large area of meanings, issues and problems—as well as many other queries. (5)

1. What kinds of phenomena are the sciences, the arts and religion (including theology), concerned with respectively? (6)
2. Does the term "datum," or "data," have significant meaning in all of these fields? If so, the same meaning? If not, why not? (7)
3. What kinds of "matter" do the sciences, arts and theology deal with respectively? (8)

4. Do concepts play similar, and equally important, roles in these fields? What kinds of concepts are characteristic of each? Do they also have nonconceptual, or ineffable, elements? (9)
5. Are there "functional" relationships or dependencies only in science? (10)
6. When has anything been "explained" in the three different fields? What needs explaining in each? Does theory contribute to explanation? Could there be explanation without theory? Is there theorizing in art and religion? If so, what for? In the same sense as in science? (11)
7. What kinds of problem situations are encountered and solved in the three different fields? When does a given problem belong in the domain of science, or art or religion?
8. How are these three groups of disciplines different or similar in their basic attitudes, purposes and goals?

Analysis of Dynamic Interactions and Cultural Interdependence

Another powerful teaching tool for the identification of significant reciprocal relations is the *analysis of dynamic interactions*. How have science, art and religion, as well as other components of our culture, affected one another in the course of their history and to what extent is such interaction still operative in society today? How do they interact in people's minds?

These questions are important because science is something big and momentous, with ramifications and influence far beyond its more narrowly conceived self. Indeed it is so far-flung and intertwined with virtually all of contemporary thought and culture that it is utterly impossible to understand it adequately unless it is known in relation to them rather than in isolation. Moreover such intertwining and interaction goes on also in the minds of individual persons—with powerful effects and serious consequences in personal thought and action, and in social relations. Not to understand such cultural and psychological relations is not to understand significant aspects of science. Again we present a few typical discussion topics.

1. Has there been linguistic or conceptual interaction between science and religion? If so, has this been mutually beneficial? In what sense? Has there been methodological interaction? If so, what kind? With what effects? How about philosophical interaction? (12)
2. It is well known that there has been "warfare" between science and Christian theology. In what sense? How did this come about? Might it have been avoided? Does it still exist? Has it in the long run made for the enrichment or impoverishment, strengthening or weakening, of each? (13)
3. Is it defensible to assert, as it often is asserted, that the Judaeo-Christian tradition prepared the soil on which science has grown and thrived? Or that many of the thought patterns of science were drawn from theology? And that this may be one reason why science has grown so much more rapidly in the West than in the East? (14)
4. It is often asserted that the Christian church has been largely suppressive and retarding in its influence upon the growth of science. In what sense? Is this assertion defensible?
5. Are science and religion indebted to each other for fundamental presuppositions? If so, to what extent? (15)
6. How do they interact psychologically in the thought of individuals and communities? Do the critical, analytical and other attitudes and habits characteristic of science react upon the habits and modes of thought characteristic of religion? How? Does scientific study react upon people's conception of, faith in and worship of God? With what results? Are there also inverse effects, e.g.

do religious attitudes, commitments and thought patterns react upon men's science and upon their understanding or acceptance of it? Consider these questions from the viewpoint of humanistic as well as deistic, theistic and other faiths and beliefs. (16)

7. Can, and does, thorough knowledge of the one aid the understanding of the other?

Questions like these are the subject of frequent discussion by many people. Unfortunately, however, they are answered altogether too often in terms of uncritical personal opinions or of pseudo-psychological notions. Good teaching should, of course, insist on facts—derivable from history, biography, autobiography, and case history records. Whatever a student's personal attitude may be toward religion and its relationships with science, his learning to insist on actual evidence will, of course, do much to give a more adequate picture of the scientific process, as well as of its relations to religion. If sufficient evidence is not immediately at hand—as is often the case—discussion should at least point up the need to postpone the drawing of conclusions and to reject mere opinion.

The Recognition and Analysis of Complementary Relations

A potent approach that may be especially effective in connection with our general subject is to explore the possibility of complementary relations from a positive, constructive point of view. Here are some typical questions for this approach:

1. Do science and religion, or, say, science and philosophy complement each other in a significant way?
2. Without both would our knowledge be necessarily incomplete? Our experience? Our world view?
3. Do religious and scientific methodology supplement each other? Does each contribute anything that the other cannot?
4. Does science furnish concepts that fill in gaps in other-

wise incomplete theological systems? Does the reverse of this obtain?

This approach is particularly helpful because it stresses positive values and relationships, encourages thinking in terms of wholes, and starts with the supposition—subject to confirmation or denial—that science and religion each has something unique and valuable to offer for the common good. It helps the student to realize that it is the business of the scholar whenever possible deliberately to try to produce and maintain unitary views—even in the face of what at some stages of inquiry may seem contradictory or incompatible—and to strengthen centripetal tendencies toward fusion and synthesis and to resist the centrifugal ones tending to shatter wholeness. The student cannot learn too soon that relationships are not only discovered, but that they may also be created, i.e. brought into being by the thinker. "Finding relationships" means not only looking around to see what relations may exist in some sense independent of us, but it means also the conscious, active relating of things in our thought. He should know that with regard to many relationships there are elements of intellectual choice. The concept of complementarity has inherent in it the notion of two things belonging together as indispensable parts of a whole and having meanings which derive at least in part from their being parts of the same whole. To discover the actual complementarity of science and religion, if it exists, or to establish their complementarity in one's thinking if this can be shown to be desirable, would be a significant intellectual undertaking. (17)

SOME OF THE VARIOUS ASPECTS AND MODES OF SCIENCE

We must now ask how educators should think of "natural science." (18) When has a science been "*taught*" or "*learned*" adequately? How broad a conception of science is requisite to the kind of perspective called for here? Are such conceptions of science as we might adopt on this basis consonant with the views held independently on other grounds within the science community itself? As might be expected, we feel that a student should realize that no one definition of science is accurate or inclusive enough to give an adequate conception of it in all its aspects. It must be known in many ways, or it is not *known*. It exists in at least six significantly different aspects or modes. The chart on the last page of this chapter portrays this in over-all perspective. (Since this chart will be referred to many times, it is suggested that it be left opened out for ready reference during the first reading of the chapter.) As it suggests, science may be thought of (A) as a body of organized knowledge, (B) as a way of knowing, (C) as an area of experience with nature and in creative work, (D) as a foundation of technology, (E) as an intellectual and moral influence in our culture, and (F) as a social enterprise. The chart indicates under each of these headings the kind of subject matter it represents. In discussing these various modes I shall suggest relationships to religion that seem significant, and provide, as I did in the preceding section, illustrative lists of topics, questions and propositions (which do not necessarily represent my own point of view) that may be suitable for class discussion. Again I shall not discuss the issues involved, except to make clear the kind of problem I have in mind, and the meaning of the teaching materials to which I refer. I am not proposing that any one science course in college or school include all, or *nearly all,* of the material suggested here. Such comprehensiveness is manifestly impossible. My purpose is only to indicate what subject matter is pertinent and what a wealth of opportunity the study of the natural sciences presents for teaching reciprocal relations with religion.

In referring to our chart, a notation such as Ch. C 2 f indicates: *theories* under Science as an Experience in "Creation." Similarly, Ch. B 3 b means: Chart, column B (Science as a Way of Knowing), subheading 3 (Methods), item b (General Methods).

Science as a Body of Organized Knowledge

This aspect of science is without doubt covered more adequately than any other in conventional courses and textbooks. Indeed most of the traditional course content is represented by items 1 to 8 under this heading (Ch. A). It is here that the teacher finds it especially difficult to see how reference to religion could contribute to the understanding of science itself as well as of its relations with religion. Nevertheless, I suggest that this particular field does offer many such possibilities, especially for the teacher committed to emphasizing basic meanings.

It is important in science education some time—if not at the very beginning—to study the scope, avowed purpose and unique task of a given science, and of science in general. Since this is difficult to do without involving questions of methodology, the material considered here will overlap that of the next section. In the following list of typical questions and propositions for discussion the specific references to physics are intended to be merely illustrative of similar ones relative to the other natural sciences.

1. In the total quest for knowledge what in particular is the task of physics? Or of natural science in general? Can a sharp distinction be drawn between physics and chemistry? Between physical and biological science? Between physics and philosophy? Are there problems of basic interest to both physics and chemistry, to physics and philosophy, to physics and art, physics and religion?
2. In defining a science, or any other discipline, or in specifying its scope or area of responsibility and competence, this may be done (a) by referring to its internal structure and noting its subdivisions, (b) by bounding

it with reference to its external neighbors, (c) by identifying the kinds of inquiry it does, and does not, undertake, (d) by pointing out what its methodological resources and competencies are and what therefore it can, and cannot, do successfully, (e) by asking what kinds or aspects of experience and reality it endeavors to investigate, describe and interpret. Are there still other approaches? Compare science and religion in this manner.

3. Natural science's realm of interest is nature. What do we mean by "nature"? When scientists look at a part of nature, they see there a bewildering array of objects and phenomena with many aspects and components, and with exceedingly complex patterns of relationships. They find it impossible to describe all of it in a systematic and intellectually satisfying manner. Therefore they "abstract" out of the total situation those parts or aspects that they can handle with some degree of facility and disregard the rest, leaving it to other disciplines. What does a physicist abstract from a rainbow for his study? From a symphony? From a magnet? A tree? What does he disregard and leave to others? Does the artist abstract anything from the rainbow or symphony or tree? Does the theologian?
4. Consider the experience of "space" and "time," and such concepts as distance, dimension, extension, duration, near, far, past, future, fast, slow. Do physicists, poets, philosophers and theologians think of spatial and temporal experience in the same way and from the same point of view? Are the meanings they attach to these concepts the same?
5. Are there different kinds of time? Is the time concept of physics the same as that of the ancient Hebrews and Greeks? Of modern psychology or metaphysics? Is the "eternity" concept of theology directly related to the time concept of science? (19)

6. Are the subjects of origins and possible future temporal termini—of the universe, earth, life, species, atoms, nuclear particles—within the realm of competence of the natural sciences? In what senses and to what extent?
7. In physics there is the important Principle of Least Action. It was first proposed by Maupertuis on theological grounds. His thinking in that connection illustrates a kind of interaction between science and theology leading to an important scientific concept that has not been at all uncommon in the past. Would scientists and theologians regard such reasoning legitimate today? Why? Consideration of this question can shed much light not only on the nature and temper of science and religion, but also on their past and present relationships. (20)

Science as a Way of Knowing

Probably no question is more important and fruitful for present purposes than that of methodology, of how we can or do "know." Perhaps nowhere else is the ignorance and misunderstanding of both science and religion more abysmal than in this area. To illustrate, it is believed widely that science is completely self-sufficient, self-confirming and self-correcting methodologically, that it employs only its own unique criteria by which it can and does decide between "truth" and "error" on the basis of purely scientific reasons. It is supposed that when confronted, for instance, by two alternative hypotheses its choice is determined solely by the extent to which they can be verified by observation or experiment. But this common belief is by no means sound. Science has other criteria of acceptability, and many have been drawn from outside experimental science (Ch. B 4 b).

Throughout the history of science some of its hypotheses and theories have been accepted, and others rejected, for reasons other than simply their conformity to nature. Among the criteria of acceptability that have actually been used widely in science are those of (a) simplicity, drawn from metaphysics, (b) elegance, from aesthetics, (c) rigor and consistency, from logic, (d) economy of thought, (e) fruitfulness in prediction, (f) reasonableness in terms of common sense, (g) social value, (h) moral value, (i) conformity to theological or political doctrine and others. (21) This fact illustrates the important truth that methodologically science has been inseparably a part of the very warp and woof of life and culture, not independent and isolated from it—not at all self-sufficient.

A similar misconception lurks in the popular notion of "The Scientific Method" (Ch. B 6) which is alleged to consist of a few standard "steps" by which scientists are able inevitably to arrive at infallible truth. It is commonly thought of as a sort of intellectual machine that magically solves problems by an automatic, foolproof system which only science possesses. But this is a gross exaggeration—to say the least. Science has many characteristic methods (Ch. B 3), not *one*, and they are so varied that reference to them en masse by such a stereotype as "The Scientific Method" is thoroughly misleading. What many, and probably most, scientists think about this is expressed pointedly by Professor P. W. Bridgman of Harvard University, Nobel prize winner and one of the world's most distinguished physicists, in the following oft-quoted, provocative quotation:

> The scientific method, as far as it is a method, is nothing more than doing one's damnedest with one's mind, no holds barred. What primarily distinguishes science from other intellectual enterprises in which the right answer has to be obtained is not method but the subject matter. (22)

Pedagogically this statement is extremely valuable because when presented to a class it always arouses much discussion. It is illuminating both negatively and positively. On the one hand, it denies the existence of such a unique thing as "The Scientific Method," and, on the other, it affirms the methodological continuity between science and the rest of scholarship.

For many persons this view comes as a disconcerting intellectual surprise—if not shock.

Of course, we should hasten to say that not all scientists subscribe to Bridgman's views on this subject. This disagreement in itself illustrates another important fact about science, namely that scientists are by no means unanimous in their views about science, not even about method. Many of them insist that science does have *a characteristic method,* that it has certain indispensable components—if not "steps"—such as the gathering of data, the inductive formulation of general relationships, and the deductive application of generalizations to particular situations. Others point out, however, that scientific method thus defined, i.e. in terms of very general methodological processes, is essentially indistinguishable from that which characterizes all of scholarship, and is therefore not at all unique. Of course, this is tantamount to saying, as Bridgman and others do, that the *primary* difference between science and the other disciplines is not one of method, but of subject matter.

The unfortunate stereotype of "The Scientific Method" has tended to obscure one of science's most potent sources of strength, namely that of human intuition (Ch. B 7)—and herein it is remarkably akin to religion, and, of course, to art and mathematics. There can be little doubt that most of the truly great and revolutionary ideas of science came into being intuitively during periods of revelatory insight, rather than as the result of the calculated, systematic, sequential manipulation of logical elements of thought. Therefore it has been suggested that if there are any typical "steps" in scientific method they may well be designated as preparation, incubation, illumination and verification. (23)

The prevalence of the misconceptions and stereotyped notions of the nature of science has had other serious consequences also. Not the least of these is that when students think of science in such terms not only is their understanding of science itself sadly warped, but so is their perspective of its relations to other enterprises and fields of knowledge. Frequently they develop undesirable attitudes, such as the intellectual snobbishness that is so often evident when immature science students look with disdain upon the arts, philosophy and theology because to them they appear inferior. This malady is likely to disappear when science is seen in its true light as very much more like other disciplines than the popular stereotype seems to suggest it is. In this area comparative studies become very valuable.

Again I present some typical questions and propositions for discussion:

1. Are all the methods listed under Ch. B 3 b (and many others a class might add) characteristic of all the natural sciences? Which, if any, could (or could not) be used in the social sciences, arts, philosophy and religion?
2. The methods scientists use are largely *ad hoc* in nature, (24) i.e. devised for particular purposes, problems and circumstances, and vary with the investigator and his inclinations, ingenuity and knowledge. Illustrate—if true. Is this an aspect of the continuity of science with the humanities and religion?
3. Is emphasis on measurement and quantitative considerations equally characteristic of all the natural sciences? May it be regarded as a distinguishing mark of science?
4. In what sense, and to what extent, is the knowledge which science yields unimpeachable, true, certain, permanent? More so, or less so, than in other disciplines?
5. What, if any, limits and limitations apply to the operations of science in its search for knowledge and understanding? If so, are the limits by design or necessity? Why? Are there similar or analogous ones in other fields —including theology? (25)
6. In what sense do the methods of science enable it to reveal reality? What aspects of reality? What might the

term "physical reality" mean, as distinguished from, say, "artistic reality," or "divine reality"? Is a molecule real? In what sense? Are energy, light rays, light waves, light quanta, neutrons, functional relationships, Boyle's law, color and pitch real?

7. In what sense do the methods of science yield "objective truth"? Are there also elements of the subjective in scientific method? It has been said that scientific objectivity rests at least in part, on what has come to be called "intersubjective testability." (26) Is there a legitimate sense in which objectivity may be claimed also in the realms of art and religion, as well as science?
8. The methodologies of science and religion are said to be radically different with respect to "reason," "faith" and "revelation." In what sense of these terms is this belief true or false? (27)
9. A religious creed is said to be a statement of something believed to be true (credo—I believe). Does science employ statements of the "I believe this to be true" kind, i.e. creeds? If so, illustrate. What are the methodological use and value of such credal statements in science, in religion, in other fields? (28)

Within this broad field of methodology a particular subject area of tension between science and religion-theology is that of determinacy and indeterminacy, and the related subjects of cause and effect, predictability, certainty versus probability, and natural law. Here the science teacher can contribute mightily to the deeper understanding of science itself, as well as to the minimizing of some of these tensions by taking special care to clarify the meanings of these terms in various fields, including religion. This difficulty seems to be twofold. First, the meanings these terms convey from a common sense point of view are not those of some of the modern sciences, especially physics. Second, these concepts have different semantic content in different fields.

The situation may be illustrated by reference to the idea of cause. In contemporary physics the meaning of this concept is far removed from that of popular usage. Indeed, the whole point of view about causality in modern physical science is radically different from the so-called common sense view of it. This difference is pointedly expressed by a very able physicist-philosopher, Professor Victor F. Lenzen, (29) of the University of California:

> Causality is a relation within the realm of conceptual objects. The relation of cause and effect refers to conceptual events regardless of the relation of the latter to reality. In the prescientific stage of experience causality is attributed to an intuitively given world which confronts the observer. In the sophisticated stage of science causality must be attributed to a model which the scientist constructs out of concepts.

If this be correct the common sense conception of causality —and the one usually found in textbooks—is prescientific or, at any rate, very different from that of twentieth century physics. According to the latter a cause is not something precisely identifiable in the laboratory, i.e. something known to be physically coercive in bringing about one event or state as a necessary consequence of another. Rather it is a concept that applies strictly speaking only to the simplified, abstract, theoretically created world of models or mental constructs —which conceptual world is so ordered, by deliberate postulation, that causality reigns rigorously within it.

Another view worth quoting here is that of the late philosopher, Ernst Cassirer: (30)

> We find the essential significance of the causal relation, if interpreted in a critical rather than in a metaphysical sense, to be that it contains a statement not immediately about things but about experience, by which and in virtue of which alone things, as objects of knowledge, can be given us. It expresses something about the structure of empirical knowledge; it determines the individual phases of the path by which empirical knowledge strives toward its goal, the goal of knowledge of objects.
>
> . . . We formulate the principle of causality in all strictness as a

> proposition concerning cognitions, instead of trying to understand it as one concerning things and events. . . . Every genuine causal proposition, every natural law, contains not so much a prediction of future events as a promise of future cognitions.

We do not present these quotations as "proof" of a particular point of view, but as evidence that such a view exists. Actually several different meanings of the concept of cause are current in physics today. And there are still others in the other sciences. Not only are modern science's sophisticated concepts of cause-and-effect different from that of common sense, but they are apparently quite unlike those of theology,(31) in both meaning and purpose. In considering causes theistic theology seems to have been interested mainly in active "personal" agents thought to have a will and in some sense determinative power, viz. gods, angels, devils, and human beings. Its concern is with purpose and with so-called "primary" rather than "secondary" causes, with aspects of happenings that are of no direct concern to science. Theologians do not seek, as scientists do, functional "causal" relationships that make precise prediction possible. Many of the perplexities and tensions of "science vs. religion" are due to (a) the uncritical transfer of such words as cause from science into theology, or vice versa, without recognizing that this should involve a change of its conceptual content, and (b) the confounding of technical meanings with primitive and common sense usages.

Two other important aspects of scientific methodology should be considered here, namely the roles of logic and language in natural science. One convincing way to see science as clearly continuous with other disciplines—including religion—is to note the common components of their methodologies (Ch. B 3 a). With regard to logic two aspects seem especially significant for present purposes. First, the sciences do not in general demand of their devotees that they be experts in logic. Such logic as is required for success in science is for the most part of a surprisingly simple kind, and even that is largely hidden in the more or less automatic processes of mathematical manipulation. It is not correct to say, as it so often is said, that science is essentially logical while religion-theology is not. Second, the struggles of scientists (notably physicists) and theologians with the highly refractory problems facing them today have accelerated their acceptance of the view that logic is instrumental in nature, something that has developed for purposes of investigation and thought, rather than being a system of immutable laws of the mind embedded in the nature and structure of the world. Since both science and theology lean heavily upon logic, an understanding of these developments will shed much light upon their basic nature as disciplines, their contemporary aspects and their reciprocal relations.

Language, too, is a tool used by all disciplines. Unfortunately, however, the huge success of the scientific enterprise has created the impression in the common mind that only literal, discursive language, the language of precise logical denotation that is used with such power by the natural sciences is capable of communicating "objective truth" and that the expressive or depth language of song and myth is meaningless. Thus again over-all perspectives have become badly warped, with consequent impairment of the correct understanding of science itself, and of its interdisciplinary relations. The analysis of contemporary insights regarding the nature of language, the kinds of language, myth and symbol, as well as of the particular functions of language in science, the arts and religion can therefore be very helpful. (32)

There are, of course, many other important topics under the heading of ways of knowing that are worthy of discussion for present purposes. Practically every item of Ch. B, if considered thoroughly, will be seen to have relevance for the subject of this chapter.

Science as an Area of Experience

We shall consider this mode of science under two headings: experience directly with nature, and experience in discovery and creative thought.

Perhaps nowhere are we more truly in the territory of science—at least natural science—than when we are in direct contact with natural phenomena themselves. While recognizing that the concepts of "nature" and "experience" have rather sophisticated connotations in science and philosophy, we stipulate in this connection merely their common sense meaning. Nature shall refer to the concrete world, to physical objects and phenomena such as heat, light, sound, gases, solids and liquids, the planets and skies, plants and animals, the rainbow and sunset, magnets, musical instruments, cyclotrons, electrons, and so on. We thus include in it some elements of our cultural, man-made environment. Experience with nature shall mean our perceiving it with our senses and instruments, and our responses and reactions to it in experimentation, theoretical interpretation, and the control and transformation of nature.

As I see it, the most basic meaning of natural science is that it is experience with nature. Certainly the most fundamental purpose of natural science is to explore and explicate nature. Many, probably most, scientists have entered science because of their deep interest in, or even love of, nature. He who does not become excited about a newly discovered phenomenon, or who does not have a passion to unravel or interpret its meaning, is probably not a scientist. One way to distinguish science from other disciplines is by the kind of experience which it offers its devotees.

Moreover, one of the most important aspects of science is its insistence that if we would learn about nature we must address our questions about it to nature itself—not to metaphysics, or theology, or to some sort of "authority." While science teaching today certainly does not go to such sources for its information, and certainly is not authoritarian in that sense, it has to a disconcerting extent allowed itself to become far removed from direct contact with nature. In a sense the undergraduate student learns about nature mostly from textbooks and the pronouncements of teachers rather than from nature itself. It seems to me that a student's understanding of phenomena, or associated concepts, does not usually derive directly to any large extent from first-hand basic experiential knowledge. Most of his experience is usually not *with* nature, but with second-hand knowledge *about nature*.

Of course, these remarks do not apply equally well to all the sciences. The prevailing teaching practices of some of them typically offer many more opportunities for such direct experience than do those of others. Moreover, there are good reasons why much of the student's knowledge of nature should come to him initially via the abstractions of science. Nevertheless, there can be little doubt that rather extensive direct contact with nature is requisite to an adequate understanding of the concepts and methods of science and of the fundamental drives and attitudes of scientists.

Thinking of the educational objectives espoused here, it would seem especially important then that the beginning student himself have as many direct experiences with nature as possible, specially such as would make clear to him explicitly what the role of direct experience is both in science itself and in interdiscipline relations.

Let me illustrate this with reference to the particular problem of identifying the specific task (Ch. A 1) of physics. I suggest that no amount of reading or reflection can of itself make clear what aspects of our experience of sound are the business of the physicist as distinguished from that of, say, the psychologist. It is doubtful that the distinction between the physical properites of intensity, frequency and wave form and the psychological ones of loudness, pitch, and timbre, ever becomes truly meaningful and clear until it has been explored empirically. Not until one has listened to sounds with critical and discriminative awareness and manipulated them systematically is one likely to understand that they have aspects that are not accessible to exploration and analysis with instruments only, i.e. without the ear, and therefore fall outside the area of competence of physics. Similarly, only direct experience can fully clarify the difference between those aspects of light that are of interest primarily to the psychologist and those mainly the concern of the physicist. What I am suggesting for present purposes is that we need many more teaching materials, e.g. carefully planned laboratory situations, explicitly designed to provide opportunities for such directly experiential, discriminatory analysis. I suggest further that until the student has had a considerable number of such experiences he is not in a position to appreciate that science is a "symbolic representation of experience," and to understand what it means to say that the task and procedure of science is in part "selecting or constructing a pattern of relations between temporal experiences of individuals." (33)

It is doubtful also that the need for, and the true significance of, many of the more specific concepts of science can be understood adequately by any one for whom they are not anchored in direct empirical data of their own (Ch. C 1 c). One reason for this is that there intervenes, between the initial basic perceptual experience and its eventual conceptualization, the mediating process of abstraction, referred to earlier in section A. While this process is absolutely necessary and indispensable, the abstraction it yields is easily misused or misunderstood—especially by him who bases his thinking upon the abstraction rather than upon the experienced concrete situation.

There seem to be at least three aspects, or possibly stages, in the process of abstraction in science. First there is extraction, from the totality of an experienced object or phenomenon, of certain components thereafter to be kept in view, while all others are to be deliberately disregarded. Thus when studying the motions of many different kinds of objects, such as marbles, bullets, cars, raindrops, snowflakes, dogs and birds, the physicist concentrates simply upon their masses, i.e. thinks of them as undifferentiated masses subject to physical forces, without regard to their being alive or inanimate, hard or soft, black or white, fragrant or smelly, beautiful or ugly. Second, there is the process of abstracting the concrete out of the situation and then dealing with purely idealized mental constructs. This is the kind of abstraction, going a step beyond the first, which led to Newton's laws of motion stated basically in terms not merely of masses, but of abstract, geometrical bodies with imagined masses, but no other physical properties. It was this step that enabled Galileo and Newton to think successfully in the abstract, i.e. not only of the motion of physical bodies but of motion itself. This liberation of the human mind from the bondage of thinking in the concrete was one of the greatest of all human achievements. (34) The third aspect of abstraction consists of postulating imaginary "bodies" or entities, properties or models to take the place of and theoretically explain the ones known empirically. This is what happens when for large, continuous bodies we substitute in our thinking a swarm of tiny molecules and atoms, and for beams of light corpuscles of energy.

Now in these processes, remarkable as they are, reside certain potential dangers. The first and second kinds of abstraction, if not anchored in or continually referred back to the underlying experience, often result in the mistaken impression that only the abstracted part of experience is real and meaningful and that the other parts are meaningless, or even nonexistent. Thus he who is overly preoccupied with the "physical reality" that has been abstracted from the rainbow, viz. its electromagnetic radiation, its wave lengths, the indices of refraction, the refraction and reflection effects of the raindrops, is likely to forget that there are other aspects of the rainbow which are just as real, though in a different sense. Such preoccupation, over-abstraction, may lead also to the notion that only science deals with the objectively real, that art and religion do not. The danger in the third type of abstraction is the tendency to regard one's mental constructions as themselves, in some sense, objectively real. Thus many students think of magnetic lines of force, or optical rays or Bohr orbits in atoms as concretely real when they are not, just as no doubt many people once regarded the Ptolemaic system of epicycles as concretely real. This tendency, evident in both science and theology, to regard one's theoretical models or constructs as "true" or "real" rather than only as symbolic devices of thought and interpretation, has been the cause of much misunderstanding and tension. Again we suggest that maintaining direct experiential contact with nature is a potent guard against such unfortunate tendencies. In this vein we propose the following topics for discussion:

1. When are empirical data valid? (Ch. C 1 d) In science? Religion? Just what is meant by illusion and delusion? What safeguards do science and religion have against them? (35) (Ch. C 1 e)
2. What kind of order (Ch. C 1 f) do we recognize experientially in nature? Is there also disorder in nature? (Ch. C 1 g) How does the experience of order in nature find expression in scientific theory? Is there anything analogous in religion and theology? Is the order disclosed by science significant for theology? (36)
3. Are there aspects of physical reality that cannot be perceived by the human senses alone? What about electricity, magnetism, radioactive radiations, X-rays? Others?
4. In what sense and to what extent is nature predictable? Unpredictable? Does your answer come out of scientific experimentation or out of its theorizing?
5. Science is said to concern itself with the typical and repetitive in nature, not with the unique and unrepeated. Is this true? Illustrate with examples. (Ch. C 1 h) Does

the totality of human experience reveal both the repetitive and the unique?

6. One cannot turn to science to learn whether there is in nature any metaphysical purpose, or ultimate mystery and unpredictability, or "objective" beauty (Ch. C 1 i, j, k, l) because science has, in the process of abstracting, or carving out, its domain, deliberately disregarded such matters. Is this a true statement? May one conclude that *because* science does not recognize or deal with them they are therefore nonexistent, or meaningless and unreal?
7. The phrase "inherent cussedness of inanimate nature" was first made famous, apparently, by James B. Conant in his delightful little book *On Understanding Science.*(37) What does it mean? Is it an *attribute of nature* revealed by the theoretical, conceptual content of science? By the scientific experience? Is it real?
8. In what sense should scientific theory be determined by empirical findings? Should there be any analogous relationship between theological theory and religious empirical findings?
9. Does scientific theory affect one's scientific empirical findings? Do theological concepts affect one's religious experience?
10. Does scientific experience ever have aesthetic and religious dimensions? What kind of evidence, if any, might be pertinent and valid here?(38)
11. Have any scientists found that their science strengthened their religious faith? Or weakened it? Might this depend in part upon the nature and significance of such faith? If so, how? Is such interaction valid? Desirable? Are all religious faiths (as distinguished from beliefs) equally "good"?

However a teacher may personally think of or react to all this, it does constitute a body of significant facts about the experiential aspects of science and of the actual interactions between science and religion. He should be prepared to discuss it factually.

We now turn to science as experience in discovery and creation. It is important that students get a taste of science as a search, discovery and exploration, i.e. as an uncovering or unveiling of the unknown that already exists. It is equally important for them to realize that to a tremendous extent it is also artistic, creative and productive, bringing into being what has not previously existed. An understanding of the latter is especially effective in revealing otherwise unrecognized similarities, interactions, reciprocal relations and continuity between the sciences and the arts, as well as between science and religion. The outline appearing on the chart (Ch. C 2) suggests how science is creative. There seem to be two kinds of scientific creation: those in the realms of thought and those in the concrete world. In both cases the important human ability at work is that of the imagination. Few undergraduates ever come to appreciate how much of the world the physicist speaks of is the product of his own mental construction: the abstract, simplified world in which his concepts, laws and principles hold rigorous, theoretical sway, but which is in many ways different from that encountered in concrete experience. Still fewer realize with what imaginative ingenuity this idealized, schematic world is used to predict and often control the much more complex, actual observable events and phenomena. Finally, even less do they understand how this conceptual world is employed in actually bringing into being new components of the concrete world.

What a transformation our physical, objective world has indeed undergone since the advent of the electrical age, and later of the "atomic age"! We do not refer so much to the new gadgetry and technology so evident on all sides, as to the utterly new basic phenomena nonexistent before. We have today a newly *created,* not merely discovered, world of sound, audible and inaudible, and of light, visible and invisible, of new solids, liquids and gases. Then there is the phenomenon once declared to be impossible, namely the transmutation of mass and energy and its many allied effects. The boundaries not only of what we know, but also of what exists, have been expanded immeasurably—largely by the *creative* activity of scientists.

In the classroom attention can be called to this aspect of science—and other disciplines—by such provocative questions as the following:

1. Is the "electron" an invention or a discovery? Or . . . ?
2. How did the concept of energy come into being? Was it by discovery, or mental construction, or both?
3. Were Newton's laws of motion "found" or "produced"? Or . . . ?
4. Consider the ancient question: Does a sculptor find the statue in the rock or put it there by a creative act? A modern counterpart of this question might be: Are natural laws found in nature or put there by the creative act of the scientist? Or . . . ?
5. Are concepts of theology thought of as mental constructs like corresponding ones in science, i.e. do creative processes enter into theology as they do into art and into science? In the same sense?
6. What new tools of thought has science developed in its history? More particular during the present century? Has there been such creative development in theology also?
7. What types of new phenomena are the product of scientific creation?

Science as a Foundation of Technology

This aspect of science has received a great deal of attention from all science teachers for obvious reasons. It is in its "applications" to "practical problems" that the effects of science upon life and culture are most easily recognized. Certainly it is a profitable field for the discussion of reciprocal relations between science and other fields of endeavor, such as the social sciences, the arts, government, labor, business and even religion. (39)

As far as religion is concerned, some of the most obvious effects science has had upon it through its technological applications have been in the realm of ethics and morals. Tremendously difficult and consequential problems now face the moralist and religionist as the result of the so-called industrial revolution, and more recently, the advent of the "atomic age" —and the "space age." Men of affairs are asked to make decisions today that involve incredibly complex alternatives and frightening consequences. Under these impacts both scientists and religionists are gaining new insights in the realms of ethics, morals and human relations. (40)

Not only have science and technology brought on new problems, but they have placed at the disposal of men new devices for solving some of them. Operations research and modern computational devices and methods make it possible more clearly to analyze and define many kinds of problems and situations calling for decision by taking into account many more relevant variables and data. In many cases, too, they offer more accurate prediction of possible consequences of particular lines of action and therefore provide more meaningful bases for decision making.

Science and technology also offer powerful means of combating and alleviating certain kinds of ills and evils, thus by preventive measures removing basic causes of problems, tensions and controversy, or even immorality.

Aside from the implications of science and technology for ethics, morals and social service, there are others which some thinkers regard as even more specifically religious. One of these is, as Professor John Baillie, (41) of the University of Edinburgh, suggested in an address before the British Association for the Advancement of Science in 1951, "the measure of control over natural processes which it (science) seeks to put into the hand of man. Bacon . . . concludes his *Novum Organum* by expressing the belief that man's dominion over nature, which was compromised by the Fall, may be partially restored by the development of the new science leading to the progressive improvement of his estate." Many scientists who are religiously within the Judaeo-Christian tradition have therefore regarded their work as contributing to the realization of "God's purposes for man on Earth," namely that of "subduing the Earth" and making it more habitable, and more conducive of the good life. For them the application of scientific principles to the eradication of disease, the improvement of the soil for better crops, the impounding of waters for power and the utilization of minerals constitutes in itself a part of their religion, a religious act, one way of worshipping and serving their God and "carrying out His will." (42)

Examples of topics for discussion:

1. Are science and technology synonymous? If not, how do they differ basically?
2. According to the chart, science contributes to technology by virtue of at least eight of its different roles or functions (Ch. D, 1–8). Discuss the meaning of each of these and illustrate with specific examples how technology is served by science in these ways.
3. Science is able to perform the basic services considered above by providing the fundamental principles underlying the development of materials, devices and systems such as are referred to in the chart as items Ch. D, 9–13. Illustrate.
4. Items Ch. D 14 are examples of broad areas of need which technology, and through it science, seeks to meet. Are there others? Does science also have negative effects? (Ch. D 15)

5. Where do perplexing ethical or moral problems arise as the result of technological developments, i.e. as the result of the practical applications of science? Problems for whom? For society as a whole, for the nation and nations, the local community, the individual consumer of goods and services, the producer and distributor of goods and services, the soldier, the statesman, the scientist, the theologian?
6. Is it defensible for the scientist to (a) remain completely neutral as to the ethics of the application of scientific principles to technology, or of the use of technological devices based on science, (b) demand a voice in decisions regarding the use of scientific devices for, say, war, (c) refuse to participate in the development of devices that can conceivably, or are deliberately designed to, be used for destructive purposes, (d) become a lobbyist or politician for the purpose of influencing legislation that might affect society's use of scientific and technological products? Are other alternatives open to him?

Science as an Intellectual and Moral Influence

Life and culture have been profoundly influenced by science in its thought forms and habits. The chart indicates that its effects have been at least two-fold. First, it has been a curative and cleansing influence, combating authoritarianism and dogmatism, magic and superstition, intolerance and persecution (Ch. E 1, 2, 3). It has shown the value of and fought for freedom of inquiry and commitment to truth regardless of consequences (Ch. E 4, 5). It has helped bring about widespread appreciation of the importance of certain habits of mind, such as insistence upon adequate evidence, precision in language and honesty in reporting (Ch. E 7, 8, 9). Second, it has contributed positively certain elements of the thought patterns and intellectual attitudes of our culture, such as experimentation and operational and phenomenological points of view, the seeking for functional relationships in the analysis of nature and society; the critical awareness of error, uncertainty and intellectual limitations, and methods of identifying and evaluating these (Ch. E 10, 11, 12).

In all such ways the influence of science upon religion, religious philosophy and theology, as well as upon religious institutions, has been especially significant and far reaching, for altogether too often and persistently have intolerance, dogmatism and superstition been propagated and defended in the name of religion. It should be noted, however, that there is much historical evidence that science is also in debt to religion with regard to many of these very benefits attributed to science. A good, though perhaps not a completely convincing, case can be made for the claim that many of the values just enumerated have to a large extent gained acceptance and been meaningful because of the mutual, not merely unilateral, interactions between science and religion, and that each is indebted to the other for sharpening its insights and understanding of these matters.

Not only has science been a general intellectual and spiritual influence upon religion historically, but it has powerfully affected the religion of individual persons. This is one reason why it has so much to offer as a component of education (Ch. E 14, 15). Thus it supports and reinforces those influences within religion which tend toward open-mindedness and the kind of genuine understanding that characterizes the truly liberal spirit. It helps to liberate the mind from blind, uncritical adherence to inherited beliefs and communal prejudices. It emphasizes the importance of both reason and faith—in the most basic and significant meanings of these terms. It guards against fanatical excesses and unbridled speculations and self-deception (Ch. E 13).

Science provides an almost indispensable tool for both secular and religious education as these are directed toward the development of character and the disciplined mind. (43) (Ch. E 15) Caldin has suggested that "it trains the will by compelling a certain contact with 'brute force and iron law' . . . Scientific research can be a great school of patience and even of humility . . ." Hocking has developed the thought that "character comes chiefly in dealing with nature," asserting that "There is no such thing as character in men apart from nature in objects. For character forms itself on the reliabilities of the world." Von Huegel, great Catholic mystic and scholar, speaks of "The shock, friction, contrast, the slow continuous discipline" experienced when science deals with nature, as being "an essential part of the soul's spiritual fertilization." In interpreting Von Huegel, Baillie attributes to him the view that "it was only *modern* science which, recognizing fully the impersonality of nature and the autonomy of nature's laws, provided the life of the spirit with the necessary resistance."

Moreover, there can be no doubt that many people, including many scientists, have found that the perspective of and the experience with nature provided by science have profoundly affected their religious faith and beliefs. For some the picture of inexorable lawfulness and of the tremendous ranges of magnitudes, from the extremely small to the incredibly large, encountered in nature, has strengthened their faith in a God. Also the conception of the physical universe presented by science has led men to modify many of their cosmological ideas in terms of which their theological doctrines have been formulated—to the profound enrichment of the latter. On the other hand, the study of science has frequently led also to loss of faith and even to complete abandonment of religious beliefs. While for many persons the order and grandeur of nature point convincingly to a divine being or essence, for others the very same aspects of nature and science suggest the self-sufficiency of nature and an intolerable remoteness or even utter uselessness of any God. Whatever a teacher's own personal views and experience may be in this area, he surely should be aware of these facts regarding the influence of science upon religion.

Examples for discussion:

1. What is the meaning of the term "dogma"? Does science, as well as religion, have dogma? Illustrate. Discuss the following quotation from A. N. Whitehead: "The dogmas of religion are the attempts to formulate in precise terms the truths disclosed in the religious experience of mankind. In exactly the same way the dogmas of physical science are the attempts to formulate in precise terms the truths disclosed, in the sense-perception of mankind." (44)
2. Does "to be dogmatic" mean to have and use dogma? Or . . . ? When can religion or science be said to be dogmatic? Are there desirable and undesirable ways of being dogmatic? Illustrate.
3. What are the meanings of "superstition"? Illustrate. In what sense, or under what conditions, can science, or religion, be said to be an influence opposed to superstition?
4. What is "magic"? Discuss the thesis that religion grew out of magic; that science did. (45) Aside from the question of origins, what have been their interactions in history?
5. In what sense, if any, can science be regarded as a "spiritual influence" in history; in the development of personality; in personal religion?
6. What are the various meanings of the terms "faith" and "belief" in religion? Can they be used meaningfully in science?
7. How, in detail, are people's faiths and beliefs affected by science? Illustrate.

For the student desiring to build a meaningful philosophy of life an understanding of these reciprocal relations can be extremely helpful. And, of course, to understand this means understanding science itself in a dimension not appreciated as widely as it should be.

Science as a Human and Social Phenomenon and Enterprise

Altogether too often is science thought of only as an impersonal, intellectually automatic self-directing machine or device that operates at a level distinctly above that of ordinary human life and affairs and which is immune to the inroads of the vagaries, foibles, sins, shortcomings of ordinary humans. Actually, of course, it is a thoroughly human enterprise, inextricably intertwined with other such enterprises, and showing all the typically human characteristics they possess (Ch. F 1). Not only is it a human phenomenon, but also a social phenomenon and a communal enterprise. In these respects science and religion are much alike, and understanding of the one facilitates understanding of the other.

There is relatively little in print about this aspect of science. (46) Therefore without going into details we present the following brief paragraphs to suggest how this subject could be developed further.

That science is a typically human phenomenon is evidenced by its great inhomogeneities and contrasts. There is the science of the frontier and of the interior, of the pioneer and of the colonizer, of guesses and hunches as well as of logical sequiturs, of great successes and abysmal failures.

There is the science of the great masters, and that of the common men of science. Science progresses by great daring leaps of the imagination of a few geniuses, *and* by the plodding, cautious, hesitant, short steps of many ordinary, mediocre men.

Science is human in that it presents not only a picture of many fundamental agreements and common understandings among scientists, but also of many radical disagreements about many aspects of its nature, purpose, method and content.

Science is a sharing of experience (Ch. F 2, 3). A one-man

science is impossible, since inter-personal checks and balances in observation, experimentation and theorizing are indispensable. Science may be called a social enterprise because it requires group action and thought.

It may be called a social phenomenon because it is an integral, inseparable component of society, is dynamically related to all of its parts and is determined and conditioned to a large extent by the culture of its time (Ch. F 7, 8).

Science is communal (Ch. F 4). The science community has the usual attributes that characterize other kinds of communities. It has its own ideals and characteristic way of life; standards, mores and conventions, language and jargon, signs and symbols; professional ethics and moral code; authority, controls and sanctions; institutions and organizations, means of communication and publications; creeds and beliefs, orthodoxies and heresies; politics, pressure groups and maneuverings; schools of thought, divisions and schisms; personal loyalties and rallying cries, jealousies and hatreds; fads, fashions and fancies.

The enterprise of science requires the cooperation of many kinds of participants (Ch. F 5). The science community needs many talents, abilities and skills. It therefore includes many kinds of scientists and many persons ordinarily not regarded as "scientists," as illustrated by the following partial list of typical components of the community: experimentalists and theorists; the lone researcher and the team researcher; the critic and referee; the philosopher, historian and teacher of science; the recorder, report writer, translator, editor and librarian of science; the personnel officer, research business officer and research director; the liaison and the publicity officer; the instrument designer, instrument maker and science engineer; and the science-conscious secretary.

Members of the scientific community recognize each other, as "belonging" fellow scientists, to a considerable extent by "smell," i.e. by translogical, undefined feelings, common insights, intuitions and a sense of values, that develop, mostly unconsciously, as scientists live together and go about the business of their community.

While both science and religion are social phenomena and enterprises, they are, of course, much more than that. To a large extent there is a significant and instructive parallelism between them in this regard (a parallelism not of analogy but, as I see it, of fact), so much so that an understanding of the one enhances understanding of the other. When someone objects to religion because it has become "institutionalized," or fails to see the need for, say, a church, it may be helpful to consider the analogous situation with respect to science. A church is a religious community and its role relative to religion is much like that of the science community relative to science. From science one can learn the inevitability of institutions and communal organization, and learn how very useful they can be—witness the tremendous value and potency of the many learned and professional societies dedicated to the propagation and advancement of science.

When a religionist objects to the technical jargon of science, he should reflect upon how impossible it would be to make progress in his own field without a technical vocabulary. When the scientist objects to theological concepts and terms, he will do well to reflect on why correspondingly the science community has its own communal language.

The role of the religious community in the identification and confirmation of the truth of religion can be better understood by one who appreciates the parallel function of the science community with respect to scientific truth. When it seems difficult to see why religion emphasizes *both* the individualistic and communal aspects of religious life and practice, it may help to consider how important the parallel emphases have become in the science enterprise.

I submit that careful, critical, comparative analyses and studies of science and religion as social enterprises—and indeed of all their analogous aspects—will produce *deeper understanding* not only of the interrelations of science and religion, but of *science itself*—and of religion itself.

Having thought of natural science as an *enterprise*, emphasizing especially the meanings and attributes implied by the adjectives *human, social* and *communal,* we should now consider how it is different from all others. I suggest that it is a unique enterprise (Ch. F) which has resulted from man's compelling curiosity about certain aspects of himself and his environment, and from his desire to "understand" his experience with that environment (Ch. C), and has led him to develop powerful methods (Ch. B) of analyzing such experience and producing organized "knowledge" (Ch. A). This knowledge man has used for purposes of control and transformation of his physical (Ch. D), as well as intellectual and spiritual world (Ch. E).

Now in the study of science from this point of view we come upon an exceedingly significant relationship between it and religion, namely their common interest in one of the most important questions in the realm of thought: What is man? Or, to put it somewhat differently, what is the nature of man? Or what are man's attributes, capacities and predilections? A controversial issue is whether either science or theology can yield a complete answer. Do we need the contributions of both?

Some of the questions listed hereafter will suggest the directions a discussion of this issue may well take. Without going into much detail, we suggest that the natural sciences can furnish two kinds of pertinent information. First, they tell us *directly* that man is a mechanical system of, say, levers, a thermodynamic system of thermal sources and sinks, insulators and conductors, a "cybernetic" electrical network, a chemical system, a particular sort of vital organism and so on. Second, they reveal *indirectly,* i.e. when looked at as themselves objects of analysis and investigation, that man is the kind of being who measures, experiments, devises certain types of symbolization, hypotheses and theories, who is critical about the power and limitations of his methods and the adequacy and meaning of his "knowledge." (47)

Philosophy and theology (48) have turned rather consistently to both natural and social science for such insights. To realize this and to understand critically what science has to offer here is to know science in one of its most significant aspects.

Topics for discussion:

1. What is a social enterprise, as distinguished from an individual enterprise?
2. Could a man with unlimited longevity, intelligence, ingenuity and material resources living in complete isolation, i.e. without communication with other persons, conceivably develop in time a science such as physics? Assuming that he would develop instruments, make observations and experiments, discover many laws of nature, engage in theorizing, and that he could develop unlimited automation in his experimental and computational facilities, what element of the physics enterprise as we know it would still be lacking?
3. What is meant by "community"? By "science community"? By "religious community"? Is it merely, or more than, an aggregate of individuals? To assert that science, or religion, is a communal enterprise is to claim what about its nature?
4. Does a science community, say the chemistry community, accept as true what is claimed to have been observed or experienced scientifically by only one person, i.e. has not been cross-checked or verified by others? Does a religious community accept as true what has been claimed as experienced religiously by only one person? What is the role of the community, as distin-

guished from that of the individual, in the identification and verification of "truth"?

5. When does a scientist speak "as a scientist"? When "only" as a human being? When he writes a book about science, or about the philosophy of science, or gives an address interpreting science, or accepts the presidency of a professional science society, or advises the government about how to spend funds for science research?

   Of course answers depend upon definitions of science. What definitions? For our purposes, which ones are most useful as we endeavor to gain or transmit a complete view of science as it is known existentially by the practicing scientist?

6. What is meant by the expression "science says this or that," or "science proceeds thus and so"? Corresponding expressions about religion?
7. Is science completely impersonal, beyond passion and controversy? Should it be? Can it be? (49) How does it compare with religion in this regard?
8. In what sense, and to what extent, is science, or religion, institutionalized? Is this desirable? Necessary?
9. What have been the interactions between the science community and other components of society (Ch. F 7)?
10. How have science and religion been culturally conditioned (Ch. F 8)?
11. Under what conditions do the science and religion communities flourish (50) (Ch. F 9)?
12. What capacities and tendencies of man are basic to natural science? Art? Religion?
13. To what extent—if any—would the study of sacred scriptures reveal those aspects of man's nature that are basic to the natural sciences? Would such study disclose those human predilections which have led man to formulate laws of nature and theories to explain them?

Would it lead one to suspect specifically that man is the kind of being who would explore the internal behavior of atomic nuclei or seek out invisible stellar objects by "invisible" light, i.e. by radio astronomy?

14. Does the "nature" of a particular human being depend upon his particular cellular structures or chemical constituents? Can it be changed say, by chemical or physical treatment, e.g. shock treatment? In what sense of the word *nature?* Could, and does, theology appeal to science for enlightenment along these lines?
15. At various stages of the development of science the scientific images of man have changed. What analogies has man used to describe or explain his capacities and behavior? To what extent have these depended upon the concepts of science and technology? Consider, for instance, the notions of man as machine, or of the brain as a computer, as communications control center (e.g. telephone exchange), as a self-directing and self-controlling cybernetic system. (51) To what extent—if any—are these modes of thought about man adequate? Do they, for instance, yield adequate insights or explanations of man as artist, or as philosopher, or as lover, or as worshipper?
16. Can, or should, one conclude from reflection upon the actualities of science as a human quest that the achievement of adequate understanding of nature leads to, or requires, the recognition of intangibles, immeasurables, and non-conceptuals as actual aspects of reality?

AREAS OF PERPLEXITY AND TENSION; "SCIENCE VS. RELIGION"

While for many persons the so-called warfare between science and religion no longer exists, for many others the area of contact between science and religion still is one of great perplexity and serious tension. There are certain questions which come up almost invariably, at least in beginning science courses, because students are genuinely puzzled or disturbed by them and turn to their science teachers for help in answering them. Therefore it is desirable that prospective teachers be forewarned about them and be prepared to deal with them in a professionally defensible manner. Some questions are so foreign to the purposes of a given course that their discussion cannot be justified in class. The teacher may then offer to discuss them in private. Some should, no doubt, be referred to a religious counsellor. In most cases, however, the science teacher should not hesitate to accept the responsibility of discussing at least the scientific aspects of the issues involved. In doing this he should, of course, be careful to distinguish carefully between the factual, theoretical and hypothetical elements of the evidence and the scientific argument, to present any alternative points of view that may prevail within science itself, to evaluate the present state of knowledge as to its adequacy or completeness, to point out where science is or is not competent to speak.

Many of the problems and issues arising from real or apparent contradiction between scientific and religious beliefs have already been identified earlier in this chapter. Illustrative of those that have not, including some that are hardy perennials, are the following ones: (a) evolution vs. creation, (b) the age of the earth, (c) the "supernatural," (d) miracles of various sorts, (e) the virgin birth of Christ, (f) the resurrection of Christ, (g) the "hereafter," (h) determinism vs. human freedom, (i) prayer, in the light of natural law, (j) the nature of disease, (k) vaccination, (l) sex and contraception.

Many of these would not naturally arise in a science course at the initiation of the teacher, but they are often brought up by students.

The study of the relations between science and religion has come to be a field in its own right, referred to as that of "science and religion." Not a few books have been devoted to it explicitly.(52) A study of some of them should give the prospective teacher some idea of the problems and issues, and suggest how they may be resolved or otherwise dealt with.

SUMMARY

This chapter has had six specific goals: first, the development of a point of view about the relation of science education to religious thought; second, the consideration of practical methods of approach in the classroom; third, a survey of so-called natural science in six of its different aspects or modes; fourth, the identification of significant reciprocal relations between the natural sciences and religion (considering theology to be the interpretive part of religion); fifth, the listing of typical questions and topics that may be suitable for class discussion, term papers or independent study projects; and sixth, a brief introduction to relevant bibliographic resources.

The audience I have had in mind primarily is the fraternity of college teachers of natural science, and especially those participating in the education of future science teachers—though I hope that teachers of religious thought may also find something of value in the chapter. The topics and questions suggested for discussion are intended mostly for college classes—though it may be that many of them can be adapted profitably to use at the secondary school level, and a few in the elementary school.

The point of view is expressed in two sets of educational principles, the first pertaining to the meaning of teaching in general, and to science teaching in particular, and the second to the question of the propriety of including non-scientific subject matter in individual science courses and in the curriculum of science education. According to the first, the goal of science teaching is not only to communicate items of scientific information, but to help the student attain deep insight and broad perspective through acquaintance with science in all its important aspects, through understanding its fundamental nature and through seeing it in relation to other fields of knowledge and method. The second set of principles sets forth conditions under which non-scientific subject matter can and should be included in science courses and curricula, in order to make possible the attainment of such broad educational purposes.

Integral to this point of view is my conviction that the study of religion is one of the intellectual disciplines and should in the curriculum of education be given the same recognition, rights and obligations as the others. Therefore its relations to the natural sciences should be as much the concern of the science curriculum as those to any other discipline.

The methods of approach in the teaching situation which I feel can be most effective are those that stress teaching for deep understanding and are related naturally to the kinds of relations between natural science and religion that are most significant. These relations are those of similarity, difference, complementarity, common concern, dynamic interaction and cultural interdependence.

Most of the chapter is devoted to an analysis of natural science in terms of the following of its modes: science as a body of organized knowledge, as a way of knowing, as an area of experience, as a foundation of technology, as an intellectual and spiritual influence, and as a typically human, social enterprise. This detailed survey has revealed many important reciprocal relations between science and religion. These have been pointed up by series of questions and propositions designed to stimulate and guide class discussion. Every effort has been made to recognize various points of view that are likely to be encountered in the college classroom. No one philosophy or theology is espoused consciously in this chapter, and no answers have been provided to the questions raised. My purpose here has been only to identify important relations and issues.

Finally I have provided bibliographic notes indicating where

A. Science as a Body of "Organized Knowledge"

1. Purposes and tasks of science
2. Its structure
3. Phenomena and "effects"
4. Functional relationships
5. Concepts and definitions
6. Explanations and theories
7. Typical problem situations
8. Instrumentation
9. Historical perspectives
10. Its great names
11. Its literature
12. Its present scope and limits
13. Discovered but unexplored areas
14. Unsolved problems within the present known
15. Basic potentialities and limitations

B. Science as a Way of Knowing

1. Knowing what?
2. Knowing in what sense?
3. Methods
   - *a. Universal tools*
     - mathematics
     - logic
     - language
     - symbolism
   - *b. General methods*
     - observation
     - experimentation
     - measurement
     - classification
     - abstraction, various types of
     - curve fitting
     - postulation
     - conceptualization
     - definition
     - construction (mental)
     - generalization
     - theorizing
     - explanation
     - prediction
     - confirmation
   - *c. Techniques*
     - dissection
     - mapping
     - excavation
     - magnification
     - amplification
     - irradiation
4. Criteria of acceptability and adequacy
   - *a. Criteria regarding*
     - method
     - technique
     - data
     - concept
     - principles
     - hypotheses
     - theories
     - predictions
   - *b. Sources of criteria*
     - science
     - logic
     - aesthetics
     - economics
     - philosophy
     - politics
     - theology
5. Accuracy, precision, approximation
6. The stereotype of "The Scientific Method"
7. The role of intuition
8. Presuppositions
9. Scientific "faith" and "creeds"

WHAT IS SCIENCE? SOME OF ITS ASPECTS AND MODES

These lists are suggestive and are not intended to be exhaustive.

C. *Science as an Area of Experience*

1. Direct experience with nature
   - *a. Aspects pertinent to science*
   - *b. "Scientific" experience*
   - *c. As a basis for understanding*
   - *d. Validating knowledge empirically*
   - *e. Illusion and delusion*
   - *f. Order and predictability*
   - *g. Non-uniformity and non-predictability*
   - *h. The unique and unrepeated*
   - *i. Purpose and interdependence*
   - *j. Vastness and mystery*
   - *k. Observables and measurables*
   - *l. Beauty, form, symmetry, rhythm*
   - *m. Ugliness, chaos, catastrophe, brutality, stern impersonality*
   - *n. The "cussedness" of nature*
   - *o. The unexpected*
2. Experience in discovery and "creation"
   - *a. Of concepts*
   - *b. Of constructs*
   - *c. Of models*
   - *d. Of relationships*
   - *e. Of hypotheses*
   - *f. Of theories*
   - *g. Of problems*
   - *h. Of experiments*
   - *i. New tools of thought*
   - *j. New methods*
   - *k. New instruments and devices*
   - *l. New phenomena*
   - *m. New orders of reality and*
   - *n. New experience*

D. *Science as a Foundation of Technology*

1. In its transformative role
2. In its exploratory role
3. In its diagnostic role
4. In its preventive role
5. In its curative role
6. In its instrumental role
7. In its informational role
8. Conservation
9. Communication systems
10. Computation and analysis
11. Controls
12. New materials
13. New methods and techniques
14. Areas of positive responsibility:
    - *a. Food*
    - *b. Clothing*
    - *c. Shelter*
    - *d. Climate*
    - *e. Medicine*
    - *f. Weaponry*
15. Areas of negative effects:
    - *a. Destruction (e.g. war)*
    - *b. Health hazards (e.g. smog)*
    - *c. Displacement of labor (automation)*

Science as an Intellectual and Moral Influence

1. Upon authoritarianism and dogmatism
2. Upon magic and superstition
3. Upon intolerance
4. For freedom of inquiry
5. For commitment to truth regardless
6. [illegible] thinking
7. In insistence upon adequate evidence
8. In insistence upon precision of language
9. In insistence upon honesty in reporting
10. In recognition of functional relationships
11. In estimation of uncertainty and error
12. In recognition of limitations
13. Way of life:
   a. Devotion to truth
   b. Devotion to experimental approach
   c. Devotion to rational approach
14. Toward philosophical unity
15. As component of education for:
   a. Character—moral competence
   b. Social competence
   c. Intellectual competence

F. Science as a Social Enterprise

1. Intensely, typically human
2. "Sharing" of experience
3. Checks and balances
4. The science community
   a. Its way of life
   b. [illegible]
   c. [illegible]
   d. Sanctions and controls
   e. Autonomy
   f. Organizations and institutions
   g. Politics
5. Many kinds of participants
6. Communal insights and criteria
   a. Tradition, presuppositions
   b. Faith
   c. Confidence
7. Relations and interactions with other components of society
   a. Educational community
   b. Industry and business
   c. Government
   d. Religious communities
8. Its cultural continuum; its debt to:
   a. Philosophy
   b. Art and literature
   c. Mathematics and logic
   d. Language
   e. Religion
   f. Politics
   g. Economics
9. Conditions under which it flourishes:
   a. War, peace
   b. Dictatorship, democracy
   c. Wealth, poverty
   d. Secrecy, restrictions
   e. In the face of opposition

. Science as an Intellectual and Moral Influence

1. Upon authoritarianism and dogmatism
2. Upon magic and superstition
3. Upon intolerance
4. For freedom of inquiry
5. For commitment to truth regardless
6. For critical thinking
7. In insistence upon adequate evidence
8. In insistence upon precision of language
9. In insistence upon honesty in reporting
10. In recognition of functional relationships
11. In estimation of uncertainty and error
12. In recognition of limitations
13. Way of life:
    - *a. Devotion to truth*
    - *b. Devotion to experimental approach*
    - *c. Devotion to rational approach*
14. Toward philosophical unity
15. As component of education for:
    - *a. Character—moral competence*
    - *b. Social competence*
    - *c. Intellectual competence*

F. Science as a Social Enterprise

1. Intensely, typically human
2. "Sharing" of experience
3. Checks and balances
4. The science community
    - *a. Its way of life*
    - *b. Standards and conventions*
    - *c. Language and jargon*
    - *d. Sanctions and controls*
    - *e. Authority*
    - *f. Organizations and institutions*
    - *g. Politics*
5. Many kinds of participants
6. Communal insights and criteria
    - *a. Tradition, presuppositions*
    - *b. Faith*
    - *c. Conscience*
7. Relations and interactions with other components of society
    - *a. Educational community*
    - *b. Industry and business*
    - *c. Governments*
    - *d. Religious communities*
8. Its cultural conditioning; its debt to:
    - *a. Philosophy*
    - *b. Art and literature*
    - *c. Mathematics and logic*
    - *d. Language*
    - *e. Religion*
    - *f. Politics*
    - *g. Economics*
9. Conditions under which it flourishes:
    - *a. War, peace*
    - *b. Dictatorship, democracy*
    - *c. Wealth, poverty*
    - *d. Secrecy, restriction?*
    - *e. In the face of opposition?*

information on the various subjects, and possibly even answers to the questions I have posed, can be found. To the beginner in this field the extent of these notes may seem formidable. He who is genuinely interested in these matters will soon discover, however, that this is actually a short bibliography—for a vast field in which the possibilities for fascinating study, adventurous thinking and rewarding teaching are unlimited. And the expert will know how inadequate is this bibliography—and how, in spite of my good intentions to the contrary, my own prejudices and points of view have affected my choices of references.

As a final challenge to all science teachers we quote the following wise words of a very distinguished scientist and teacher, Sir Hugh S. Taylor, Professor of Chemistry and Dean of The Graduate School, Princeton University:

> In the pursuit of wisdom the teacher of science must find the opportunity to convince the student that beyond the areas covered by science and scientific conclusions, beyond the testimony of history there are areas of truth which supplement those of knowledge to yield *sapientia.* These embrace art, literature, philosophy and religion. They include emotional and symbolic conclusions which require discipline and training no less than those activities practised in the laboratories, require a critical appreciation that can estimate the ultimate work of an art, of music, of literature, of all forms of effort that can lead to valid emotional reactions. The emotions will need to be fortified by a disciplined capacity for ethical, philosophical and religious conclusions. The urgent need is not for the science specialist but for the liberally educated man. (53)

6

Techniques and Processes[*]

The differences between initiating and continuing a study of the relationship of teacher education and religion and other campus curricular studies are very little. If a college or university faculty and administration have had a history of successful cooperative action in other types of activities, this college or university group will be successful in its study of teacher education and religion. Negatively stated, a college or university faculty or administration which finds it difficult to work as a cooperative unit in other collegiate activities will have difficulty in achieving success in a teacher education and religion study. Work in the area under consideration will resemble that in which faculty and administration have engaged in other curricular enterprises.

ATTITUDES TOWARD A TEACHER EDUCATION AND RELIGION STUDY

A working team to study teacher education and religion on any campus, by necessity, must be made up of the personnel

* This chapter prepared by Dr. A. L. Sebaly, Professor of Education, Western Michigan University, Kalamazoo.

of that particular institution. The study will be susceptible to the weaknesses and strengths of these individuals. Further, the material resources of the institution will condition, to a degree, the rate of progress which that institution will make. The attitudes which the individuals on the campus take toward the study will determine the direction it will go. Hence, anyone who is contemplating a study for a campus should give some consideration to how the faculty and administration on that campus feel toward such a study.

The extent to which the following attitudes exist on a given campus should be a matter of exploration. They do exist, and because they do, faculty and administrators are likely to react in a variety of ways to the thought of a study of the relationship of teacher education and religion.

1. One attitude is that of complacency by the local faculty and administration with the way it is carrying on its own activities. This inertia can prove to be a major stumbling block to curricular effort.

2. A second attitude is found among those who are not opposed to the study and are willing to work, but feel because of the current activities on the campus there is no room for another program. On the basis of necessity the contemplated study must give way to those with higher priorities.

3. A third attitude, varying from indifference to resentment, arises from a supposed implication that the college or university staff is not doing what it should. Individuals who hold this point of view will state that they have always been doing what the study advocated. They will maintain that the climate of opinion to teach about religion has always been friendly on their campus.

4. A fourth group will feel that the study is so subjective that any attempt at experimentation is doomed to failure. Individuals in this classification will view the study as one which is too sensitive to lend itself to exploration.

5. A fifth group of faculty members and administrators will be disturbed that any one should believe that they have a responsibility on their campus beyond the job for which they were hired. These individuals will state that they realize that the study is important, but that they do not have time to do adequately what needs to be done in their field of work. They are perturbed if they feel that they have an implied or real responsibility to contribute to activities beyond their own classes or department.

6. A sixth group will confuse the study with planned religious activities which exist on the modern collegiate campus. When a study of the curricular offerings of the college or university is proposed, these individuals classify planned religious activities in the same category with the study of materials about religion, intrinsic to the various subjects.

Conditions necessary for the operation of a teacher education and religion study on a college or university campus. The following conditions seem necessary if a college or university campus is to carry on a study of teacher education and religion.

1. The campus as a whole should accept the idea that it has a responsibility to improve teacher education in all of its aspects—general, special, and professional.

2. The faculty and administration should agree in general that it is the proper function of colleges and universities preparing teachers to teach intelligent understanding of the role of religion in human affairs.

3. The broad area of religion as a phase of man's development should be recognized whenever and wherever appropriate in the various disciplines.

4. There should be genuine concern by the faculty and administration for curricular enrichment and improvement in all areas.

5. There should be acceptance of the idea that the coopera-

tive self-study is an integral and continuing part of a collegiate institution's program.

6. Individual faculty members should be willing to initiate through study and experimentation enrichment and change in the course they are teaching.

7. Administrators should be willing to support the study not only with interest but with material resources as well.

8. Any program of action proposed should fit into the present and anticipated collegiate program.

9. Faculty members and administrators should avoid any effort to propagandize in the study.

ROLE OF THE ADMINISTRATOR

The administrator will be a key person in all stages of the study. From the beginning he should be convinced of the necessity of the study. The experienced administrator, however, is not deluded that because he wishes to have a particular study pursued on the campus the faculty will be anxious to engage in it. The probability exists, however, that the faculty will take their cues from the administration and be more willing to pursue it if they are convinced that the administration is for it.

The administrator must not expect quick returns from a committee's work in a curricular area such as this. Experience indicates that progress in the study will be slow. The administrator should encourage discussion but avoid high pressure tactics. The administrator should keep in mind that what is sought by this study is to promote not religion, but a better teacher of humanities, social science, science, professional education, or whatever the field may be. The administrator in his role should support the study in all phases of its development.

ROLE OF THE COORDINATOR

The administrator may wish to keep the leadership for the study of teacher education and religion. If he chooses to do this, he should realize that his being the committee chairman does not insure that work will be done. His committee will be susceptible to the same difficulties which are common to all group activities. More than likely he will appoint, on a tentative basis at least, someone to carry leadership for the contemplated study. This person should be a well-qualified leader who as a minimum has these characteristics: 1. knows the campus and its operation; 2. has interest in the subject; 3. has some ability to organize; 4. has tact and ability to work with people; 5. has some knowledge of the place of religions in the American society. If this individual does have prestige with the rest of the faculty, so much the better.

ESTABLISHING A COMMITTEE

Let it be assumed that the administrator is convinced that there should be a curricular study of the relationship of teacher education to religion. Some way must be established to put this idea into operation. The following plan is one which has been successfully used in several of the pilot institutions: 1. The study was discussed at a meeting to which invited representative faculty personnel came. 2. The nature of the study was explained to them. 3. Some concensus of opinion was sought to see if this group felt that the study was a desirable one for the campus as a whole. 4. Either an interim or a more permanent committee was appointed (if the group were in favor of the study).(1) 5. As needed, subcommittees were formed. 6. Committee membership was drawn from as broad a departmental representation as possible. 7. Provisions were made for individuals to volunteer to work on the committee.

In actual operation the administrator may leave the presentation of the idea to someone else. He may even absent himself from the preliminary discussion. Whatever procedure he follows the staff should realize that his interest in the study is genuine and that he is willing to lend administrative support to it.

COMMITTEE MEMBERSHIP

The ideal committee would be one which is composed of interested individuals from a wide variety of departments in the college or university. Interest and voluntary participation are essential for committee membership. The strength of this approach is that it will bring together interested individuals to work on a common concern. Purpose of the committee in the final analysis will determine the type of membership sought. If the local group decided that it wished only to have an informal discussion group, there may not even be any formal committee organization. In actual practice potential committee members will come from any area of the campus. Consideration, however, should be taken in having committee members from these areas at least: humanities, natural science, social science, and professional education.

RELATIONSHIP OF THE COMMITTEE TO THE COLLEGE OR UNIVERSITY

Committee purpose and collegiate structure will determine this relationship. The committee may be so informal as to have no relationship with collegiate structure. The membership is then individual. It may be a highly coordinated committee which is integrated into the power structure of the campus. The advantage of a separate committee is that it gives committee members a specific task to do. The disadvantage is that the committee may become extraneous to the rest of the campus. If the committee is to be more than a discussion group, then jurisdictional problems should be anticipated. For example, the relationship of this committee to a general curriculum committee should be clarified early in the study.

ROLE OF A CONSULTANT

After a committee is organized and ready for operation the members will find that the services of a consultant can be useful. The consultant is used when local committee members face problems which either require more knowledge and experience than local committee members have to offer, or which provide an opportunity for them to use an off-campus resource to strengthen a position which they have already taken. If a decision is made to use a consultant, the local group should clarify its own thinking as to what is expected from the consultant when he visits the campus. The consultant, on his part, has a responsibility for preparing himself for the visit. This means that through one means or another he should become acquainted with the campus and what is expected of him when he visits it. He will need to know the local committee's point of emphasis in its work if he is to serve as a satisfactory consultant.

POSSIBLE USE OF CONSULTANTS

1. *Process persons.* In this capacity the consultant will assume the responsibility of a discussion leader in helping the local group clarify problems, identify new problems, and, in general, carry thought processes forward. When the consultant plays this role, it is assumed that he will have had some experience as a discussion leader.

2. *An expert.* In this capacity he is asked to point out relationships between his subject matter specialty and religion; to give definite answers to questions; to propose methods of doing things. The consultant who plays this role assumes he knows what the answers are.

3. *An evaluator.* The consultant gives opinions of what he thinks about the local program. Too, he may be asked to give an opinion of how the local situation compares with others he has seen. Tact is needed if the consultant plays this role.

4. *As status person.* The consultant is used to bring prestige to the committee's work. He may be used as a speaker to faculty and students alike. He may be used at a workshop or din-

ner meeting as a speaker, and outsiders may be invited to hear him.

The local committee members must decide how they will best use the services of a consultant. In actual practice they may want him to play all of the roles at the same time. However, if the consultant plays a different role from what the local group expects, they will be dissatisfied with his visit.

SELF-CORRECTION BY DISCUSSING THE PROBLEM

The job of a teacher preparation institution is to prepare teachers. The study of the relationship of teacher education to religion is concerned with the improvement of teacher education. Its concern, in a curricular sense, is with suspected substance gaps in course content. The assumption is that if the course gaps are filled, the prospective teacher's education in an academic, substance sense, or knowledge way, will have been improved. This point is a slippery one for some because of the apparent lack of agreement by many faculty and administrative groups as to what religion or curriculum is.

The following discussion is taken from the discussion notes of a group which was attempting to clarify its thinking as to the purpose of the study. It is presented because it is typical of the discussion which occurred in pilot institutions and in all probability will re-occur from time to time as faculty groups study the relationship of teacher education to religion. (2)

> X—Sometimes we have been talking about *general education in the sense of a common education.* Sometimes we have turned aside and said general education is a liberal education which is needed by all. Sometimes we have talked about what everybody knows—that teachers teach what they are. If teachers are to teach and do their jobs, they should know their own convictions. We have said in a variety of ways that the purpose of the Project is not to aid religion but to have religion aid education. This statement does not mean religion *per se* but only as religion improves literature, art, music. This is distinct from religious literacy and commitment.

Y—We are concerned with education in a broader sense than state institutions. Our concern is with every college or university which prepares teachers.

Q—I come to the problem from a naturalistic point of view. Our failure, or unwillingness to define what we mean by religion means in most instances that theism will be assumed by habit.

Z—Some of us are saddened by no attention to commitment.

X—Many serious people want religious organizations to grow out from this Project. Good as this is, it is not the purpose of the Project.

Z—Everyone who runs into the Project seems to have a semantic difficulty. Are member institutions in the Association clear as to what the Project is about?

X—No. Of original concern to us is that materials about religion are important. But our concern in the Project is only in as much as they further the intent of the course. We are concerned whereby materials can aid courses. We are not interested in commitment, or religious literacy as such. When we talk about specific activities, we can see how purposes have been blurred. We have had surveys, inventories, workshops on our campus. We have learned that the problem is subject to approach. We have learned that the process of delimiting the field is a painful one.

Z—In a sense aren't we trying to reaffirm an educational ideal that religion is all important over other areas?

X—I would like to say this is a point of departure for us in this institution. The Project may not limit us in our activities in the future. I myself do not see these limitations. If intellectual conviction is achieved in the study, then perhaps all areas of it are strengthened.

Q—What is it that we are after? I am afraid that some want an acceptance of their religions; or, at the least, they want it made clear that the source of values lies beyond the going experiences of man, that man lives in some relationship to a Creator, to a plan.

X—If any college teacher teaches religion then there are those who would be united against it. Our business is educational.

A—How would you answer the criticism that you are not asking for anything else than what a good course is already doing?

X—There are a good many answers—*Moby Dick, The Scarlet Letter,* T. S. Eliot. It is a shortcoming to think only in terms of the religious dimension.

Z—The problem is discovering and spreading the best practice.

B—When I attended the —— meeting, I was led to see what goes on in teacher training and what teachers do in their teaching. Anything which aids the teacher to do his job better is good.

C—What is good teaching in a specific field? Or are we thinking about teachers in elementary and secondary schools? What is the meaning of religious dimension and experience?

X—We are not concerned with teaching moral and spiritual values of religion. We are concerned with a substance gap and not methods.

Z—The more you follow this Project, the more you can see similarities with other projects.

A—If we weren't primarily concerned with religious content, where would prospective teachers get this adequacy? Where would they learn about the role of religion in the culture?

X—They would get this information from the courses they take in college.

Q—At this point, I lose interest, so far as the problem of public education is concerned. Frankly, I do not see where this Project may lead, beyond the advantages gained where staff members give themselves freely to discussion if the critical question, what religion is to mean, is continually passed over. I especially dislike those situations where the question is not raised but in which action is dictated by the answer that would have been given had it been.

A—Your position would be widely accepted in teacher education institutions. Yet the area gets no tangible focus.

Z—It is a matter of practical advantage. I believe there is a value in directly facing up to the place of religion in the culture. When you have them all—science, mathematics, history—they might not be facing up to the total content of the field.

X—The committee's concern is not through courses, in my mind, or commitment, or through extracurricular activities. Does a teacher weasle when he is talking about religion?

X—To separate religion is not good. It is better to say there is a reciprocal relationship between religion and other elements in the human culture. It is our job to seek it and prepare teachers who have the ability to teach in the schools of this country.

A—It is a matter of practical judgment.

Y—What questions would the Project answer? Are we doing what can't be done directly by doing it indirectly? Isn't the real purpose of the Project to strengthen religion?

X—I think you propose a dilemma. I don't want to appear to dodge your question, but we shouldn't engage in any activity which will strengthen religion. Our job is to prepare teachers. There is an assumption that teachers lack this knowledge of where religion is intrinsic to the disciplines which they teach. We need to strengthen teacher education.

B—I imagine we are suspect and our role needs clarification. Are we clear in our own thinking that we don't have any ulterior motives in attending this seminar? What is authentic higher education anyway?

X—I am sure there is this suspicion. This is a Project to broaden and deepen American education. The long-range view is more defensible. The result of this seminar may leave a person more at sea.

A—If we find ourselves with two values—education and religion—is there a higher commitment? If one is engaged in values which involve self-sacrifice, might this not lead to the worship of an unknown God?

X—Aren't you constructing an artificial dilemma? Aren't we as people associated with education concerned with enlightenment? I can see no reason why a complete agnostic couldn't work on the Project at our college.

A—But when the chips are down, may he not have an ultimate set of values?

X—But you get into more difficulty by asking this question. Our proposition is that education is incomplete if it leaves reference to religion out. I mean education in an academic, substantive sense or in a knowledge way. The charge that the public schools are godless seems irrelevant to the purposes of my teaching.

B—I am not clear as to what you mean by knowledgeableness. Is this not the religious dimension? The attitudinal?

X—I see it this way. At the operational level what aspects of religion fit into education, humanities, the social sciences?

Any college group which enters into study of the relationship of teacher education to religion can expect a similar discussion to take place. There seems to be no substitute for the self-corrective process of talking the problem out. This conclusion implies that adequate provision should be made for discussion groups to explore the study on a campus.

METHODS OF APPROACH TO GET THE JOB DONE

For the college which is carrying on an all-campus approach to the study, the following methods seemed to be the better ones to bring about change: 1. committee meetings, 2. consultants, 3. conferences, 4. faculty meetings, 5. faculty seminars. These approaches may be satisfactory for the group, but the individual teacher will find little solace in them unless he is stimulated to do something about the study as he faces his students in his classes. The significant point of contact in teaching is that point between teacher and student. The previous writers in the fields of science, social science, humanities and professional education have pointed out ways whereby teachers in these areas can approach the study.

The teacher must come to grips with what determines course content in the area in which he is teaching. Among others, these items should be considered: 1. his frame of reference; 2. course objectives as defined by the department; 3. purposes of the course within the college picture; 4. what scholars in the field state about the subject matter in that area; 5. the needs of the students for general, specialized and professional preparation in becoming competent teachers.

Where a local campus will begin is a matter of local decision. The pilot institutions began in different places. In one, the faculty felt that it was important that there be discussion groups only. In another, the college as a whole felt that the work could be best done by experimental classes in the humanities. In another the sociology department took the leadership in developing and teaching a unit on contemporary religions. In another the experimental class in contemporary religions was offered as an elective. In another the need was to find out what teachers in the elementary and secondary schools felt their problems were. Several felt they needed to check students and teachers in the field to see if in a knowledgeable way they were conscious of the role that religions have played in the development of civilizations. *The important thing is that the program go beyond the discussion stage alone.* Failure to have an action program of some kind will cause individuals to lose interest in the study.

SOME OF THE GAINS WHICH A COLLEGE OR UNIVERSITY CAN EXPECT FROM A STUDY OF TEACHER EDUCATION AND RELIGION

1. *Curricular offerings will be re-examined.* There will be a re-examination of the curricular offerings in the general education sequence. This re-examination will be concerned with not only the relationship of materials about religion to general education, but the place of general education in higher education.

2. *Faculty changes in attitude.* Some faculty will become aware of situational opportunities where materials about religion are intrinsic to the disciplines which they are teaching. Others will look for hidden motives behind the study. The end result will be increased discussion and a healthy exchange of opinions and points of view.

3. *Personal and professional growth of the staff.* Through informal discussion and faculty seminars individual staff members will be encouraged to study the area of concern on their own initiative. There will be a greater awareness on the part of the faculty of the role of religion in human affairs.

4. *There will be many by-product gains* such as increased contacts by the college staff and administration with other groups and institutions; new ideas for research problems; more objective teaching.

5. *The teacher education program of the institution as a whole will be strengthened.* All segments of a campus are brought together to work on a common problem. Teacher education is viewed not only in terms of professional sequence but in its general education aspects as well.

SUMMARY

1. The study of the relationship of teacher education to religion is similar to other campus curricular studies.

2. Faculty attitude toward such a study on a given campus will vary from extreme indifference to emotionalized attitudes, *pro* and *con*.

3. For a campus to carry on a study successfully the campus as a whole should accept the idea that it is important that prospective teachers receive the best general, specialized and professional education possible.

4. The faculty and administration must accept the idea that it is the proper function of colleges and universities preparing teachers to teach an intelligent understanding of the role of religion in human affairs.

5. The administrator is a key person in initiating a program, but for it to continue successfully the faculty must not only favor it but be in on the plans for it from the beginning.

6. The study leader should be one who has tact, patience, persistence, is creative, and knows the campus and its operation.

7. Committee membership should be on the basis of interest and broad departmental representation.

8. The study should be one which is primarily concerned with suspected substance gaps in curricular offerings and at the same time is one which is equally opposed to the injection of materials in a course where there is no relevancy.

9. Definition of the committee's task will be difficult. There must be much self-correction of ideas through discussion.

10. The methods used to carry on a campus-wide operation are the same ones used to carry on any other curricular study.

11. Definite gains will follow from a study: curricular offerings will be re-examined; there will be changes in faculty attitude; there will be personal and professional growth of the staff; and the teacher education program as a whole will be strengthened.

7

Summary and Problems *

To attempt fully to summarize the materials of the earlier chapters of this book would be as presumptuous as it would be futile. The writers of the several chapters represent a wide range of scholarship in their specializations, in diverse fields. Their chapters are at once detailed and fundamental, specialized and comprehensive. The reader has presumably already followed each of them through the closely-knit fabric of his exposition. This last chapter makes no attempt to restate what has already been said.

Some few strands, however, run through all the earlier chapters, and need to be tied together. Separate as the chapters are, they have a common origin, share a common concern, acknowledge a common purpose and a common hope. In sum, the chapters reflect certain outcomes of a Project in the modification of the curriculum for the education of teachers; this Project reflects a concern that teachers, no matter what their field, teach incompletely, if they omit the materials drawn

* This chapter prepared by Dr. Evan R. Collins, President, State University of New York College for Teachers, Albany.

from the field of religion which are intrinsic to their teaching field.

But also, because this is a story of a Project which, with the planning stages, spanned some eight years, it is more than an account of the Project itself. It illustrates fundamental changes in the curriculum and the climate of teacher-educating institutions during this period, especially in the field with which this Project has been concerned. And because these institutions have themselves changed, this account illustrates certain changes in the total complex of American higher education, especially in the last ten years. Third, because we are concerned in all types and levels of education with learning from experience—our own and others'—we may derive from these accounts of a Project, set in the context of higher education, some inferences which suggest directions and potentials for the future. This, then, is the plan for this chapter—a view of the book as an account of a Project, as an illustration of certain far-reaching changes in American higher education, and as a predictor and promise of what these changes presage.

THE TEACHER EDUCATION AND RELIGION PROJECT—A CURRICULAR STUDY

Obviously, this book is first and foremost an account of a project centering on the curriculum for teacher education. Through this Project, the American Association of Colleges for Teacher Education explored for five years the relationship between the curricular materials of religion and of various subject matter disciplines. The basic motivation for the Project lay in the AACTE's concern that the teachers being prepared for the country's elementary and secondary schools be themselves as well educated as possible. There seemed reason to believe that a substantial portion of these teachers were beginning their work incompletely informed in the field of religion and that this inadequacy would show itself in the teacher's own classroom.

When the Project was designed, there seemed no reason to question this assumption. None of the experience during the Project suggests any basis for questioning it. This Project has not undertaken any broad scale survey or measurement of this apparent lack of preparation among teachers and there still seems real need for measuring and specifying these suspected inadequacies in the preparation of teachers.

This concern with the materials of religion as they are intrinsic to the subjects taught in the classroom is simply stated: the teacher's responsibility is to purvey the culture. Religion is a part of the culture. To omit the religion intrinsic in the subject field taught is to teach incompletely, and therefore falsely. Hardon interpreted this idea in the following manner:

> The forms of this relation are myriad. They can be purely informational, as in a historical study of Ancient Greece and Rome; or causal, as in tracing the religious inspiration of the Crusades; or reflective, as in the poetry of John Milton; or interpretative, as in the origins of the Reformation; or motivational, as in civics and the social sciences. (1)

In short, the education of a teacher is incomplete if it avoids or ignores the materials drawn from the field of religion that are implicit in the academic subject matter field and intrinsic to it. The teacher, as purveyor of the culture, must be prepared to convey more than a partial view.

The teacher at any level is in a very real sense a curriculum builder, no matter what the syllabus or course of study, nor by whom prepared and provided. The teacher not only shapes the formal statement of the program or course he teaches; he then interprets it and selects from it at every class session. He cannot avoid influencing the scope, the sequence, the emphasis, the effect, even though this influence may often be unintentional or unconscious. Often the teacher exerts this influence in unaware reflection and propagation of the incomplete elements in his own education. The teacher, then, needs knowledge about religion in order that his knowledge of his own subject field may be complete. Justice Jackson in the McCollum case made this point clearly.

> We would tear history and literature into shreds if we tried to remove all traces of religion. (2)

Clearly, however, he is here talking about teaching history or literature, not religion, in the schools.

LIMITATION OF THE PROJECT

Limitation of the materials drawn from religion to those which are intrinsic to the subject taught, has been an important characteristic of the Project. It has needed repeated emphasis to forestall misunderstanding. The concern of the Project has been curricular; that is, it has considered the subjects of the teacher education program; the materials of the study of religion have a place in this program only as they illuminate and contribute to the understanding of the academic field of study. The primary aim of the study was from the beginning

> to deal directly and objectively with religion whenever and wherever it is intrinsic to learning experience in the various fields of study. (3)

It was not the aim of the study to stimulate individual commitment, nor to encourage students to explore the resources of religion as a basis for durable convictions. Some who have read this account of the Project may regret this rigorous limitation, which excludes those elements of the religious experience that many find most significant. This limitation, however, permitted attention to be focused on the critical area where the propriety of the Association's concern is clearest. In addition, this limitation acknowledges the restrictions so well described in their application to the public school, by Sister Mary Nona, the limitations which are not alone those imposed by law, by policy of the system and school, by parental convictions; but most important, by each pupil's freedom of conscience, which must be respected. (4)

Two other aspects of the Project should be noted briefly. The Project, though limited to the area already specified, is not limited in time; it is not self-terminating. The pilot institutions which began this activity, under the stimulus of the Association's leadership, will certainly continue their interest and activity in this field; they will undoubtedly be joined by others. This report, then, is in the nature of a progress report only; more will develop.

Secondly, it should be noted that this has been at once a Project in religion in teacher education, and an exercise in curricular change. The procedures developed in the stimulation of course and program changes in the specific area of religion in teacher education are readily subject to application to other curricular change. The role of the consultant, the local administrator, the local coordinator, the committee member—these have been the subject of separate study and analysis in the course of the Project, and yield results readily adaptable to the general field of curricular change. Discussion of these processes is not appropriate in this volume, but discussion of the Project without mention of these valuable by-products would be incomplete.

In its first aspect, then, this book is the story of a project in enriching and completing certain aspects of the curriculum for the education of teachers, by including materials drawn from the field of religion. This Project has been carried on at fifteen pilot institutions, representing the membership of the American Association of Colleges for Teacher Education.

GROWING EMPHASIS ON THE STUDY OF VALUES IN AMERICAN HIGHER EDUCATION

In a larger sense, however, the experience of this Project is not limited to the fifteen pilot institutions, nor even to the full membership of the AACTE. The basic motivation of the study is directly traceable to the changes of the last decade common to all colleges and universities, especially at the undergraduate level. These changes reflect the social climate, and center in the acceptance of a search for enduring ethical values as a function of the undergraduate curriculum, usually through the studies classified as general education.

Only in the last twenty years or so would it have been possible to generalize from the experiences of a group of teacher-preparing institutions any broad findings generally valid for higher education as a whole. Especially in the period up to World War I, when the specialized normal school was the characteristic institution preparing teachers, particularly for the elementary schools, such generalization would have been unjustifiable. The colleges and universities of this country accepted their social responsibility for preparing teachers late in their history, and reluctantly, and incompletely. Only in approximately the last thirty years have these institutions fully accepted the lesson learned early in the teachers colleges, that professional preparation, too, is a necessary element in the teacher's education. In the same period, the specialized colleges for teachers have been developing appropriate general education and truly college-level subject matter courses. In consequence, the institutions of both types, once only distant academic cousins, now look more and more like brothers, if not twins.

There is ample documentation of this current in educational history, and it need not be detailed here. As one result of it, however, the group of institutions which participated in this Project may truly be considered to mirror the changes in the academic climate of American higher education during the last ten years. The heart of those changes, as has been indicated, has been the growing emphasis on the study of values, this study usually designated as a part of the program of general education.

Some of the reasons for this development were suggested in the first chapter: the desirability of including in common or general education a sampling truly representative of the culture, not excluding the religious dimension in human experience; the increasing concern with interpersonal relationships in a period of tension, and the accompanying interest in the bases for ethical judgments and moral values. Certainly the period since the last declared war has been one of strain, with an attendant groping for certainties or enduring values. To use an illustration outside the colleges, the tremendous increase in religious activity and interest, as evidenced by participation, during this period, is interpreted by many observers as a reflection of this quest for certainties, for a basis of ethical judgments.

The problem of values is as old as education. Yet it is new, too; the post-war years have seen a resurgence of interest in this aspect of higher education. This rediscovered need is not well met by the traditional courses, most colleges apparently feel. General education, by which is usually meant common education, has been developed in an attempt to avoid the narrowness of specialization inherent in the traditional divisions of subject matter, while preserving their values. This general, or common education, has assumed a position of increasing importance in the undergraduate liberal arts curriculum as the colleges and universities have felt the impact of mass increase in enrollment, and now prepare for a second and long-continuing rise. Indeed, as many have pointed out, the increase in the significance of general education is a function of the availability of higher education to an ever-wider fraction of the population.

The gradual but very substantial shift in the emphasis and concern of the undergraduate general education program described here is reflected and exemplified in the development of the Project this book describes. The Project began with the conditions prevailing in 1949 and 1950, the conditions well represented in the publications of the Educational Policies Commission on Moral and Spiritual Values in the Public Schools, and of the American Council on Education's Committee on Religion and Education. The first group, while not precluding a broader concern, emphasized that

> To omit from the classroom all references to religion and to the institutions of religion is to neglect an important part of American life. Knowledge about religion is essential for a full understanding of our culture, literature, art, history, and current affairs. (5)

The second group limited itself and the schools less sharply to the religion intrinsic in other subject matters, and included as a basic responsibility of the schools the teaching of the role of religion in human affairs.

> The first obligation of the school with reference to religion is, we believe, to facilitate intelligent contact with it as it has developed in our culture and among our institutions. (6)

These statements were, of course, drawn to apply to the public elementary and secondary schools, rather than to the college. The college or university which prepares teachers, however, is never far removed from the requirements of the schools for which it is preparing its students, and tends, therefore, to reflect without major change such limitations as those regarding religion.

ANALYSIS OF THE WRITERS' POSITIONS IN THIS BOOK IN RELATIONSHIP TO RELIGION IN TEACHER EDUCATION

The committee of the AACTE, in any case, accepted the limitation and, indeed, the very wording of the narrower delimitation, and announced in its first report that the Project's primary aim was

> to deal directly and objectively with religion whenever and wherever it is intrinsic to learning experience in the various fields of study. (7)

Not for several months, and then after prolonged and earnest deliberations, did the committee extend the definition of its concern to include the discovery and development of

> ways and means to teach the reciprocal relation between religion and other elements in human culture in order that the prospective teacher . . . be prepared to understand, to appreciate, and to convey to his students the significance of religion in human affairs. (8)

The difference between these two statements of position will not disturb many readers, and fewer now than it would have even five years ago. Yet the difference is noteworthy. It is the difference between the position taken by Cooper, for example, and that expressed by Justice Jackson in the McCollum case. The position taken by Schilling is about midway between the two. Cooper, in his discussion of the social sciences, holds closely to the "intrinsic" limitation. His basic assumption he announces as "knowledge about religion is an important aspect of the scholarly study of human society." He is concerned with "the place which knowledge about religion should have in the social sciences in order that they may realize their own purposes as scholarly disciplines." Schilling, however, goes a little further; he seeks the reciprocal relations between science as a field and religion as a field which will further the objectives of science teaching. He is not concerned with religion's significance in all human affairs, but only in those affairs he teaches —science. "It is proper to consider (religion) in a (science) course whenever, but only when, this is logically or psychologically necessary or desirable from the viewpoint of the objectives of the course." Although he finds many and marvelous ways in which the two disciplines are mutually reinforcing, his primary concern is still the teaching of science. Justice Jackson's position was further on:

> And I should suppose it is a proper, if not an indispensable part of preparation for a worldly life to know the roles that religion and religious have played in the tragic story of mankind. . . . One can hardly respect a system of education that would leave the student

> wholly ignorant of the currents of religious thought that move the society for a part in which he is being prepared. (9)

This is the position that does not stop with saying that the teacher is responsible to purvey the culture, and that religion is a part of the culture, so that the education of the teacher is incomplete without the materials intrinsic to his field. This position includes the logical next statement, that the schools should teach that religion is indeed a part of the culture, should teach the reciprocal relationships between religion and other aspects of human affairs, should teach, again in Justice Jackson's words that

> . . . nearly everything in our culture worth transmitting, everything which gives meaning to life is saturated with religious influences, derived from paganism, Judaism, Christianity—both Catholic and Protestant—and other faiths accepted by a large part of the world's peoples. (10)

There is a third state, still further from the starting-point of "intrinsic only." This position would, of course, hold the education of the teacher incomplete unless it included the materials from religion intrinsic to his field, and unless it taught also the role of religion in human affairs. It would stress the part which organized religion has played in establishing the moral and ethical values that the schools must develop and transmit. Giving due respect to the principle of valuing differences in a free society, it would not seek to equate religion and morality, by suggesting that religious convictions or sanctions alone undergird moral principles or ethical imperatives. It would, however, acknowledge the resources found by most people in religion as a basis for durable convictions and moral and ethical imperatives.

This third position reflects the extent of the shift in emphasis during the years of the Project. It has already been noted that the original committee of the AACTE only with difficulty and after deliberation made the transition from "intrinsic" to "reciprocal relationships." Five years later the analogous committee, in a corresponding statement of policy, was not content with asserting these responsibilities; they saw as the concern of the teacher the additional need to stress the relationship of religion and values. It is to this point that both Hill and Kircher speak, although from viewpoints somewhat different. Hill is concerned with the humanities as liberalizing studies.

> Humanities are capable of liberalizing the mind by making it sympathetic, intelligently and positively sympathetic, to any human aspiration which is sincerely and intelligently expressed.

The study of the humanities should, therefore, extend the capacity for "positive sympathy"—not merely negative tolerance—for the expressions of religious literature, art; humanities should help the student appreciate the "civilizing power of religions." Hill is clearly addressing himself to the problems of values, of the emotions, of judgments of beauty and of rightness. He is concerned with the encouragement of intelligent commitments regarding religion, and with the development of an intelligent, a constructive tolerance toward the commitments of others.

Kircher extends the context of his discussion of professional education into the whole realm of the university's basic purposes and philosophy; he is, then, dealing with the essentials of the general education ideal. In doing so, he combines the several strands we have been tracing: the breadth of truly professional education for teachers, legitimately a concern of the university; the university's increasing acknowledgment of the search for values as a function of the undergraduate liberal arts program usually in the general education or required common core; the change in the climate of discussion of the place of religion in higher education. The essence of Kircher's chapter—the potentials of constructive pluralism—is the basic element in much of general education—the synthesizing of subject fields to permit non-specialists to share in their values. The liberal university, in Kircher's view, is the best counterbalance for the many groupings of men committed to a single common commitment or cause—church groups, unions, lodges, political parties. As an agency dedicated to diversity, to the creative accommodation of differences, it can seek the mutual accommodation of man to man. "A true university is unalterably pluralistic not because it doesn't know better, but because this is the best it knows." Accepting diversity as desirable, it furthers religious enlightenment so it can teach mutual respect, and manifests in its methodology the "implicit religion" of creative, constructive accommodation. Kircher's chapter, indeed, might well be considered the summary section for this aspect of the book. And in one sense he brings us full circle. Just as for centuries theology was the unifying study in the universities of the Western world, the element of coherence that unified diverse disciplines, so now general education, common education, in an age of greater complexity and diversity of knowledge, seeks in a secular curriculum to perform the same function of reconciliation and unification. Yet, in the publicly supported higher education institutions at least, there seems to be no agreement at present as to what the integrating principle of general education should be.

PROBLEMS OF THE TEACHERS OF TEACHERS

Teacher educators face many problems as they consider where materials about religion are intrinsic to the sets of disciplines essential for the prospective teacher's preparation. Three of these are listed for discussion purposes, as of major importance:

Problem 1: It is the role of a liberal college or university preparing teachers to teach in a free society to see that prospective teachers have a knowledge of the role which religion has had and is having in that society.

The teacher, for his professional preparation, needs to have an awareness of the influence which religion, in its various manifestations, has had and is having upon the society in which he finds himself. The answer to the problem of how this preparation should best be done is unclear. The nature of the educational process is such that it is difficult, if not impossible, for the prospective teacher or the teacher educator to escape ego-involvement in that which he experiences. However, within the range of professional scholarly competency, it is necessary for a teacher to have not only a knowledge of how individuals grow, but also of how society influences the type of educational experiences which each has.

The writers of this book have suggested avenues of approach to teaching about religion based on the thought that if teachers are better informed regarding the role of religion in human affairs, they can do a more scholarly job of teaching in the various content fields. The AACTE Teacher Education and Religion Project, as it has been previously noted, operated on a limited basis. But even a limited operation can become snarled between desires of the teacher educator to give objective recognition to religion, in a generic sense, as one of the motivating forces in men's lives, and the lack of knowledge of how to do the job. The challenge to the teacher educator who accepts the proposition that a prospective teacher in a free society should have a knowledge of the role which religion plays in that society is to analyze the discipline which he is teaching to see where materials about religion are intrinsic to it.

Problem 2: Workable inter-disciplinary structures are needed on the university and college campus which will allow teacher educators to work comfortably and effectively to improve teacher education.

An increasing number of the studies engaged in by faculty and administration tend to be team projects. The Teacher Education and Religion Project was an example of a team study. It cut across departmental, divisional, and college lines. A team approach is not without its difficulties because organizational structure inherent within the academic community makes it difficult for faculty and administration in one area to work easily, comfortably and effectively with faculty and administration in another.

Within the academic disciplines there are recognized specialties. And apparently the fields of specialization are increasing. This movement is occurring in professional education as well as in other areas. The trend toward specialization has a tendency to separate the specialist in one field from the specialist in another. Consequently, even if the specialists of various fields wish to work together, they find it difficult to understand each other's language and frames of reference.

The curricular studies done by faculty and administration in the pilot institutions proved for the greater part, at the action research level, at least, that constructive inter-disciplinary curricular studies could be done. These individuals demonstrated repeatedly that the nature of teaching and learning in a free society is such that departmental, divisional, and college lines will be crossed if individuals work on common problems of common concern. When they entered fields of specialization other than their own, however, they were working against academic structure which by and large has placed a premium upon specialization. It must be recognized that not all faculty or administrators were able to work with specialities other than their own. This difficulty, however, did not seem inherent in the nature of the study as much as it was the difficulty of one specialist working comfortably and effectively with another within the same academic community.

It is sound practice for teacher educators, whether specialist or generalist, to advocate an inter-disciplinary approach to curricular study. Curricular studies of the relationship of religion to teacher education lend themselves to the team approach. The challenge to the academic community is whether a university or college preparing teachers can establish workable structures which will allow faculty and administrators to work comfortably and effectively together for common purposes.

Problem 3: Research is needed in the area of teacher education and religion.

There is need for much research in the area of teacher education. The following problems are part of a list developed by the AACTE committee in the course of its work; it is suggestive of the kinds of information which scholars in the field might seek. No attempt has been made to be definitive. If the list stimulates thinking about possible research problems, it will have served its purpose.

1. Research in the philosophy of the relation of education to religious thought and experience in a pluralistic society, and its implications for teacher education.
   a. What are the specific educational objectives in this area of teacher education in terms of particular measurable outcomes to be sought?
   b. How does knowledge and understanding of religion (both empirical and theoretical) contribute to general education? To specializing education?
   c. When is it legitimate and desirable to discuss religion in courses devoted to the various disciplines? How and to what extent does understanding of religious experience and thought contribute to adequate understanding of the arts and sciences? And vice versa?
2. What knowledge about religion should a teacher possess in order to understand his pupils and community? The approach here may be from:
   a. Philosophical analysis
   b. Factual studies of actual situations and problems (including the use of case histories and anecdotal records).

      There are at least four areas or dimensions of such knowledge:

      (1) Factual knowledge of the history, basic concepts

and major beliefs, practices, ritual, institutions of religions.

(2) The perspective of the influence and significance of religion in history and cultures.

(3) The personal qualities characteristic of the "religious person," or that characterize the "religious sentiment." (This may be regarded as an existential definition of religion.)

(4) The religious dimension, or components, of the arts.

3. The psychology (and sociology) of child development with particular reference to religion. (What should the teacher know about this, with special reference to stages of development attained at different age levels?)
   a. At what stages of growth and development do the various reciprocal relations between religion and the various disciplines become meaningful to the child?
   b. At what stages of development do certain perplexities and tensions arise that the teacher should be aware of and be able to cope with?
   c. To what extent, and how, do various religious attitudes and beliefs affect ethics and morals? Undergird or undercut spiritual and moral values?

4. How and to what extent do, or do not, extra-curricular religious activities contribute to the educational process? And to teacher education?

In carrying on such research the following more specific investigations are basic:

5. Status studies (by surveys) of:
   a. The present situation regarding courses devoted to the role of religion in public education.
   b. In-service training projects relating religion to teaching.
   c. Courses in religion in teachers colleges.

d. Courses or course units in cognate fields, or devoted to the relations of religion to other fields.
e. Areas of public education where questions about religion are asked by pupils.
f. Practices and points of view from abroad.

6. The development of instruments and techniques for education measurement and evaluation (including longitudinal investigation).
7. The development and evaluation of teaching methods relative to the teaching of reciprocal relations between religion and the various disciplines.
8. The development and/or accumulation of appropriate teaching materials appropriate for students at different age levels.

THE FUTURE

The culture in the United States is pluralistic. The social dimensions of living in a constricted physical world require the communality, the communication, and communicability of a common education; this is the general education that buttresses our specializations. This general, common education is socially unifying in its purposes; its philosophy is that of cultural pluralism, the constructive accommodation of differences. The expression of this philosophy in the teaching of colleges and universities requires the inclusion of the materials drawn from religion but intrinsic to the subject fields supporting the common core of general education. It requires the recognition of the role of religion in human affairs, and of the reciprocal relations between religion and other disciplines. And it requires the acknowledgment and the teaching of the part played by religion in the development of those moral and ethical imperatives which guide, restrain, and inspire men—which make life and education possible and precious.

This study was undertaken because there had been for a

long time a desire to get these problems out in the open and deal with them in free discussion by all concerned, and with all the resources of trained scholars.

At this stage, it was considered less important to attempt to solve problems than it was to see clearly of what they consist. To attack problems of this size and complexity requires imagination, boldness and courage. More than these individual qualities, it requires cooperative effort by scholars from many backgrounds, and patient attention to the constructive accommodations of diversity. The Project described in this book is a mere beginning. Perhaps its most important product is the conviction that the potential results are so far-reaching as to demand and to justify the best efforts of us all.

long time a desire to get these problems out in the open and deal with them in free discussion by all concerned and with all the resources of trained scholars.

At this stage, it was considered less important to attempt to solve problems than it was to see clearly of what they consist. To attack problems of this size and complexity requires imagination, boldness and courage. More than those good qualities, it requires cooperative effort by scholars, institutions, foundations and government to the extent that the program now contemplated may be carried out. The Project described in this book is a mere beginning. Perhaps its most important product is the conviction that the potential returns are so far-reaching as to demand and to justify the best efforts of us all.

Appendix: Notes and Bibliography

CHAPTER 1

Notes

1. (p. 1) Pilot Institutions, see p. xi of preface.
2. (p. 2) American Council on Education, Committee on Religion and Education, *Function of the Public Schools in Dealing With Religion;* A Report on the Exploratory Study Made by the Committee. p. 76. Washington: American Council on Education, 1953.
3. (p. 2) ———, Cooperative Study of Evaluation in General Education, *General Education: Exploration in Evaluation;* The Final Report of the Study, Paul L. Dressel and Lewis B. Mayhew. p. 4. Washington: American Council on Education, 1954.
   Will M. French and Associates, *Behavioral Goals of General Education in High Schools.* p. 26. New York: Russell Sage Foundation, 1957.
4. (p. 3) Chalmer A. Gross, *Implementing Programs of General Education for Teachers.* p. 9. Oneonta, New York: American Association of Colleges for Teacher Education, 1953.
5. (p. 3) Maurice E. Troyer and Robert C. Pace, *Evaluation in Teacher Education.* p. 95. Washington: American Council on Education, 1944.
6. (p. 3) *Ibid.*

7. (p. 3) Ernest C. Johnson, "Summary of Policies and Recommendations of the American Council on Education Committee on Religion and Education," *Study of Religion in the Public Schools; An Appraisal,* ed. Nicholas C. Brown. p. 7. Washington: American Council on Education, 1958.

8. (p. 4) William H. Vaughan, "Religious Practices in State Teachers Colleges," *Twenty-Sixth Yearbook,* AATC. p. 114–18. Oneonta, New York: American Association of Teachers Colleges, 1947.

9. (p. 5) *Moral and Spiritual Values in the Public Schools.* p. 77–8. Washington: Educational Policies Commission of the National Education Association, 1951.

10. (p. 5) American Council on Education, Committee on Religion and Education, *Relation of Religion to Public Education; The Basic Principles.* p. 49. Washington: American Council on Education (Studies Series 1, No. 26, V. XI), 1947.

11. (p. 6) *Ibid.*

12. (p. 6) *Ibid.*, p. 16.

13. (p. 6) *Ibid.*, p. 35.

14. (p. 6) *Ibid.*

15. (p. 6) *Function of the Public Schools in Dealing with Religion, op. cit.*, p. 83.

16. (p. 6) *Ibid.*, p. vii.

17. (p. 6) *Ibid.*

18. (p. 6) *Ibid.*, p. 11.

19. (p. 7) Vivian T. Thayer, *Religion in Public Education.* p. 184–90. New York: Viking Press, 1947.

20. (p. 7) George F. Thomas, "Religious Perspectives in College Teaching; Problems and Principles," *Religious Perspectives in College Teaching,* ed. Hoxie N. Fairchild. p. 13. New York: Ronald Press Co., 1952.

21. (p. 7) Evan R. Collins, "Teaching About Religion in Teacher Education Institutions; An *Ad-Hoc* Committee Report," *Sixth Yearbook,* AACTE. p. 109–10. Oneonta, New York: American Association of Colleges for Teacher Education, 1953.
Prospectus of the Teacher Education and Religion Project. p. 1–6. Oneonta, New York: American Association of Colleges for Teacher Education, 1953.

22. (p. 8) *Ibid.*

23–36. (p. 10–25) Submitted by Local Coordinators of the Teacher Education and Religion Project. (See individual footnotes at bottom of each page.)

37. (p. 28) American Jewish Committee, *Religion and Public Education; A Statement of Views*. p. 7–10. New York: American Jewish Committee (Revised, 1957).
Philip Perlmutter, "Teaching About Religion: Solution or Confusion," *Reconstructionist*, XXII (March 9, 1956), 23–5.
Religion and the Public Schools; A Statement of Policy and Position Jointly Adopted by the Synagogue Council of America and the National Community Relations Advisory Council. p. 7. New York: Joint Advisory Council, 1956.
Study of Religion in the Public Schools; An Appraisal, op. cit., p. 18–32, 204.

38. (p. 28) Eugene E. Dawson, "The Next Decade of Research and Experimentation Relating to Religion and Public Education," *Study of Religion in the Public Schools; An Appraisal, op. cit.*, p. 187–200.

39. (p. 30) Isaac B. Berkson, *Ideal Mind and Community: A Philosophy of Education*. New York: Harper and Brothers, 1958. 302 p.
R. Freeman Butts, "The Relation Between Religion and Education," *Progressive Education,* 33 No. 5 (September, 1956), 140–42.
John L. Childs, *American Pragmatism and Education;* An Interpretation and Criticism. New York: Henry Holt and Co., 1956. 373 p.
Joseph L. Costanzo, S.J., "Religion in Public School Education," *Thought*, XXI No. 121 (Summer, 1956), 216–44.
Ernest Johnson, "Religion and Education," *Progressive Education,* 33 No. 5 (September 5, 1956), 143–48.
Alfred Jospe, "Religious Perspectives in Higher Education—Some Unresolved Issues," *Reconstructionist,* XXIV No. 3 (March 21, 1958), 7–15.
William H. Kilpatrick, "Some Issues in Religion and Education," *Progressive Education,* 33 No. 5 (September, 1956), 135–38.
Robert M. MacIver, *Academic Freedom in our Time* (A Study prepared for the American Academic Freedom project of Columbia University). p. 134–46. New York: Columbia University Press, 1956.
Jerome Nathanson, "Religion in Public Education," *Progressive Education,* 33 No. 5 (September, 1956), 151–60.
Religious Perspectives in College Teaching, ed. Hoxie N. Fairchild. New York: Ronald Press Co., 1952. 460 p.
Selected Readings in the Philosophy of Education, ed. Joe Park. New York: Macmillan Co., 1958. 440 p.
Teaching of Religion in American Higher Education, ed. Christian Gauss. New York: Ronald Press Co., 1951. 158 p.

CHAPTER 2

Notes

1. (p. 37) Robert E. Fitch, "Faith of a University," *New Republic,* 138 (May 19, 1958), 22.

2. (p. 50) *Minutes of the General Assembly of the Presbyterian Church in the United States of America,* Part I. p. 94. Office of the General Assembly, Witherspoon Building, Philadelphia 7, Pennsylvania, 1957.

3. (p. 50) *Ibid.,* p. 99.

4. (p. 50) Sarvepalli Radhakrishnan, "Religion of the Spirit and the World's Need," *This Is My Philosophy,* ed. Whit Burnett. p. 357. New York: Harper and Brothers, 1957.

5. (p. 52) Robert Ulich, *Human Career—A Philosophy of Self-Transcendence.* p. 164–65. New York: Harper and Brothers, 1955.

6. (p. 58) *Minutes of the General Assembly, op. cit.,* p. 100.

7. (p. 60) Martin Buber, *Between Man and Man,* tr. Ronald Gregor Smith. Boston: Beacon Press, 1955. 211 p.

8. (p. 61) Philip E. Jacob, *Changing Values in College.* New York: Harper and Brothers, 1957. 174 p.

9. (p. 68) Seymour A. Smith, "Religious Instruction in State Universities—A Report of Recent Trends," *Religious Education,* LIII (May, 1958), 290–94 (published by Religious Education Association, New York).

10. (p. 69) *Philosophies of Education,* Forty-First Yearbook of the National Society for the Study of Education, Part I. Chicago: University of Chicago Press, 1942. 321 p.
Modern Philosophies and Education, Fifty-Fourth Yearbook of the National Society for the Study of Education, Part I. Chicago: University of Chicago Press, 1955. 374 p.

11. (p. 72) R. Freeman Butts, "What Image of Man Should Public Education Foster?" *Religious Education,* LIII (March, 1958), 114–20.

12. (p. 79) Pitirim A. Sorokin, "Integralism Is My Philosophy," *This Is My Philosophy,* ed. Whit Burnett. p. 179. New York: Harper and Brothers, 1957.

13. (p. 79) *Ibid.,* p. 181.

14. (p. 80) *Ibid.,* p. 188–89.

15. (p. 84) Erich Fromm, "Love In Psychotherapy," *Merrill-Palmer Quarterly* (Spring, 1958), 131.

16. (p. 85) *Ibid.,* 132.

17. (p. 85) *Ibid.,* 133.

18. (p. 85) *Ibid.,* 135.

19. (p. 86) Everett J. Kircher, "Religion and the Liberal University," *Progressive Education,* 33 (July, 1956), 97–103.

20. (p. 90) Bernard Meland, *Higher Education and the Human Spirit.* p. 106–07. Chicago: University of Chicago Press, 1953.

21. (p. 91) *Ibid.*, p. 106.
22. (p. 91) *Ibid.*, p. 135.
23. (p. 92) Floyd H. Ross, *Addressed to Christians*. p. 20–1. New York: Harper and Brothers, 1950.
24. (p. 93) *Ibid.*

Bibliography

Bernstein, Philip Sidney. *What the Jews Believe*. New York: Farrar, Strauss and Young, 1951. 100 p.

Brubacher, John S. *College Reading and Religion*. New Haven: Yale University Press, 1948. 345 p.

———, ed. "The Public Schools and Spiritual Values," *Seventh Yearbook*, The John Dewey Society. New York: Harper and Brothers, 1944. 222 p.

Buber, Martin. *Between Man and Man*, tr. Ronald Gregor Smith. Boston: Beacon Press, 1955. 211 p.

———. *I and Thou*, tr. Ronald Gregor Smith. New York: Charles Scribner's Sons, 1937. 132 p.

Burnett, Whit. *This Is My Philosophy*. New York: Harper and Brothers, 1957. 378 p.

Butts, R. Freeman. *American Tradition in Religion and Education*. Boston: Beacon Press, 1950. 230 p.

———. "What Image of Man Should Public Education Foster?" *Religious Education*, LIII (March, 1958), 114–20 (published by Religious Education Association, New York).

Cottrell, Donald P. *College Reading and Religion*. New Haven: Yale University Press, 1948. 345 p.

Dewey, John. *Common Faith*. New Haven: Yale University Press, 1934. 87 p.

Ehlers, Henry, ed. *Crucial Issues in Education*. New York: Henry Holt and Co., 1955. 277 p.

Emerson, Ralph Waldo. "Education," *Selected Prose and Poetry*. New York: Rinehart and Co., 1950. 485 p.

Fitch, Robert E. "Faith of a University," *New Republic*, 138 (May 19, 1958), 22.

Fromm, Erich. "Love in Psychotherapy," *Merrill-Palmer Quarterly* (Spring, 1958), 131.

Function of the Public Schools in Dealing With Religion. Washington: American Council on Education Committee on Religion and Education, 1953. 145 p.

Hocking, William E. *Living Religions and a World Faith.* New York: Macmillan Co., 1940. 293 p.

Jacob, Philip E. *Changing Values in College.* New York: Harper and Brothers, 1957. 174 p.

Johnson, Frederick Ernest, ed. *American Education and Religion: The Problem of Religion in the Schools,* Institute for Religious and Social Studies. New York: Harper and Brothers, 1952. 211 p.

———. *Patterns of Faith in America Today,* Institute for Religious and Social Studies. New York: Harper and Brothers, 1957. 192 p.

Kircher, Everett J. "Religion and the Liberal University," *Progressive Education,* 33 (July, 1956), 97–103.

Maynard, Theodore. *Catholic Church and the American Idea.* New York: Appleton Century, Inc., 1953. 309 p.

Meland, Bernard Eugene. *Higher Education and the Human Spirit.* Chicago: University of Chicago Press, 1953. 204 p.

Minutes of the General Assembly of the Presbyterian Church in the United States of America, Part I. Philadelphia: Office of the General Assembly, Witherspoon Building, 1957.

Moral and Spiritual Values in the Public Schools. Washington: Educational Policies Commission of National Education Association, 1951. 100 p.

Niebuhr, Reinhold. *Reinhold Niebuhr: His Religious, Social and Political Thought,* ed. C. W. Kegley and R. W. Bretall. New York: Macmillan Co., 1956.

———. *Pious and Secular America.* New York: Charles Scribner's Sons, 1958. 105 p.

Relation of Religion to Public Education—The Basic Principles. Washington: American Council on Education Committee on Religion and Education, 1947. 54 p.

Religion and Freedom of Thought, Perry Miller, Robert L. Calhoun, Nathan M. Pusey, Reinhold Niebuhr. Garden City, N. Y.: Doubleday and Co., 1954.

Religion and the Free Society. New York: Fund for the Republic, 60 East 42nd Street, 1958.

Religion and the Public Schools, Synagogue Council of America, National Community Relations Advisory Council. New York: Joint Advisory Council, 1956.

Ross, Floyd H. *Addressed to Christians (Isolationism vs. World Community).* New York: Harper and Brothers, 1950. 154 p.

Smith, Thomas Vernon. *Abraham Lincoln and the Spiritual Life.* Boston: Beacon Press, 1951. 95 p.

State and Sectarian Education. Washington: National Education Association Research Bulletin, Vol. XXXIV No. 4 (December, 1956), 167–215.

Thayer, Vivian Trow. *Attack Upon the American Secular School.* Boston: Beacon Press, 1951. 257 p.

Ulich, Robert. *Human Career—A Philosophy of Self-Transcendence.* New York: Harper and Brothers, 1955. 255 p.

———. "Problems and Principles," *Religious Perspectives of College Teaching,* ed. Hoxie N. Fairchild. New York: Ronald Press Co., 1952. 460 p.

CHAPTER 3

Notes

1. (p. 102) George Santayana, "Brief History of My Opinions," *Contemporary American Philosophy;* Personal Statements, Vol. II, ed. George P. Adams and William P. Montague. p. 239–57. New York: Macmillan Co., 1930. (Quoted with permision of the publisher.)

2. (p. 115) It is not the case that the spirit of positive tolerance destroys a man's capacity to reject things which ought to be rejected. Positive tolerance is not equivalent to willingness to accept anything. If this were so it would also be impossible for the intelligent humanist of catholic taste to reject certain works of art as aesthetically inferior. Intelligent appreciators of the arts do tend to develop catholicity in their tastes; but they also tend to become very discriminating—they reject many things as bad or trivial; their aesthetic intelligence is displayed by the grounds they can give for such rejections. The truly tolerant man will not be led by his tolerance to tolerate superstition. He will reject many things. He has an advantage over the negatively tolerant man, whose rejections are all of the same sort; the latter tends to argue that all doctrine is superstition, and he thus becomes unable to find one form of "superstition" better or worse than another. He must accept them all, or he will not appear to be tolerant.

3. (p. 118) I do not mean to draw a hard and rigid line between the functions of scholarship and of teaching. The best teachers must to some extent share the interests and activities of the professional scholar, and should have time available for pursuing these. Also, few scholars can afford to separate sharply their scholarly activities from teaching. This is only a question of emphasis. Some academic careers are bound to emphasize one of these things, and other careers the other.

4. (p. 121) Nevertheless, I have much sympathy for the view which regards the great works of the humanities as foolproof. It is better, of course, if students read with the guidance of intelligent and devoted teachers, but people often exaggerate the amount of harm that may be done when students read exotic works without professional help. I have heard learned men argue that students should not be allowed to read Oriental literature except under the guidance of men as learned as themselves. This supposes a high priesthood in the teaching of the humanities which the great original artists would have despised.

Bibliography

Allport, Gordon W. *Individual and His Religion.* New York: Macmillan Co., 1953. 147 p.

Axtelle, George E. "Religion, Education and Culture," *Educational Forum,* XXI (November, 1956), 5–17.

Berkson, Isaac Baer. *Education Faces the Future.* New York: Harper and Brothers, 1943. 345 p.

Bradley, A. C. *Ideals of Religion.* London: Macmillan Co., 1940. 286 p.

———. "Poetry for Poetry's Sake," *Oxford Lectures on Poetry.* London: Macmillan Co., 1950. 395 p.

Bradley, F. H. *Ethical Studies,* 2d ed. Oxford: Clarendon Press, 1927. 344 p. (See especially: "Concluding Remarks," p. 313–44.)

Brown, Kenneth I. *Not Minds Alone.* New York: Harper and Brothers, 1954. 206 p.

Cohen, Morris R. "The Dark Side of Religion," *Faith of a Liberal.* New York: Henry Holt and Co., 1946. 497 p.

———. "Epilogue: In Dispraise of Life, Experience and Reality," *Reason and Nature.* New York: Harcourt, Brace and Co., 1931. 470 p.

Collingwood, R. G. *Principles of Art.* Oxford: Clarendon Press, 1938. 347 p. (See especially: Book III, "The Theory of Art," p. 273–336.)

Cotton, J. Harry. "Religion in the Liberal Arts Curriculum," *Association of American Colleges Bulletin,* XLI (May, 1955), 234–38.

Dewey, John. *Art as Experience.* New York: Minton, Balch and Co., 1934. 355 p. (See especially: Chapters 12–14, p. 272–355.)

———. *A Common Faith.* New Haven: Yale University Press, 1934. 87 p.

Educational Freedom in an Age of Anxiety, ed. Henry Gordon Hullfish. New York: Harper and Brothers, 1953. 229 p.

Hartshorne, Charles, and Reese, William L. *Philosophers Speak of God.* Chicago: University of Chicago Press, 1953. 535 p.

James, William. *Varieties of Religious Experience.* New York: Longmans, Green and Co., 1902. 534 p.

———. "The Will to Believe," *Philosophic Problems,* ed. Maurice Mandelbaum, Francis W. Gramlich and Alan Ross Anderson. New York: Macmillan Co., 1957. 762 p.

Kircher, Everett J. "Religion and the Liberal University," *Progressive Education,* XXXIII 4 (July, 1956), 97–103.

Langer, Susanne. *Philosophy in a New Key.* Cambridge, Mass.: Harvard University Press, 1942. 313 p.

Lewis, C. S. *Allegory of Love: A Study in Medieval Tradition.* London: Oxford University Press, 1938. 378 p.

Madden, Ward. "Religion and Educational Progressivism," *Progressive Education,* XXXIII (September, 1956), 135–38.

———. *Religious Values in Education.* New York: Harper and Brothers, 1951. 203 p.

Maritain, Jacques, and Cocteau, Jean. *Art and Faith.* New York: Philosophical Library, 1948. 138 p.

Maritain, Jacques. *Art and Scholasticism,* tr. J. F. Scanlan. New York: Charles Scribner's Sons, 1949. 177 p. (See especially: Chapters VII–X, p. 40–94.)

———. *Creative Intuition in Art and Poetry.* New York: Meridian Books, 1955. 339 p.

Miller, Perry, and others. *Religion and Freedom of Thought.* New York: Doubleday and Co., 1954. 64 p.

Ortega y Gasset, José. *Dehumanization of Art.* Garden City, N. Y.: Doubleday and Co. (Anchor Books), 1956. 187 p.

———. *Mission of the University,* tr. Howard Lee Nostrand. Princeton: Princeton University Press, 1944. 103 p.

Religious Perspectives in College Teaching, ed. Hoxie N. Fairchild. New York: Ronald Press Co., 1952. 460 p.

Santayana, George. *Interpretations of Poetry and Religion.* New York: Harper Torchbooks, 1957. 290 p.

———. *Reason in Religion* (*The Life of Reason,* Volume III). New York: Charles Scribner's Sons, 1945. 279 p.

———. *Sense of Beauty.* New York: Charles Scribner's Sons, 1936. 210 p.

Scott, Nathan A., Jr. "Poetry, Religion, and the Modern Mind," *Journal of Religion,* XXXIII (July, 1953), 182–97.

———, compiler. "Religion and Literature; A Selected Bibliography," *Christian Scholar,* XLI (March, 1958), 7–76.

Tawney, R. H. *Religion and the Rise of Capitalism.* New York: Harcourt, Brace and Co., 1926. 337 p.

Tolstoy, Leo. *What Is Art?* tr. Aylmer Maude. London: Oxford University Press (for the Tolstoy Society), 1929. 399 p. (See especially: Chapter XX, p. 276–88.)

Walsh, Chad. "Religion in Liberal Arts Education," *Association of American Colleges Bulletin*, XLI (May, 1955), 239–45.

Wilder, Amos N. *Modern Poetry and the Christian Tradition.* New York: Charles Scribner's Sons, 1952. 287 p.

———. *Spiritual Aspects of the New Poetry.* New York: Harper and Brothers, 1940. 262 p.

Zitner, Sheldon P. "Some Comments on the Relations Between Poetry and Religion," *Journal of General Education,* XI, No. 4 (October, 1958) 197–201.

CHAPTER 4

Notes

1. (p. 128) Delivered at Strasbourg in 1862.
2. (p. 128) *Varieties of History,* ed. Fritz Richard Stern. p. 182–83. New York: Meridian Books, 1956.
3. (p. 128) *Ibid.,* p. 185.
4. (p. 129) Fustel de Coulanges, *Ancient City.* p. 10. Boston: Lee and Shepherd, 1874.
5. (p. 129) Stern, *op. cit.,* p. 185.
6. (p. 129) Fustel de Coulanges, *op. cit.,* p. 11.
7. (p. 129) Stern, *op. cit.,* p. 186.
8. (p. 129) James Westfall Thompson, *History of Historical Writing.* Vol. II. p. 365–66. New York: Macmillan Co., 1942.
9. (p. 130) John H. Hallowell, "Political Science," *Religious Perspectives in College Teaching,* ed. Hoxie N. Fairchild. New York: Ronald Press Co., 1952. (Also published as a pamphlet by the Hazen Foundation.)
10. (p. 131) J. Milton Yinger discusses the different functions of a definition in *Religion, Society and the Individual.* p. 3–7. New York: Macmillan Co., 1957. (Quotations referred to in notes 31, 35, 36 and 41 in this section used with permission of the publisher.)
11. (p. 132) Elizabeth K. Nottingham, *Religion and Society.* p. 10–11. New York: Random House, copyright 1954. (Quoted with permission of the publisher.)
12. (p. 132) Steven Runciman, *History of the Crusades.* 3 vols. London: Cambridge University Press, 1954.
13. (p. 132) *Ibid.,* Vol. III, p. 130.

14. (p. 134) Harry Elmer Barnes, *Survey of Western Civilization.* p. 415. New York: Thomas Y. Crowell Co., 1947.

15. (p. 134) *Ibid.*, p. 416.

16. (p. 134) The use of this phrase provides an interesting illustration of how a historian may select material when writing a general textbook. In his *Survey of Western Civilization,* from which this is taken, Dr. Harry Elmer Barnes cites as the basis for his judgment an old article by Preserved Smith, "Luther's Early Development in the Light of Psycho-Analysis," published, in 1913, in *American Journal of Psychology,* XXIV (July, 1913), 360–77. In this article Smith states that Luther "inherited a taste for drink from his father," that "his childhood was very unhappy," and that "Luther is a thoroughly typical example of the neurotic, quasi-hysterical sequence of an infantile sex-complex." It is interesting to note that Smith did not include this interpretation of Luther seven years later in *Age of the Reformation* (New York: Henry Holt and Co., 1920). Instead he wrote concerning the young Luther, "For the sudden change that came over his life at the age of twenty-one no adequate explanation has been offered" (p. 64). Smith also merely described how "During the first ten years in the cloister he underwent a profound experience" without speculating about the subconscious causes of this experience (p. 64–7). Evidently Smith had had second thoughts about the wisdom of psycho-analyzing Luther at the distance of some centuries.

17. (p. 135) Margaret Mead, *New Lives For Old.* p. 5–6. New York: William Morrow and Co., Inc., © 1956 by Margaret Mead.

18. (p. 136) Herbert Butterfield, *Christianity and History.* p. 46. New York: Charles Scribner's Sons, 1950.

19. (p. 136) *Ibid.*, p. 4.

20. (p. 136) *Ibid.*, p. 45–6.

21. (p. 139) Carleton Stevens Coon, *Reader in General Anthropology.* p. v. New York: Henry Holt and Co., 1948.

22. (p. 139) By permission from *Preface to the Social Sciences,* by Raymond Flavius Bellamy and others. p. 13. Copyright 1956. New York: McGraw-Hill Book Co., Inc.

23. (p. 140) Carl Lotus Becker, *Everyman His Own Historian.* p. 235. New York: Appleton-Century-Crofts, 1935.

24. (p. 141) For examples of how religion is treated in the history of civilization, see: Joseph Swain, *Harper History of Civilization.* New York: Harper and Brothers, 1958.
Edward Burns and Philip Ralph, *World Civilization.* New York: W. W. Norton and Co., 1958.
For United States history, see:
Leland Baldwin, *Stream of American History.* New York: American Book Co., 1952.

S. E. Morison and H. S. Commager, *Growth of the American Republic*. New York: Oxford University Press, 1950.

25. (p. 141) *Puritanism in Early America*, ed. George M. Waller. *Problems in American Civilization* Series. Boston: D. C. Heath and Co., 1950. 115 p.

26. (p. 141) *Transcendentalist Revolt Against Materialism*, ed. George F. Whicher. *Problems in American Civilization* Series. Boston: D. C. Heath and Co., 1949. 107 p.

27. (p. 141) *Pragmatism and American Culture*, ed. Gail Kennedy. *Problems in American Civilization* Series. Boston: D. C. Heath and Co., 1950. 114 p.

28. (p. 141) *Evolution and Religion: The Conflict Between Science and Theology in Modern America*, ed. Gail Kennedy. *Problems in American Civilization* Series. Boston: D. C. Heath and Co., 1957.

29. (p. 143) William James Durant, *Reformation*. Vol. 6, *Story of Civilization*. p. 3. New York: Simon and Schuster, 1957.

30. (p. 143) James Harvey Robinson, *New History*. p. 9–11. New York: Macmillan Co., 1918. (Quoted with permission of Bankers Trust Co., New York.)

31. (p. 144) Yinger, *op. cit.*, p. 18.

32. (p. 144) Edward B. Tylor, *Anthropology: An Introduction to the Study of Man and Civilization*. p. 342. New York: D. Appleton and Co., 1881.

33. (p. 144) *Ibid.*

34. (p. 144) Herbert Spencer, *Study of Sociology*. p. 294. New York: D. Appleton and Co., 1874.

35. (p. 145) Yinger defines the sociology of religion as "the scientific study of the ways in which society, culture, and personality (or, in another sense, societies, cultures, and personalities), influence religion —influence its origin, its doctrines, its practices, the types of groups which express it, the kinds of leadership, etc. And, oppositely, it is the study of the ways in which religion affects society, culture, and personality—the processes of social conservation and social change, the structure of normative systems, the satisfaction or frustration of personality needs, etc." *Religion, Society and the Individual*, p. 20–1.[10*] So broad a definition makes plain his statement that sociology was a "shorthand way of writing 'anthropology-social psychology-sociology'."

36. (p. 145) Yinger, *op. cit.*, p. 4.

37. (p. 145) William L. Kolb, "Values, Positivism, and the Functional Theory of Religion: The Growth of a Moral Dilemma," *Social Forces*, XXXI (May, 1935), 305–11.

* Superscript refers to earlier footnote number in this section.

38. (p. 145) *Ibid.*, p. 305.
39. (p. 145) *Ibid.*
40. (p. 145) *Ibid.*, p. 307.
41. (p. 146) Yinger, *op. cit.*, p. 309.
42. (p. 146) A. L. Kroeber and Clyde Kluckhohn, *Culture: A Critical Review of Concepts and Definitions*. Papers of the Peabody Museum of American Archaeology and Ethnology, Harvard University, XLVII No. 1 (1952), p. 178.
43. (p. 146) *Ibid.*, p. 175–76.
44. (p. 146) *Ibid.*, p. 177.
45. (p. 146) *Ibid.*
46. (p. 147) Ashley Montagu, *Man: His First Million Years*. p. 14. Cleveland: World Publishing Co., 1957.
47. (p. 147) ———, *Direction of Human Development*. p. 247. New York: Harper and Brothers, 1955.
48. (p. 148) *Ibid.*, p. 289.
49. (p. 148) *Ibid.*, p. 309.
50. (p. 148) *Ibid.*, p. 310.
51. (p. 148) Frederick Rogers Fairchild, Edgar S. Furniss, and Norman S. Buck, *Elementary Economics*. p. 8. New York: Macmillan Co., 1926. (Quoted with permission of the publisher.)
52. (p. 150) Howard Rothmann Bowen, *Christian Values and Economic Life*. p. 195. New York: Harper and Brothers, 1953.
53. (p. 150) George Shorey Peterson, *Economics*, p. 32. New York: Henry Holt and Co., 1949.
54. (p. 150) Donald Fulton Putnam in *Geography in the Twentieth Century*, ed. Thomas Griffith Taylor. p. 221. New York: Philosophical Library, 1951.
55. (p. 151) Richard Hartshorne, "The Nature of Geography—Reexamined." Unpublished manuscript.
56. (p. 151) Ellen Churchill Semple, *Influences of Geographic Environment*. p. 1. New York: Henry Holt and Co., 1911.
57. (p. 151) James Watson discusses this aspect of geography in the chapter, "The Sociological Aspects of Geography," *Geography in the Twentieth Century*, ed. Thomas Griffith Taylor (New York: Philosophical Library, 1951). Watson admits that some geographers would exclude from the field the study of non-material phenomena. Watson states the reasons for a "social geography," and shows how it differs from sociology.
58. (p. 152) Harley Harris Bartlett in *Man's Role in Changing the Face of the Earth*. p. 711. Chicago: University of Chicago Press, 1955.

59. (p. 152) Earl Emmet Lackey and Esther Sanfreida Anderson, *Regions and Nations of the World*. p. 259. New York: D. Van Nostrand Co., 1946.
60. (p. 152) *American Geography: Inventory and Prospects*, ed. Preston Everett James and Clarence Fielden Jones. Published for the Association of American Geographers by Syracuse University Press, 1954. *Geography in the Twentieth Century*. New York: Philosophical Library, 1951.
61. (p. 152) Frank Fraser Darling in *Man's Role in Changing the Face of the Earth, op. cit.*, p. 401–08.
62. (p. 153) Alfred de Grazia, *Elements of Political Science*. p. 4. New York: Alfred A. Knopf, 1952.
63. (p. 153) Frank J. Goodnow quoted by Raymond G. Gettell, *Readings in Political Science*, p. 1. Boston: Ginn and Co., 1911. (Quoted with permission of the publisher.)
64. (p. 153) Stephen Butler Leacock, *Elements of Political Science*. p. 3. Boston: Houghton Mifflin Co., 1913.
65. (p. 155) Kenneth Scott Latourette, *History of Christianity*. New York: Harper and Brothers, 1953. 1516 p.
66. (p. 156) *Catholic Historical Review*, XL (April, 1954), 63–4.
67. (p. 156) *Church History*, XXII (March, 1954), 87.
68. (p. 156) *Church History*, XVIII (September, 1949), 184.
69. (p. 156) Philip Hughes, *Popular History of the Catholic Church*. New York: Macmillan Co., 1949. 294 p. (Also available in a paperback Image Books edition. Garden City, N. Y.: Doubleday and Co., 1954.)
70. (p. 156) John Tracey Ellis, *American Catholicism*. Chicago: University of Chicago Press, 1956. 207 p.
71. (p. 158) William Seward Salisbury and Frank A. Scholfield, "Teaching Sociological Concepts by Learning About Religion," *Religious Education*, LII (November, 1957), 453 (published by the Religious Education Association, New York).
72. (p. 159) Used in Introductory Sociology at State University of New York Teachers College at Oswego, as described by Salisbury and Scholfield, *op. cit.*, p. 452.
73. (p. 160) This technique has been used in political science courses at North Texas State College, Denton, Texas. See *Project on Religion in Teacher Education*. Bulletin issued by North Texas State College, August, 1955.

Bibliography

Listed below are selected works dealing with the relationships between religion and various social science disciplines, especially as they relate to college teaching. No effort has been made to compile a bibliography of the separate fields such as the history of religion or the sociology of religion.

Abrams, Ray Hamilton. "Organized Religion in the United States," *Annals of the American Academy of Political and Social Sciences*, 256 (March, 1948), 1–172.

Becker, Howard Paul. "Supreme Values and the Sociologist," *American Sociological Review*, VI (April, 1941), 155–72.

Bennett, John Coleman; Bowen, Howard R.; Brown, William A., Jr.; and Oxnam, G. Bromley. *Christian Values and Economic Life*. New York: Harper and Brothers, 1954. 272 p.

Bernard, Luther Lee. "The Sociological Interpretation of Religion," *Journal of Religion*, XVIII (January, 1938), 1–18.

Boulding, Kenneth. "Economics," *Religious Perspectives in College Teaching*, ed. Hoxie N. Fairchild. New York: Ronald Press Co., 1952. p. 360–83.

Butterfield, Herbert. *Christianity and History*. New York: Charles Scribner's Sons, 1950. 146 p.

Carlson, Leland H. "European History," *College Reading and Religion*. New Haven: Yale University Press, 1948. 345 p.

Casserley, Julien Victor Langmead. *Morals and Man in the Social Sciences*. New York: Longmans, Green and Co., 1951. 230 p.

Childs, Marquis William, and Cater, Douglass. *Ethics in a Business Society*. New York: Harper and Brothers, 1954. 191 p.

Dynes, Russell R. "Toward the Sociology of Religion," *Sociology and Social Research*, XXXVIII (March, 1954), 227–32.

Ellwood, Charles A. "Implications for Religion of Current Trends in the Social Sciences," *Religion in Higher Education*, ed. Milton Carsley Towner. Chicago: University of Chicago Press, 1931. 327 p.

Ferré, Nels Frederick Solomon. *Christian Faith and Higher Education*. New York: Harper and Brothers, 1954. 251 p.

Hallowell, John H. "Political Science," *Religious Perspectives in College Teaching*, ed. Hoxie N. Fairchild. New York: Ronald Press Co., 1952. 384–422.

Harbison, E. Harris. "History," *Religious Perspectives in College Teaching*, ed. Hoxie N. Fairchild. New York: Ronald Press Co., 1952. p. 67–97.

Hintz, Howard William. *Religion and Public Higher Education*. New York: Brooklyn College, 1955. 62 p.

Kolb, William L. "Values, Positivism, and the Functional Theory of Religion: The Growth of a Moral Dilemma," *Social Forces*, XXXI (May, 1935).

Latourette, Kenneth Scott. "The Christian Understanding of History," *American Historical Review*, LIV (January, 1949), 259–76.

Lee, Dorothy D. "Anthropology," *Religious Perspectives in College Teaching*, ed. Hoxie N. Fairchild. New York: Ronald Press Co., 1952. p. 338–59.

Mead, Margaret, and Rhys, Jean. "Cultural Anthropology," *College Reading and Religion*. New Haven: Yale University Press, 1948. 345 p.

Muelder, Walter G. "Norms and Valuations in Social Science," *Liberal Learning and Religion*, ed. Amos Niven Wilder. New York: Harper and Brothers, 1951. 338 p.

Niebuhr, Reinhold. *Faith and History*. New York: Charles Scribner's Sons, 1949. 257 p.

Nottingham, Elizabeth Kristine. *Religion and Society*. New York: Random House, 1954.

Orton, William A. "Economics," *College Reading and Religion*. New Haven: Yale University Press, 1948. 345 p.

Parsons, Talcott. "Sociology and Social Psychology," *Religious Perspectives in College Teaching*, ed. Hoxie N. Fairchild. New York: Ronald Press Co., 1952. p. 286–337.

Rosenthal, Henry M. "On the Function of Religion in Culture," *Review of Religion*, V (January and March, 1941), 148–71 and 290–309.

Salisbury, William Seward, and Scholfield, Frank A. "Teaching Sociological Concepts by Learning About Religion," *Religious Education*, LII (November, 1957), 451–54 (published by Religious Education Association, New York).

Shinn, Roger Lincoln. *Christianity and the Problem of History*. New York: Charles Scribner's Sons, 1953. 302 p.

———. "Religious Faith and the Task of the Historian," *Liberal Learning and Religion*, ed. Amos Niven Wilder. New York: Harper and Brothers, 1951. 338 p.

Sperry, Willard Ledroyd. *Religion in America*. New York: Macmillan Co., 1946. 317 p.

Sutherland, Robert L. "Sociology," *College Reading and Religion*. New Haven: Yale University Press, 1948. 345 p.

Tillich, Paul. *Interpretation of History*. New York: Charles Scribner's Sons, 1936. 284 p.

Toynbee, Arnold Joseph. *An Historian's Approach to Religion*. New York: Oxford University Press, 1956. 318 p.

———. *Christianity Among the Religions of the World*. New York: Charles Scribner's Sons, 1957. 116 p.

UNESCO. "Sociology of Religions: A Trend Report and Bibliography," *Current Sociology*, V (1956).

Yinger, John Milton. "Present Status of the Sociology of Religion," *Journal of Religion,* XXXI (July, 1951), 194–210.

———. *Religion, Society, and the Individual.* New York: Macmillan Co., 1957. 322 p.

CHAPTER 5

Notes and Bibliography

1. (p. 163) It is assumed that science teachers are aware of and can locate in the literature various definitions of *science.* For alternative definitions or views as to the meaning of *religion* and related concepts see such standard reference works as: *Oxford Dictionary, Universal Jewish Encyclopedia, Catholic Encyclopedia, Encyclopaedia of Religion and Ethics, New Schaff-Herzog Encyclopedia of Religious Knowledge, Twentieth Century Encyclopedia of Religious Knowledge* (especially about "profound changes in man's thinking in the field of religion" during the past fifty years—in article "Religion"), and the general purpose encyclopedias, such as the *Britannica.* These sources refer to many other works considering various aspects of the subject at length.
Among the related subjects are the following: theology, religious institutions, faiths and beliefs, religious practices, symbols, rites and rituals, magic, comparative religion, psychology of religion, history of religion, denominations and sects, humanism, naturalism, deism, theism.
Various kinds of definitions of religion place emphasis respectively upon God, man, nature, cosmos; upon faiths and beliefs, religious experience, attitudes, sentiments and emotions; practices, ceremonies and institutions; chosen peoples; commitment; the moral law; destiny, ultimates, absolutes, spirit, spirits, unity, One, All and other key concepts or aspects of being. An unusual, thought-provoking discussion of the meaning of religion is presented in the following book:
Philip Phenix, *Intelligible Religion.* New York: Harper and Brothers, 1954. 189 p.

2. (p. 164) The term "scientific" is commonly used in two senses. First, it may refer to the general method of intelligence which, in attempting to solve problems or answer questions, proceeds logically, basing conclusions on evidence and avoiding bias and prejudice. According to this usage any inquiry is either scientific or not. Second, it may refer specifically to the sciences. In this sense scientific methodology means the methodology that is characteristic of the sciences as distinguished from, say, the arts, philosophy and theology. Thus according to the first usage a theological or philosophical inquiry may or may not be scientific, while according to the second it would not be scientific. In this chapter the term "scientific" is employed only in the second, more restricted, sense.

3. (p. 169) While this self-education is without doubt a formidable undertaking, it is not an impossible one. A systematic course of reading followed persistently will work wonders within a few years. While many college libraries are fairly well stocked in the philosophy of science, many are not so in fields cognate to religion. To overcome this handicap it should be possible for almost any college teacher to accumulate, and work through, a modest personal library of, say, fifty or sixty books on the subject in four or five years.

A good encyclopedia is a tremendously helpful source of information in this field. The writer of this chapter recently spent several weeks in a library investigating to what extent the various subjects mentioned in this chapter could be studied profitably in the absence of specialized library resources in the fields of philosophy, art and religion. He found that there is practically no pertinent topic on which one cannot find veritable mines of information in the standard encyclopedias and dictionaries mentioned in Note 1, and which may be found in most libraries.

A self-directed study program might well begin with such articles as the following (aside from those referred to in the earlier note): science, scientific method, experiment, theory, cause and effect, metaphysics, philosophy, realism, idealism, positivism, logic, epistemology, language, symbol, myth, art, art criticism, music, aesthetics, Christianity, Judaism, other religions, God, Trinity, Christology, creeds, dogmas, faith, ethics. These lead through their copious bibliographic references to many other topics, books and papers in journals.

With regard to the study of the meaning and content of Christian theology, the following volume will help:

Walter M. Horton, *Christian Theology; An Ecumenical Approach.* New York: Harper and Brothers, 1955. 304 p.

This book attempts to help the beginner to see Christian theology from different points of view. It does not espouse a particular theology. The general bibliographic references are presented under the following headings: (I) Classic Systems of Theology; (II) Recent and Contemporary Textbooks of Theology; (III) Creeds and Catechisms; (IV) Short Surveys of the Christian Faith.

Under II the textbooks referred to are classified under the following headings: (1) Roman Catholic; (2) Non-Roman Catholic; (3) Conservative Protestant; (4) Liberal Protestant; (5) Radical Protestant (Religious Humanism and Naturalism); (6) Neo-Orthodox Protestant; (7) Anglican. Under IV the short surveys are classified in the same manner. These lists are excellent and the reader is referred to them. To save space here I offer no such lists of my own relative to Christianity in its various forms.

The following references are, I am told, representative of Jewish theology and thought:

Leo Baeck, *Essence of Judaism.* New York: Schocken Books, Inc., 1948. 288 p.

Ben Z. Bokser, *Wisdom of the Talmud.* New York: Philosophical Library, 1951. 180 p.

Philip D. Bookstaber, *Idea of Development of the Soul in Medieval Jewish Philosophy.* Philadelphia: Maurice Jacobs, Inc., 1950. 104 p.

Martin Buber, *Israel and the World.* New York: Schocken Books, Inc., 1948. 255 p.

Will Herberg, *Judaism and Modern Man.* New York: Farrar, Strauss and Young, Inc., 1951. 313 p.

Abraham J. Heschel, *Man Is Not Alone; A Philosophy of Religion.* New York: Farrar, Strauss and Young, Inc., 1951. 305 p.

———, *God In Search of Man; A Philosophy of Judaism.* New York: Farrar, Strauss and Young, Inc., 1955. 437 p.

Jews, Their History, Culture and Religion, ed. Louis Finkelstein. 2 vols. New York: Harper and Brothers, 1949. 744 p.; 745–1431 p.

Mordecai M. Kaplan, *Judaism as a Civilization.* New York: Thomas Yoselof, Inc., 1957. 601 p.

Solomon Schechter, *Some Aspects of Rabbinic Theology.* New York: Macmillan Co., 1909.

A. H. Silver, *Where Judaism Differed.* New York: Macmillan Co., 1956. 318 p.

Milton Steinberg, *Basic Judaism.* New York: Harcourt, Brace and Co., 1947. 172 p.

In recent years there have been numerous summer conferences, institutes and seminars conducted for the purpose of helping teachers in the various disciplines to explore the reciprocal relations between their fields and religion. These, as well as faculty study and discussion groups conducted in many colleges and universities, constitute potent resources for the teacher bent on self-education.
Moreover many of the resources referred to here seem altogether suitable for the education of prospective teachers.

4. (p. 171) Not only does this method have pedagogical value, but it is recognized, when formulated more precisely, as a powerful tool in modern logic and philosophy, and is frequently applied, say, in the analysis of the languages of the various disciplines. A component of this method is represented by the complementary pair of logical devices referred to as "verification" and "falsification" by which the truth of a statement can be asserted or denied. Essentially, "verification" may be regarded as saying when a statement may be regarded as acceptable or true, while "falsification" means pointing out under what circumstances it would be regarded as false, since when one asserts something to be true, one thereby (always or usually?) also asserts something else to be untrue. Certainly in everyday life, when one is not sure what a person means, one way to achieve clarity is to ask him what he does not mean. If he contends that something is true, it helps us to understand him if he says why he does not regard

it as false, or under what conditions he would consider it false. The use of this method in the clarification of theological discourse is discussed in these two volumes:

Antony G. Flew and A. C. MacIntyre, *New Essays in Philosophical Theology*. New York: Macmillan Co., 1955. 274 p.

Basil G. Mitchell, *Faith and Logic*. London: George Allen and Unwin, 1957. 222 p.

5. (p. 171) For the study of similarities and differences among science, art, religion and other fields the following may be helpful. All of them contain copious bibliographic references, thus making unnecessary a comprehensive listing here.

John Baillie, *Natural Science and the Spiritual Life*. New York: Charles Scribner's Sons, 1952. 43 p.

Edward F. Caldin, *Power and Limits of Science*. London: Chapman and Hall, 1949. 196 p. (Chapters on Beauty and Science, Ethics and Science, Society and Science, Metaphysics and Science.)

Ernst Cassirer, *An Essay on Man*. Garden City, New York: Doubleday Anchor Book, 1953. 294 p. (See especially: Part II, "Man and Culture"; with chapters on Myth and Religion, Art, History, Science.)

Richard Courant and Herbert E. Robbins, *What Is Mathematics?* New York: Oxford University Press, 1941. 521 p.

John Dewey, *Common Faith*. New Haven: Yale University Press, 1934. 87 p.

Emile Durkheim, *Elementary Forms of the Religious Life*. New York: Macmillan Co., 1915.

Irwin Edman, *Arts and the Man*. New York: W. W. Norton and Co., 1939. 154 p.

Theodore M. Greene, *Arts and the Art of Criticism*. Princeton, New Jersey: Princeton University Press, 1940. 690 p. (Note especially the following subjects: the objectivity of aesthetic quality; the nature and value of aesthetic inquiry; complementary approaches to art and the aesthetic experience: the scientific, critical and philosophical approaches; the artistic categories and the matter of art; artistic form; artistic content; artistic truth.)

Mary B. Hesse, *Science and the Human Imagination*. New York: Philosophical Library, 1954. 171 p.

Martin C. Johnson, *Art and Scientific Thought*. London: Faber and Faber, Ltd., 1944. 192 p. (Part I: Features of Resemblance and of Contrast Between the Arts and the Sciences; Part II: Examples of Imaginative Stimulus Through Structure and Symbolism; Part III: Historical Failure to Maintain a Balance Between the Scientific and the Imaginative; Part IV: Leonardo da Vinci as Scientist in Art: His Fantastic Drawings and the Prototype of Scientific Uneasiness in an Unscientific Community.)

James R. Newman, *What Is Science?* New York: Simon and Schuster, Inc., 1958. 493 p.

Filmer S. C. Northrop, *Logic of the Sciences and the Humanities.* New York: Macmillan Co., 1948. 402 p.

Alban G. Widgery, *What Is Religion?* New York: Harper and Brothers, 1953. 330 p.

6. (p. 171) Concerning the phenomena experienced in art and religion see also:

Gordon W. Allport, *Individual and His Religion.* New York: Macmillan Co., 1950. 147 p.

Friederich Heiler, *Prayer.* New York: Oxford University Press, 1932. 376 p.

Friedrich von Huegel, *Mystical Element of Religion as Studied in Saint Catharine of Genoa and Her Friends.* 2 vols. New York: E. P. Dutton, 1923.

William James, *Varieties of Religious Experience.* New York: Longmans, Green and Co., 1902. 534 p. (Also a Mentor Book, 1958, MD-221.)

Robert M. MacIver, *Hour of Insight.* New York: Harper and Brothers, 1954. 145 p.

———, *Moments of Personal Discovery.* New York: Harper and Brothers, 1952. 170 p.

Bronislaw Malinowski, *Magic, Science and Religion.* Boston: Beacon Press, 1948. 327 p.

Joseph Needham, *Science, Religion and Reality.* New York: George Braziller, Inc., 1955. 355 p.

Rudolf Otto, *Idea of the Holy.* New York: Oxford University Press, 1925.

George Santayana, *Sense of Beauty.* New York: Dover Publications, 1955. 275 p.

Roger H. Sessions, *Musical Experience of Composer, Performer, Listener.* Princeton, New Jersey: Princeton University Press, 1950. 127 p.

Paul J. Tillich, *Dynamics of Faith.* New York: Harper and Brothers, 1957. 127 p.

Evelyn Underhill, *Mysticism.* New York: E. P. Dutton, 1948.

———, *Worship.* London: Nisbet and Co., 1936. 350 p.

It should be remembered that in some religions, notably the Judaeo-Christian tradition, the phenomenology of religious experience includes not only that of individual, personal experience but also that of "the People" (hence the concept of "peoplehood" in Jewish thought) and the church, i.e., of the religious community. Reference here is, of course, to great historical events thought to have religious significance ("mighty acts of God") in the life of "the people of God."

As to the phenomenology of science, probably nothing is more instructive and enlightening for the non-scientist (aside from actually participating in scientific work) than to read the biographies and auto-biographies of scientists and to study the anecdotal history of science.

Especially helpful are:

Harvard Case Histories of Experimental Science, ed. James B. Conant. 2 vols. Cambridge, Massachusetts: Harvard University Press, 1957. 321 p.; 323–639 p.

The following is a very illuminating book on this subject:

Gerald J. Holton, *Introduction to Concepts and Theories in Physical Science*. New York: Addison-Wesley, 1952. 650 p.

7. (p. 171) About data: Webster defines "datum" as "something given or admitted, as a fact on which an inference is based."

Concerning what constitutes the data of science, consult almost any treatise on the philosophy of science.

Concerning the "givens" (data) of religion and philosophy, see the works already referred to with respect to the phenomenology of religion, as well as the following:

John Dewey, *Experimental Logic*. New York: Dover Publications, 1954. 444 p. (See Ch. IV, "Data and Meanings.")

Herbert H. Farmer, *Towards Belief in God*. New York: Macmillan Co., 1943. 252 p. (Especially Chapter IV: "The Coercive Element in Belief in God.")

John A. Hutchison, *Faith, Reason and Existence*. New York: Oxford University Press, 1956. 306 p.

Edward LeRoy Long, Jr., *Science and Christian Faith*. New York: Association Press, 1950. 125 p.

Walter R. Matthews, *God in Christian Thought and Experience*. London: Nisbet and Co., 1930. 283 p.

Richard H. Niebuhr, *Meaning of Revelation*. New York: Macmillan Co., 1941. 196 p.

James A. Pike and W. Norman Pittenger, *Faith of the Church*. New Haven: Seabury Press, 1951. 214 p.

Charles E. Raven, *Experience and Interpretation*. New York: Cambridge University Press, 1953. 226 p. (Especially Chapters

II and III: "Religious Experience: Its Origin and Character"; "Religious Experience: Its Interpretation.")

Paul Roubiczeck, *Thinking Towards Religion.* London: Darwen Finlayson, 1957. 192 p.

Milton Steinberg, *Basic Judaism.*[3*]

Paul J. Tillich, *Systematic Theology.* 2 vols. Chicago: Chicago University Press, 1951. 300 p. (Vol. 2, *Existence and the Christ,* 1957. 187 p.)

8. (p. 171) The term "matter" is used here in a philosophic sense as "the indeterminate subject of reality; the unorganized basis or stuff of experience which when combined with form gives phenomena, or real individual objects" (Webster). Students should realize that terms like "matter" and "material" and "substance" have important meanings different from those commonly used in physics and chemistry. In a philosophical sense one kind of "matter" is indeed the material of atoms and molecules. But so also are energy and electricity. A most interesting analysis of the "matter" of the several fine arts is given by Greene, *Arts and the Art of Criticism.*[5*] Thus the categories essential to artistic inquiry include "matter," "form" and "content."
"The 'matter' of a work of art is that in it which has been expressively organized. The 'form' of a work of art is the expressive organization of its matter. The content of a work of art is that which finds artistic expression through such formal organization of its matter." "Furthermore the matter of art can be analyzed with precision only in terms . . . of the 'raw material' and the 'artistic medium' (*op. cit.,* p. 32 and 39). Thus the 'primary' raw material of music is auditory sound (p. 46); that of the dance is bodily motion and rest; that of architecture includes all the physical substances (e.g. wood, brick . . .) . . . , plus their visible color and texture; plus the physical laws . . . , and the three-dimensional structural shapes . . . , plus the . . . space in which they exist . . . ; plus physical light" (p. 76). Now what meanings, if any, attach to such terms as "matter" and "substance" in religious, or theological, discourse? When a student asserts that "only matter is real," just what does he mean? Quite aside from the question of reality he should certainly be aware of meanings of "matter" other than those current in physical science.

9. (p. 172) Many of the books referred to in previous notes shed light upon the role of concepts and conceptualization in science, art, religion and philosophy—as well as upon the non-conceptual.
A much-quoted assertion of Lord Kelvin is that when one measures, one knows. Is it true that one knows only what one measures? Does one know only what can be expressed conceptually? Many musicians, for instance, would assert that much of music can be expressed only

* Superscripts hereinafter refer to earlier footnote numbers in this section.

musically, i.e., not in words or by means of concepts. The story is told that after Beethoven had played a sonata, he was asked what it meant, what message it conveyed. In reply he simply turned to the piano and played "his message" again. Are there other aspects of "reality" and life that are similarly non-conceptual? For example, is humor? Is love? Is the "holy"?

10. (p. 172) Function (or functional) here refers to a relationship between two variables (traits, qualities or facts) that depend upon and change with one another—a relationship analogous to that of a mathematical function. Without considering specific mathematical functions, in physics forces between bodies depend upon and change with the distances separating them; accelerations depend upon forces; pressures of confined gases depend upon temperatures; the heating effects of electric currents are functionally related to resistance of the current-carrying conductors. Does anything in art depend and vary with anything else, i.e., can the artist count on the variation of one factor with another to achieve specific effects? Are there analogous dependencies (co-variations) in religion? The discovery of functional relationships is one of the main goals of science and their existence one of the foundations of technology. To what extent are the arts and religion similar to or different from science with regard to these matters?

11. (p. 172) Not only do "explain" and "explanation" have different meanings in various fields, but there are often different meanings within any one field. Moreover their meanings change in time; thus in Aristotelian, Newtonian and contemporary quantum physics they have vastly different meanings. Similarly theological explanation has changed markedly in time. See:

    Richard B. Braithwaite, *Scientific Explanation.* London: Cambridge University Press, 1953. 375 p. (See also Note 30.)

12. (p. 173) Regarding linguistic, conceptual, methodological and philosophical interactions of science and religion-theology see:

    Crane Brinton, *Shaping of the Modern Mind.* New York: New American Library. (The concluding half of *Ideas and Men.*)

    Edwin A. Burtt, *Metaphysical Foundations of Modern Physical Science.* New York: Harcourt, Brace and Co., 1925.

    Herbert Butterfield, *Origins of Modern Science.* New York: Macmillan Co., 1951. 187 p. (Quotation found in note 34 in this section used with permission of the publisher.)

    Joseph Needham, *Science, Religion and Reality.*[6*] (Especially the chapters by Malinowski, "Magic, Science and Religion"; Singer, "Historical Relations of Religion and Science"; Aliotta, "Science and Religion in the Nineteenth Century.")

* Superscripts hereinafter refer to earlier footnote numbers in this section.

John H. Randall, *Making of the Modern Mind.* Boston: Houghton Mifflin Co., 1926. 653 p.

Charles E. Raven, *Science and Religion.* New York: Cambridge University Press, 1953. 224 p.

Walter T. Stace, *Religion and the Modern Mind.* Philadelphia: J. B. Lippincott Co., 1952. 285 p.

Alban G. Widgery, *Living Religions and Modern Thought.* New York: Round Table Press, 1936. 306 p. (Discusses the impact of modern thought, including scientific thought, upon eight of the great religions of the world.)

13. (p. 173) A classic in the literature of the "warfare" is:

Andrew D. White, *History of the Warfare of Science with Theology in Christendom.* New York: George Braziller, Inc., 1955. 474 p.

See also:

H. H. Price, *Some Aspects of the Conflict Between Science and Religion.* New York: Cambridge University Press, 1953.

George de Santillana, *Crime of Galileo.* Chicago: University of Chicago Press, 1955. 338 p.

Also some of the books referred to in Note 12.

14. (p. 173) This thesis has been discussed by:

Alfred North Whitehead, *Religion in the Making.* New York: Macmillan Co., 1926.

———, *Science and the Modern World.* New York: Macmillan Co., 1926. (Quotation found in note 17 in this section used with permission of the publisher.)

and by Michael Foster in articles referred to by John Baillie, *Natural Science and the Spiritual Life.*[5*]

15. (p. 173) Concerning presuppositions see:

Chas. D. Broad, *Religion, Philosophy and Psychical Research,* essays. New York: Harcourt, Brace and Co., 1953. 308 p.

Edwin A. Burtt, *Metaphysical Foundations of Modern Physical Science.* [12*]

Edward F. Caldin, *Power and Limits of Science.*[5*]

Ray H. Dotterer, *Postulates and Implications.* New York: Philosophical Library, 1955. 509 p.

Harold K. Schilling, *Concerning the Nature of Science and Religion, A Study of Presuppositions.* Iowa City: School of Religion, State University of Iowa, 1958.

16. (p. 174) John Baillie, *Natural Science and the Spiritual Life.*[5*]

* Superscripts hereinafter refer to earlier footnote numbers in this section.

Charles A. Coulson, *Science and Christian Belief*. Chapel Hill, North Carolina: University of North Carolina Press, 1955. 127 p.

Pierre M. M. Duhem, *Aim and Structure of Physical Theory*. Princeton, New Jersey: Princeton University Press, 1954. 344 p. (See Chapter "Physics of a Believer.")

Edward LeRoy Long, Jr., *Religious Beliefs of American Scientists*. Philadelphia: Westminster Press, 1952. 168 p.

Carl W. Miller, *Scientist's Approach to Religion*. New York: Macmillan Co., 1947. 127 p.

Some of the autobiographical essays in the following books will shed light upon the actual interactions of science and religion in the experience of distinguished contemporaries:

Louis Finkelstein, *Thirteen Americans: Their Spiritual Autobiographies*. New York: Harper and Brothers, 1953. 296 p.

Robert M. MacIver, *Hour of Insight*.[6*]

———, *Moments of Personal Discovery*.[6*]

See also biographies and autobiographies of distinguished scientists of the past, e.g., Boyle, Kepler, Newton, Darwin, Pasteur, Einstein.

17. (p. 175) The following quotation from Alfred North Whitehead, *Science and the Modern World*,[14*] (p. 260) is suggestive here for two reasons. First, it calls for our relating science and religion meaningfully, i.e., making a deliberate decision as to the relationship they shall have in our thinking—not merely seeing how they are, or have been in fact, related historically or in some other objective sense. Second, it expresses his view—at the time he wrote—as to the importance of the issue and of the decision regarding it.
"When we consider what religion is for mankind, and what science is, it is no exaggeration to say that the future course of history depends upon the decision of this generation as to the relations between them. We have here the two strongest general forces (apart from the mere impulse of the various senses) which influence men, and they seem to be set one against the other—the force of our religious intuitions, and the force of our impulse to accurate observation and logical deduction."

18. (p. 175) Aside from books listed earlier the following ones on the philosophy and history of science are helpful relative to the question, What is science?

Percy W. Bridgman, *Logic of Modern Physics*. New York: Macmillan Co., 1927. 228 p.

———, *Nature of Physical Theory*. New York: Dover Publications, 1949.

* Superscripts hereinafter refer to earlier footnote numbers in this section.

Jacob Bronowski, *Common Sense of Science.* London: Heinemann, 1951. 154 p.

Norman R. Campbell, *What Is Science?* New York: Dover Publications, 1952. 186 p.

James B. Conant, *On Understanding Science.* New Haven: Yale University Press, 1947. 145 p.

Sir William C. Dampier, *History of Science and Its Relations With Philosophy and Religion,* new ed. rev. New York: Macmillan Co., 1932. 514 p.

Philipp G. Frank, *Philosophy of Science.* New York: Prentice-Hall, Inc., 1957. 394 p.

Martin C. Johnson, *Science and the Meanings of Truth.* London: Faber and Faber, 1946. 179 p.

Henry Margenau, *Nature of Physical Reality.* New York: McGraw-Hill Book Co., 1950. 479 p.

Filmer S. C. Northrop, *Logic of the Sciences and Humanities.*[5*]

Fernand Renoirte, *Cosmology; Elements of a Critique of the Sciences and of Cosmology,* tr. James F. Coffey from the 2nd rev. ed. New York: Joseph F. Wagner, Inc., 1950. 257 p.

George Sarton, *Study of the History of Science.* Cambridge, Massachusetts: Harvard University Press, 1936. 75 p.

William T. Sedgwick and Harry W. Tyler, *Short History of Science.* New York: Macmillan Co., 1917.

Stephen E. Toulmin, *Philosophy of Science; An Introduction.* New York: Longmans, Green and Co., 1953. 176 p.

William P. D. Wightman, *Growth of Scientific Ideas.* New Haven: Yale University Press, 1951. 495 p.

19. (p. 178) For an excellent discussion of the time concept of the ancient Hebrews see:

Henry W. Robinson, *Inspiration and Revelation in the Old Testament.* New York: Oxford University Press, 1946. 298 p.

An interesting biographical story about psycho-physiological brain-time appears in:

Robert M. MacIver, *Hour of Insight.*[6*]

Walter R. Matthews, *God in Christian Thought and Experience.*[7*] p. 255.

See articles on "time" and "eternity" in standard reference works.

20. (p. 179) Ernst Mach, *Science of Mechanics.* Chicago: Open Court Publishing Co., 1919. p. 364. (Also Ch. IV, Sec. 11, "Theological, Animistic and Mystical Points of View in Mechanics,"

* Superscripts hereinafter refer to earlier footnote numbers in this section.

especially p. 454, "The theological kernel of the principle of least action.")

21. (p. 180) The various criteria of acceptability have been discussed at length in a series of papers in *The Scientific Monthly*. They also provide many bibliographic references.

Robert S. Cohen, "Alternative Interpretations of the History of Science," Vol. 80 (February, 1955), 111–16.

Philipp G. Frank, "Variety of Reasons for the Acceptance of Scientific Theories," Vol. 79 (September, 1954), 139–45.

Alexandre Koyré, "Influence of Philosophic Trends on the Formulation of Scientific Theories," Vol. 80 (February, 1955), 107–11.

Barrington Moore, Jr., "Influence of Political Creeds on the Acceptance of Theories," Vol. 79 (September, 1954), 146–48.

Also:

Philipp G. Frank, *Validation of Scientific Theories*. Boston: Beacon Press, 1957. 242 p.

22. (p. 180) P. W. Bridgman, *Yale Review*, 34, 444 (1945) (published by Yale University Press).

23. (p. 181) This aspect of scientific method is discussed most cogently by:

W. I. B. Beveridge, *Art of Scientific Investigation*. London: Heinemann, 1957. 171 p.

Martin C. Johnson, *Art and Scientific Thought.*[5]*

Robert M. MacIver, *Hour of Insight,*[6]* "The A-Ha Phenomenon," by H. Hoagland.

Michael Polanyi, *Science, Faith and Society*. New York: Oxford University Press, 1946. 80 p. (Chapter I)

See also for similar treatment of mathematics:

A. D'Abro, *Rise of the New Physics; Its Mathematical and Physical Theories* (formerly titled *Decline of Mechanism*). 2 vols. 2nd rev. ed. New York: Dover Publications, 1951. 426 p.; 429–982 p.

Sir Richard Arman Gregory, *Discovery*. New York: Macmillan Co., 1928.

Jacques Hadamard, *Essay on Psychology of Invention in the Mathematical Field*. New York: Dover Publications, 1954. 145 p.

Henri Poincaré, *Foundations of Science: Science and Hypothesis, The Value of Science, Science and Method*. Auth. tr. by George

* Superscripts hereinafter refer to earlier footnote numbers in this section.

Bruce Halsted, with a special pref. by Poincaré and an intro. by Josiah Royce. Lancaster, Pa.: Science Press, 1929. 553 p. (Also in 3 vols. New York: Dover Publications)

Gÿorgy Polya, *How to Solve It*. Princeton, New Jersey: Princeton University Press, 1945. 204 p.

See again Note 2 concerning "scientific."

24. (p. 182) Gerald J. Holton, *Introduction to Concepts and Theories in Physical Science*,[6*] p. 218–21, about "the lack of a single method," and p. 234–37, about guesses, cut-and-try procedures, "feeling for things," hunches; about how scientists work like artists, but talk like bookkeepers.

W. I. B. Beveridge, *Art of Scientific Investigation*.[23*]

I. B. Cohen, *Science, Servant of Man*. Boston: Little, Brown and Co., 1948. 362 p.

James B. Conant, *On Understanding Science*,[18*] about the strategy and tactics of science. The case history studies presented show convincingly the great extent to which what scientists do in their search for knowledge is governed by considerations of the moment, by nature of particular problems and circumstances, by the temperament of the scientist—rather than by general method.

25. (p. 182) Louis T. More, *Limitations of Science*. New York: Henry Holt and Co., 1915.

John W. N. Sullivan, *Limitations of Science*. New York: Viking Press, 1933. 307 p.

Regarding the limitations of theology see:

Frederick R. Tennant, *Philosophical Theology*. New York: Cambridge University Press, 1956. (Reissue 2 vols., 422 p.; 276 p.)

On limitations of knowledge consult:

Paul Roubiczeck, *Thinking Towards Religion*.[7*]

26. (p. 183) The term "intersubjective testability" seems to have been suggested first by Herbert Feigl in his essay, "The Scientific Outlook: Naturalism and Humanism," in *American Quarterly*, I (1949). Also:

Herbert Feigl and May Broadbeck, *Readings in the Philosophy of Science*. p. 11. New York: Appleton-Century-Crofts, 1953. 811 p.

Martin C. Johnson, *Science and the Meanings of Truth*,[18*] develops the concept of "communicability" as "the property which alone elevates the products of a single scientist's mind to the common body of statements acceptable by ANY worker . . . That it becomes precisely communicable, verifiable by all and not mere individual

* Superscripts hereinafter refer to earlier footnote numbers in this section.

opinion, is perhaps the most ultimate sense in which 'science is true'" (p. 91). "Scientific knowledge therefore must lose any claim to be completed in the mind of any single investigator, and becomes judged as the body of interrelated propositions, connecting the experiences of a whole community . . ." (p. 103). Polanyi, *Science, Faith and Society*,[23*] similarly shows how important a role is played in science by "communal crosschecks" and verification. Of course, *objectivity* has several standard meanings.

27. (p. 183) Reason, faith and revelation have various meanings. The *Oxford Dictionary* presents thirteen meanings of the term "faith." These books discuss the role of faith in science:

Edward F. Caldin, *Power and Limits of Science*.[5*]

Charles A. Coulson, *Science and Christian Belief*.[16*]

Michael Polanyi, *Science, Faith and Society*.[23*]

Concerning the function of faith and reason in religion see:

Antony G. Flew and A. C. MacIntyre, *New Essays in Philosophical Theology*.[4*]

Basil G. Mitchell, *Faith and Logic*.[4*]

Edward DeLos Myers, *Christianity and Reason*. New York: Oxford University Press, 1951. 185 p.

Frederick R. Tennant, *Philosophical Theology*.[25*] (Vol. I, Ch. XI)

Paul J. Tillich, *Dynamics of Faith*.[6*]

———, *Systematic Theology*.[7*]

It should be noted that doctrines of revelation have had a most interesting development and that they are still undergoing change. For an analysis of various Catholic and Protestant views see:

John Baillie, *Idea of Revelation in Recent Thought*. New York: Columbia University Press, 1956. 151 p.

Walter M. Horton, *Christian Theology; An Ecumenical Approach*.[3*] (Ch. II)

Nathaniel Micklem, *Abyss of Truth*. London: Geoffrey Bles, Ltd., 1956. 144 p.

Richard H. Niebuhr, *Meaning of Revelation*. New York: Macmillan Co., 1946. 196 p.

Able discussions of Old Testament revelation from Catholic and Protestant points of view respectively:

John L. McKenzie, *Two-Edged Sword, An Interpretation of the Old Testament*. Milwaukee: Bruce Publishing Co., 1956. 317 p.

* Superscripts hereinafter refer to earlier footnote numbers in this section.

Henry W. Robinson, *Inspiration and Revelation in the Old Testament.*[19*]

For a radically different point of view see:

Julian S. Huxley, *Religion Without Revelation.* New York: Harper and Brothers, 1957. 252 p.

28. (p. 183) Regarding the meaning of "creed" and "dogma":

Articles in *Catholic Encyclopedia, Britannica, Universal Jewish Encyclopedia*

Louis T. More, *Dogma of Evolution.* Princeton, New Jersey: Princeton University Press, 1925. 386 p.

James A. Pike and W. Norman Pittenger, *Faith of the Church.*[7*]

Harold K. Schilling, *Concerning the Nature of Science and Religion, A Study of Presuppositions.*[15*]

Arthur F. Smethurst, *Modern Science and Christian Beliefs.* London: J. Nisbet, 1955. 300 p. (Part III, Ch. II)

Alfred North Whitehead, *Religion in the Making.*[14*] (p. 58)

29. (p. 184) Victor F. Lenzen, *Causality in Natural Science.* p. 6. Springfield, Ill.: Charles C. Thomas Publisher, 1954. 128 p. (Quoted with permission of the publisher.)

To be noted are several different usages of the term *cause* within physics; those, for instance, referring to efficacy, uniformity and identity; those representing ideas of absolute necessity, dynamic regularity, statistical probability of connection. See also p. 8 regarding Comte's three stages in the development of the concept of cause, one stage being theological.

30. (p. 184) Ernst Cassirer, *Determinism and Indeterminism in Modern Physics.* New Haven: Yale University Press, 1956. 227 p. (The two quotations appear on p. 114 and 65 respectively.)

31. (p. 185) John Baillie, *Natural Science and the Spiritual Life.*[5*] (Section III)

Henry Bett, *Reality of the Religious Life.* New York: Macmillan Co., 1949. 159 p. (Ch. II, III, IV)

Edward F. Caldin, *Science and Christian Apologetic.* London: Blackfriars, 1951. (Section I)

Herbert H. Farmer, *World and God.* London: Nisbet, 1935. 315 p. (p. 157–59)

John A. Hutchison, *Faith, Reason and Existence.*[7*] (p. 138)

Frederick R. Tennant, *Philosophical Theology.*[25*] (Vol. I, Appendix, Note J; also Vol. II, Ch. III)

* Superscripts hereinafter refer to earlier footnote numbers in this section.

32. (p. 186) Ernst Cassirer, *Language and Myth.* New York: Dover Publications, 1953. 103 p.

John A. Hutchison, *Faith, Reason and Existence.*[7]* (Ch. II)

Ernest H. Hutton, *Language of Modern Physics.* New York: Macmillan Co., 1956. 278 p. (Quotation found in note 33 in this section used with permission of the publisher.)

Susanne K. Langer (Knauth), *Philosophy in a New Key.* New York: Charles Scribner's Sons, 1953. 431 p. (Also published as Mentor Book, 1953.)

Stephen E. Toulmin, *Philosophy of Science; An Introduction.*[18]*

Philip E. Wheelwright, *Burning Fountain.* Bloomington, Indiana: Indiana University Press, 1954. 406 p.

33. (p. 189) Herbert Dingle, *Scientific Adventure.* London: Pitman, 1952. 372 p. (p. 252) "Science is . . . the arranging of experience into a rational system."

Ernest H. Hutton, *Language of Modern Physics.*[32]* (p. 15) "Science is a linguistic, or symbolic, representation of experience."

Martin C. Johnson, *Science and the Meanings of Truth,*[18]* suggests that the task and procedure of science is in part "selecting or constructing a pattern of relations between temporal experiences of individuals . . ."

Michael Polanyi, *Science, Faith and Society,*[23]* (Ch. II) shows how the knowledge of scientists and their consensus is determined by communal tradition, conscience, devotion, ideals, faith. I suggest, therefore, that if all this be true, science can be understood fully only by him who has had scientific experience within that community—since nowhere else can he come under the sway of this tradition and consensus. Similarly art and religion can be understood adequately only within the communities living them.

Regarding religious experience see:

Frederick R. Tennant, *Philosophical Theology.*[25]* (Ch. XII)

Artistic experience:

Theodore M. Greene, *Arts and the Art of Criticism.*[5]*

Martin C. Johnson, *Art and Scientific Thought.*[5]*

Roger H. Sessions, *Musical Experience of Composer, Performer, Listener.*[6]*

34. (p. 190) Herbert Butterfield, *Origins of Modern Science.*[12]* (p. 72–82) "The scientific revolution . . . the great achievement was due to a transposition taking place in the mind of the enquirer himself. Here was a problem which only became manageable when in a certain sense it had been 'geometrized' . . . It depended

* Superscripts hereinafter refer to earlier footnote numbers in this section.

on the trick of seeing a purely geometrical body sailing off into a kind of space which was empty and neutral . . ."

35. (p. 191) The following terms are almost synonymous in some of their meanings: authentication, confirmation, validation, verification. Their usage in science is discussed at length in most books of the philosophy of science.

Regarding their use in religion see:

Herbert H. Farmer, *World and God.*[31*] (p. 41)

John A. Hutchison, *Faith, Reason and Existence.*[7*] (Ch. VIII, Sec. II)

Frederick R. Tennant, *Philosophical Theology.*[25*] (Vol. I, Ch. XI)

36. (p. 191) Related terms: order, regularity, uniformity, predictability, lawfulnes, structure, design, pattern. See:

Jacob Bronowski, *Common Sense of Science.*[18*] (p. 100) ". . . science is an activity of putting order into our experience." The two realms of order of special interest here are the "natural order" and the "moral order," that of natural law and of moral law.

Martin C. Johnson, *Science and the Meanings of Truth.*[18*]

Frederick R. Tennant, *Philosophical Theology.*[25*] (Vol. II, Ch. I)

37. (p. 192) James B. Conant, *On Understanding Science.*[18*] (p. 31)

38. (p. 192) Edward F. Caldin, *Power and Limits of Science.*[5*] (Ch. VIII and IX)

Charles A. Coulson, *Science and Christian Belief,*[16*] develops the thought that science is essentially a religious activity.

Martin C. Johnson, *Art and Scientific Thought,*[5*] that it is artistic and creative.

39. (p. 195) Bernard Barber, *Science and the Social Order.* Glencoe, Illinois: Free Press, 1952. 288 p.

Jacob Bronowski, *Common Sense of Science,*[18*] (Ch. IX, "Science, the Destroyer or Creator")

Edward F. Caldin, *Power and Limits of Science.*[5*] (Ch. X, "Society and Science")

James B. Conant, *Modern Science and Modern Man.* New York: Columbia University Press, 1952. 111 p.

Herbert Dingle, *Scientific Adventure.*[33*] (Ch. 19, "Science and Religion")

Eugene P. Wigner, *Physical Science and Human Values; A Symposium.* Princeton, New Jersey: Princeton University Press, 1947. 181 p.

* Superscripts hereinafter refer to earlier footnote numbers in this section.

An inexhaustible mine of information and discussion of these matters is the monthly *Bulletin of Atomic Scientists* (Chicago).

40. (p. 195) This can be seen by following such journals as:

America, Bulletin of Atomic Scientists, The Christian Century, Commentary, Commonweal, Cross Currents, Reconstructionist, The Scientific American, The Scientific Monthly, Humanist.

41. (p. 195) John Baillie, *Natural Science and the Spiritual Life.*[5*] (p. 28–31)

42. (p. 196) Two profound books dealing with the deeply religious significance of daily work, including scientific work, are:

Robert L. Calhoun, *God and the Common Life.* Hamden, Conn.: Shoe String Press, 1954. (Reissue) 303 p. (especially Ch. IV)

———, *God and the Day's Work.* New York: Association Press, 1943. 74 p.

43. (p. 199) John Baillie, *Natural Science and the Spiritual Life.*[5*] (Von Huegel and Hocking, p. 32–4)

Edward F. Caldin, *Power and Limits of Science.*[5*] (Ch. X, Section on "Science in Education")

44. (p. 200) Alfred North Whitehead, *Religion in the Making.*[14*] (p. 58)

45. (p. 200) Sir James G. Frazer, *Golden Bough; A Study in Magic and Religion.* 12 vols. New York: Macmillan Co., 1922. (Abridged edition, 1953. 864 p.)

Bronislaw Malinowski, *Magic, Science and Religion.*[6*]

Lynn Thorndike, *History of Magic and Experimental Science.* 4 vols. New York: Macmillan, vol. 1 and 2, 1929; Columbia University Press, vol. 3 and 4, 1934.

46. (p. 201) James B. Conant, *On Understanding Science.*[18*]

Michael Polanyi, *Science, Faith and Society.*[23*]

The following two books deal specifically with science as a typically human enterprise. There is much valuable material in them, though they seem sometimes to exaggerate or give a somewhat distorted picture. They should be read with the proverbial grain of salt.

Anthony Standen, *Science Is a Sacred Cow.* New York: E. P. Dutton and Co., 1950. 221 p.

David L. Watson, *Scientists Are Human.* London: Watts, 1938. 249 p.

Also:

W. I. B. Beveridge, *Art of Scientific Investigation.*[23*]

* Superscripts hereinafter refer to earlier footnote numbers in this section.

47. (p. 205) Examples of expositions of natural science's *direct* contribution to our knowledge of man are:

    Sir Charles S. Sherrington, *Man On His Nature.* 2nd ed. New York: Doubleday Anchor Book, 1953. 316 p.

    John Zachary Young, *Doubt and Certainty in Science; A Biologist's Reflection on the Brain.* New York: Oxford University Press, 1950. 168 p.

    A discussion of *indirect* contribution is presented by:

    Ernst Cassirer, *An Essay on Man.*[5*]

    Henry Margenau, "New View of Man in His Physical Environment," *Centennial Review of Arts & Science.* Vol. I No. 1 (1957)

48. (p. 205) An aspect of man's nature that is significant for philosophers and theologians is that of the "soul." The first volume of the following book is devoted to the subject of the Soul and is replete with references to science:

    Frederick R. Tennant, *Philosophical Theology.*[25*]

    See also:

    Robert L. Calhoun, *What Is Man?* New York: Association Press, 1939. 78 p.

    George P. Klubertanz, *Philosophy of Human Nature.* New York: Appleton-Century-Crofts, 1953. 444 p.

49. (p. 206) Michael Polanyi, "Passion and Controversy in Science," *Bulletin of Atomic Scientists,* XIII (No. 6), 186.

50. (p. 206) John Ulric Nef, *War and Human Progress; An Essay on the Rise of Industrial Civilization.* Cambridge, Mass.: Harvard University Press, 1950. 464 p.

    Michael Polanyi, *Science, Faith and Society.*[23*] (Ch. III)

51. (p. 207) Norbert Wiener, *Cybernetics.* New York: John Wiley and Sons, 1948. 194 p.

    John Zachary Young, *Doubt and Certainty in Science.*[47*]

52. (p. 209) A few books, not referred to earlier, devoted specifically to the subject of *Science* and *Religion:*

    Bernard Bavink, *Science and God.* New York: Reynal and Hitchcock, 1934. 174 p.

    Karl Heim, *Christian Faith and Natural Science.* New York: Harper and Brothers, 1953. 256 p.

* Superscripts hereinafter refer to earlier footnote numbers in this section.

Karl Heim, *Transformation of the Scientific World View.* New York: Harper and Brothers, 1953. 262 p.

William E. Hocking, *Science and the Idea of God.* Chapel Hill, North Carolina: University of North Carolina Press, 1944. 124 p.

Eric L. Mascall, *Christian Theology and Natural Sciences.* New York: Longmans, Green and Co., 1956. 328 p.

Kirtley F. Mather, *Science in Search of God.* New York: Henry Holt and Co., 1928. 159 p.

Max C. Otto, *Science and the Moral Life.* New York: New American Library, 1949.

Charles E. Raven, *Christianity and Science.* New York: Association Press, 1955. 96 p.

Bertrand A. Russell, *Religion and Science.* New York: Henry Holt and Co., 1935. 271 p.

Paul A. Sabine, *Atoms, Men and God.* New York: Philosophical Library, 1953. 226 p.

Edmund W. Sinnott, *Two Roads to Truth.* New York: Viking Press, 1953. 241 p.

Walter A. Whitehouse, *Christian Faith and the Scientific Attitude.* Edinburgh: Oliver and Boyd, 1952. 149 p.

The Conference on Science, Philosophy and Religion (3080 Broadway, New York, N. Y.) has issued a volume yearly since 1942. These volumes are gold mines of material on all phases of the subject, with special reference to "Their Relation to the Democratic Life."

The Edward W. Hazen Foundation (400 Prospect Street, New Haven 11, Connecticut) has published a series of excellent brochures entitled *Religious Perspectives of College Teaching.* The following are of special relevance here:

Edward McCrady, *In Biology;* H. S. Taylor, *In the Physical Sciences;* G. F. Thomas, *Problems and Principles;* R. Ulich, *In the Preparation of Teachers.*

These publications are now included in book form with other essays. See:

Religious Perspectives in College Teaching, ed. Hoxie N. Fairchild. New York: Ronald Press Co., Copyright 1952. 460 p.

As part of its national project on Teacher Education and Religion the American Association of Colleges for Teacher Education has issued a volume of essays and studies by faculty members of one of the cooperating colleges. Two essays are pertinent:

Focus on Religion in Teacher Education. Oneonta, New York: American Association of Colleges for Teacher Education, 1955. 87 p.

George Bradley, "Another Responsibility for the Science Teacher." p. 35–6.

William C. Van Deventer, "Questions Concerning Religion in Science Classes." p. 36–9.

Another of the cooperating pilot institutions has issued the following study of which the chapter indicated is pertinent:

Religion in the High School Curriculum. Greenville, North Carolina: East Carolina College, 1956. 75 p.

J. O. Derrick, "Religion in the Teaching of Secondary School Science." p. 22–9.

53. (p. 211) *Religious Perspectives in College Teaching,* ed. Hoxie N. Fairchild.[52*] (p. 34)

CHAPTER 6

Notes

1. (p. 216) In one instance the administrator went through these steps and the group reacted negatively by saying they were already doing what was wanted. This campus conducted no study.
2. (p. 219) The concern actually is a scholarly one which would be equally opposed to injection of materials into a course where there is no relevancy.

Bibliography

Anderson, Walter A. "Study of Religion in Teacher Education at New York University," *Tenth Yearbook,* American Association of Colleges for Teacher Education. Oneonta, New York: AACTE, 1957. p. 143–45.

Benne, Kenneth D. "What the Teacher Should Know About Religion," *Eighth Yearbook,* American Association of Colleges for Teacher Education. Oneonta, New York: AACTE, 1955. p. 213–21.

Berg, Hulda M. "Religion in the High School Curriculum," *Educational Leader,* XIX No. 2 (October, 1955), 36–43.

Bernhard, Harold. "Promising Practices in the Teacher Education and Religion Project at the Iowa State Teachers College," *Tenth Yearbook,* American Association of Colleges for Teacher Education. Oneonta, New York: AACTE, 1957. p. 146–50.

Collins, Evan R. "Teaching About Religion in Teacher Education Institutions, An *Ad Hoc* Committee Report." *Sixth Yearbook,* American

* Superscripts hereinafter refer to earlier footnote numbers in this section.

Association of Colleges for Teacher Education. Oneonta, New York: AACTE, 1954. p. 93–102.

Dawson, Eugene E. "AACTE Teacher Education and Religion Project," *Seventh Yearbook*, American Association of Colleges for Teacher Education. Oneonta, New York: AACTE, 1954. p. 93–102.

———. "Critical Issues and Questions Encountered in Teacher Education and Religion Project Study," *Ninth Yearbook*, American Association of Colleges for Teacher Education. Oneonta, New York: AACTE, 1956. p. 132–33.

———. "Next Decade of Research and Experimentation Relating to Religion and Public Education," *Religious Education*, LII No. 4 (July, 1957), 289 (published by Religious Education Association, New York).

———. "Summary Report of Teacher Education and Religion Project," *Eighth Yearbook*, American Association of Colleges for Teacher Education. Oneonta, New York: AACTE, 1955. p. 222–29.

Faculty Seminars; Selected Topics. Oneonta, New York: American Association of Colleges for Teacher Education, 1957.

Focus on Religion in Teacher Education. Oneonta, New York: American Association of Colleges for Teacher Education, 1955. 87 p.

Gernant, Leonard. "The Look Ahead," *Ninth Yearbook*, American Association of Colleges for Teacher Education. Oneonta, New York: AACTE, 1956. p. 134–37.

Gilbert, Arthur. "The Teacher Education and Religion Project at Mid-Point," *Reconstructionist*, XXII (February 8, 1957), 17–24.

Gladden, James W. *General and Professional Education Sequence in the College of Arts and Sciences and the College of Education at the University of Kentucky*. Oneonta, New York: American Association of Colleges for Teacher Education, 1958. 78 p.

———. "Kentucky Experiment," *Tenth Yearbook*, American Association of Colleges for Teacher Education. Oneonta, New York: AACTE, 1957. p. 151–58.

Haggard, J. D. "How General is General Education?" *Educational Leader*, XIX No. 2 (October, 1955), 26–35.

———. "Mathematics and Religion," *Pentagon*, XV No. 2 (Spring, 1956), 81–7.

Hall, T. William. "The Place of Religion in Public Education," *Educational Leader*, XIX No. 2 (October, 1955), 5–18.

———. *Three Value Theories and Their Implications Regarding the Place of Religion in Teacher Education* (Doctoral Dissertation, Boston University Graduate School, 1956).

Hausman, Jerome. "View of the Teacher Education and Religion Project from The Ohio State University," *Ninth Yearbook*, American Association of Colleges for Teacher Education. Oneonta, New York: AACTE, 1956. p. 138–41.

Hunt, Mate Graye. *Values Resource Guide; Annotated for the Elementary School Teacher*. Oneonta, New York: American Association of Colleges for Teacher Education, 1958. 108 p.

Kircher, Everett J. "Religion and the Liberal University," *Progressive Education,* 33 No. 4 (July, 1956), 97–103.

Loew, Cornelius. *Michigan's Area Conferences on Problems Relating to Religion in Public School Education.* Kalamazoo: Western Michigan University and other Michigan Regional Colleges, 1957. 12 p.

McGrath, G. D. "Teacher Education and Religion Project at Arizona State College," *Tenth Yearbook,* American Association of Colleges for Teacher Education. Oneonta, New York: AACTE, 1957. p. 160–62.

Maucker, J. W. "Administrative Problems in Teacher Education and Religion in a State-Supported Institution of Higher Education," *Eleventh Yearbook,* American Association of Colleges for Teacher Education. Oneonta, New York: AACTE, 1958. p. 160–62.

———. "We Have Learned These Things," *Ninth Yearbook,* American Association of Colleges for Teacher Education. Oneonta, New York: AACTE, 1956. p. 142–44.

Mooney, Ross L., and Barbar, Robert. *College of Education Faculty Roundtable* on "Esthetic Experiences in the Education of Teachers." Columbus, Ohio: The Bureau of Educational Research, The Ohio State University, 1957. 106 p.

National Conference and Workshop at Kalamazoo. Oneonta, New York: American Association of Colleges for Teacher Education, 1955. 67 p.

News Bulletins. Oneonta, New York: American Association of Colleges for Teacher Education. Vol. I through Vol. IV (April, 1954–September, 1958).

Perlmutter, Philip. "Teaching About Religion: Solution or Confusion," *Reconstructionist,* XXII (March 9, 1956), 23–5.

Politella, Joseph, compiler. *Annotated Bibliography; Religion in Education.* Oneonta, New York: American Association of Colleges for Teacher Education, 1956. 90 p.

Prospectus of the Teacher Education and Religion Project. Oneonta, New York: American Association of Colleges for Teacher Education, 1953. 6 p.

Rainwater, Frank P. *Attitudes and the Aspirations of Our Students.* Troy, Alabama: Troy State College, 1958. 72 p.

———. "Teacher Education and Religion Projects Undertaken at State Teachers College, Troy, Alabama." *Tenth Yearbook,* American Association of Colleges for Teacher Education. Oneonta, New York: AACTE, 1957. p. 163–65.

Religion in the High School Curriculum. Greenville, North Carolina: East Carolina College, 1956. 75 p.

Scroggs, Jack. "Teacher Education and Religion Project: An Appraisal;" *Ninth Yearbook,* American Association of Colleges for Teacher Education. Oneonta, New York: AACTE, 1956. p. 145–47.

Sebaly, A. L. "AACTE Teacher Education and Religion Project at Mid-Passage," *Religious Education,* LIX (July, 1956), p. 226–69 (published by Religious Education Association, New York).

———. "Nature and Scope of the AACTE Teacher Education and Religion Project," *Ninth Yearbook,* American Association of Colleges for Teacher Education. Oneonta, New York: AACTE, 1956. p. 126–31.

———. "Religion in Teacher Education," *National Education Association Journal,* 46 (May, 1957), 317.

———. *Role of the Administrator.* Oneonta, New York: American Association of Colleges for Teacher Education, 1957. 16 p.

———. *Role of the Consultant.* Oneonta, New York: American Association of Colleges for Teacher Education, 1957. 20 p.

———. *Role of the Coordinator.* Oneonta, New York: American Association of Colleges for Teacher Education, 1957. 50 p.

———. *Role of the Local Committee Member.* Oneonta, New York: American Association of Colleges for Teacher Education, 1957. 27 p.

———. "Teacher Education and Religion," *Tenth Yearbook,* American Association of Colleges for Teacher Education. Oneonta, New York: AACTE, 1957. p. 223–26.

Seibert, Russell H. "Administrative Problems in Teacher Education and Religion in a General Education Program," *Eleventh Yearbook,* American Association of Colleges for Teacher Education. Oneonta, New York: AACTE, 1958. p. 163–67.

Sperry, Theodore M. "Reflections on the Place of Religion in the Teaching of Science," *Educational Leader,* XIX No. 2 (October, 1955), 19–25.

———. "Voluntary Committee," *Educational Leader,* XXI No. 3 (January, 1958), 11.

Summary Report of Pilot Institution Activities in the Teacher Education and Religion Project. Oneonta, New York: American Association of Colleges for Teacher Education, 1958.

Teacher Education and Religion Project. Bulletin of North Texas State College, Denton, Texas, 294 (April, 1958), 34.

CHAPTER 7

Notes

1. (p. 228) John A. Hardon, S.J., *An Evaluation of the Teacher Education and Religion Project,* p. 5. (Speech given at Teacher Education and Religion Project Workshop, Indianapolis, Indiana, May 18–20, 1958) Oneonta, New York: American Association of Colleges for Teacher Education, 1958.
2. (p. 229) *McCollum v. Board of Education,* 333 U. S. 203 (1948).
3. (p. 229) *Prospectus of the Teacher Education and Religion Project.* p. 3. Oneonta, New York: American Association of Colleges for Teacher Education, 1953.
4. (p. 230) Sister Mary Nona, "Some Religious Aspects of Elementary American History," *Study of Religion in the Public Schools; An Appraisal,* ed. Nicholas C. Brown. p. 153. Washington: American Council on Education, 1958.
5. (p. 233) *Moral and Spiritual Values in the Public Schools.* p. 77–8. Washington: Educational Policies Commission of the National Education Association, 1951.
6. (p. 233) American Council on Education, Committee on Religion and Education, *Relation of Religion to Public Education; The Basic Principles.* p. 29. Washington: American Council on Education, 1947.
7. (p. 233) *Prospectus, op. cit.,* p. 3.
8. (p. 234) *Ibid.*
9. (p. 235) *McCollum v. Board of Education, op. cit.* (1948)
10. (p. 235) *Ibid.*

Index